Everyman, I will go with thee,
and be thy guide

THE EVERYMAN
LIBRARY

*The Everyman Library was founded by J. M. Dent
in 1906. He chose the name Everyman because he wanted
to make available the best books ever written in every
field to the greatest number of people at the cheapest possible
price. He began with Boswell's Life of Johnson;
his one thousandth title was Aristotle's Metaphysics,
by which time sales exceeded forty million.*

*Today Everyman paperbacks remain true to
J. M. Dent's aims and high standards, with a wide range
of titles at affordable prices in editions which address
the needs of today's readers. Each new text is reset to give
a clear, elegant page and to incorporate the latest thinking
and scholarship. Each book carries the pilgrim logo,
the character in* Everyman, *a medieval mystery play,
a proud link between Everyman
past and present.*

ANGLO-SAXON PROSE

Edited and translated by
MICHAEL SWANTON

Professor of English Medieval Studies
University of Exeter

EVERYMAN
J. M. DENT · LONDON
CHARLES E. TUTTLE
VERMONT

Translations and revisions for 1993 edition
© J. M. Dent 1993

This title first published in Everyman 1975
Reprinted, with revisions, 1979, 1985

This edition first published 1993

J. M. Dent
Orion Publishing Group
Orion House
5 Upper St Martin's Lane, London, WC2H 9EA

Charles E. Tuttle Co., Inc.
28 South Main Street, Rutland, Vermont
05701 – USA

Typeset by Deltatype Ltd, Ellesmere Port, South Wirral

Printed by The Guernsey Press Co. Ltd, Guernsey, C.I.

British Library Cataloguing-in-Publication Data
is available upon request.

ISBN 0 460 87341 5

CONTENTS

PREFACE

The act of translation needs no apology. The circumstances which made it desirable for Alfred and Ælfric in the ninth and tenth centuries are no less pressing in the twentieth; and the attendant problems are no less great. The difficulties that confront the translator are innumerable; whole books have been written about them. Only those who have subjected their translations to the scrutiny of a number of others will readily appreciate how a dozen different readers will make a dozen different demands on a translation at any one time. It is simply not possible to satisfy every point at all times; of its nature, translation is unsatisfactory. The number of possible interpretations, not simply of substance, but of style and tone, is often large. And the decisions which must be taken are more often than not purely subjective. Ultimately translation cannot reproduce, or even adequately reflect, the style of an original without departing from its substance considerably. I have tried to supply as close a rendering as possible without being awkwardly over-literal. And I have thought it important not silently to 'improve' the original in those cases where I felt it to be at all clumsy, repetitive or obscure. To do so would be to present as unreal a picture as it would be to reduce all the varied styles of Old English prose to my own personal style, or to the 'colloquial Modern English' beloved of the university examiner.

In the strictly limited space available, I have tried to furnish the general reader with a representative selection of some of the very different kinds of Old English prose. It would have been possible to include everyone's favourite passages only by an anthology of excerpts. But wherever possible I have chosen works which are complete in themselves, eschewing extracts in the belief that these are inherently misleading. What might at first seem a bold step in excluding passages from both Bede and *The Anglo-Saxon Chronicle* – both of which are in any case already available in inexpensive editions – allows space for less familiar material which would otherwise have had to be omitted. I have tried to

include a body of such less accessible pieces as the estate
memoranda, as well as such high-spots as the *Sermo Lupi*, which
could scarcely be avoided; and to include examples of such
ephemeral documents as land-grants and wills, as well as works of
persistent influence, like the Gospel of Nicodemus. It was clearly
desirable not to repeat more than was inevitable material already
included in Professor Whitelock's *English Historical Documents*
c. 500–1042, and to make cultural rather than purely historical
documents available, providing supplementary material of use to
students both of Anglo-Saxon history and Old English literature.
Within the limits laid down, at least some of their needs are met.
But should others better versed in the subject ever have occasion
to peruse these pages, the translator can only plead with King
Alfred

> Þæt he for hine gebidde, and him ne wite gif he hit rihtlicor ongite
> Þonne he mihte, forÞæmðe ælc mon sceal be his andgites mæðe and be
> his æmettan sprecan ðæt he spreÞ and don Þæt Þæt he deÞ.

M. J. Swanton
Exeter 1974

NOTE TO SECOND,
ENLARGED, EDITION

I have taken advantage of the call for reprinting to extend the
range of interest, adding one or two pieces that friends and
colleagues have suggested would make this anthology more
valuable as a class-book. At the same time, I have made occasional
corrections and improvements elsewhere. The principles of
translation remain the same. And the plea with which I ended the
original preface (twenty years ago) remains no less heartfelt in
increasingly hard-pressed times.

M. J. Swanton
Exeter 1993

INTRODUCTION

The Anglo-Saxons have left us the earliest, largest and most varied body of vernacular literature to have survived from medieval Europe. But its remains are both arbitrary and uneven. While there is evidence for the extensive copying of many works, the greatest number of Old English prose writings, like the verse, are known only from unique copies which were often made centuries after the work was composed; scarcely any is the author's own manuscript, or even an immediate copy of it. And because the medium of their preservation has been that of monastic or cathedral libraries, no work has had much chance of survival unless it was of interest to a church librarian. It was mere chance that the Old English *Apollonius of Tyre* should have been copied into the back of an eleventh-century collection of homilies and laws; without it we could only have guessed at the existence of an Old English romance genre. If only the library of a lay magnate could be reconstructed in the way that Bishop Leofric's can, our picture of Old English literature might have been more balanced.

But even ecclesiastical libraries have had little chance of survival. The magnificent eighth-century library Alcuin knew at York must have been sadly depleted by Viking and other ravages by the end of the tenth century. And whatever Archbishop Wulfstan could then have restored would be destroyed once more when York Minster was burnt down again during the reign of William. In any case, even during the Anglo-Saxon period itself the processes of natural wastage may have meant the loss of many works. With considerable changes in language, spelling and handwriting conventions, old-fashioned manuscripts must often have been considered of no great value. Some may have been revised and re-written then; others scraped clean for the sake of the vellum, others still, discarded altogether. The older contents of many libraries must have been continuously dispersed and destroyed. Even the fine new books of the Benedictine Renaissance would appear old-fashioned, and even unreadable by the thirteenth century. Certainly by the early 1300s the fine collection of books left by Leofric to his cathedral library at Exeter could be dismissed by the cathedral librarian as valueless and not even worth cataloguing. Probably many were already being sold off. And of those Anglo-Saxon books that survived such vicissitudes of time as these, very many must have been lost at the Reformation. It was a happy chance that took certain of the reformers like Archbishop Parker to such disputable matters as Ælfric's writings on the Eucharist. By 1556 Parker had already acquired at least one of Leofric's books – his copy of the Gospels in English translation. And in a further half-century another nine were to come into the hands of the Oxford antiquary Thomas Bodley.

The list of extant Old English prose works is therefore an arbitrary one. The survival of the manuscripts containing them has been a matter of mere chance rather than deliberate choice because of their intrinsic value. Relatively little prose sets out to be consciously 'literary' in the way that all poetry by definition must. Its most natural function is to record and communicate facts, whether formally or informally. But in many ways this can be more directly informative about the life of the community than the poetic afflatus allows. The bailiff's memorandum, the fragmentary letter, brings us close to the real, everyday concerns of men in a way that the artistic contrivance of poetry cannot.

By chance, the earliest surviving examples of Old English prose are also among the first that could ever have been documented. One of the direct benefits of the Augustinian mission was to provide the Kentish kings with a ready-made secretariat prepared to put the skills of its clerks to the service of the newly converted regal administration. Bede describes how shortly after Æthelberht's adoption of Christianity in 597 he issued laws 'in the Roman manner, which, being written in the English tongue, are kept by them and practised to this [i.e. Bede's] day'. In speaking of the 'Roman' character of Æthelberht's laws, Bede cannot refer to the substance of the code, which is clearly Germanic in every sense; it was 'Roman' only by virtue of having been written down. Simply the memoranda of ancient custom familiar to all, these early laws are naturally concise and allusive, laconic and often elliptical to the point of confusion: brief statements of penalties and compensations incurred for various offences. It is a terse and economic prose, and relatively unadorned, although bearing extensive traces of its mnemonic origins: the devices of alliteration, assonance or parallelism to reinforce the sense of the lines, and often employing the highly specialized vocabulary and phraseology of customary law. It is significant that, unlike the laws of the Germanic peoples of the continent, these should have been written down not in Latin but in the vernacular, thus initiating a tradition of English legal prose which was to last continuously for more than four centuries. Later in the period, when the pragmatic compilations of earlier times were replaced by the elaborate and sophisticated codifications of such kings as Æthelred and Cnut, the fluid and continuous style of those who drafted them is still underpinned by traditional mnemonic devices, such as from Æthelred's fifth code the phrases:

ge mid worde ge mid wedde . . . som and sib . . . word ond weorc,

although in the case of this particular code it is difficult to distinguish between the cadences traditional to legal prose and the personal style of Wulfstan, whom we know to have had a hand in its compilation. Even at the end of the period, Anglo-Saxon laws remain profoundly traditional, albeit now framed by a consummate political theoretician.

Contemporary with these early Kentish laws there seems to have developed the custom of recording such legal transactions as the transfer of estates or the granting of privileges in the form of a document based on the late Roman private deed. There are still extant well over one and a half thousand such 'charters', sometimes collected into complete cartularies belonging to a particular house, or occasionally written into the fly-leaves or blank spaces of a Gospel or other religious book for their better preservation, but most commonly found on separate parchments. Some are written entirely in Latin; others, like the eighth-century charter recording a gift of land at Crediton (p. 14), have only an introductory framework of Latin formulae, while the specific details of the estates involved are set out in the plain prose of those who knew and worked the land. Land-boundaries are often given in meticulous detail which, although often apparently elusive from a twentieth-century point of view, offer a singularly graphic picture of a landscape it is often still possible to reconstruct. In some cases, as with the Crediton example cited, the details given are sufficiently explicit for it still to be possible to trace them out on the ground, even though there is now no billy-goat at the ford and the wolves have long gone from the hollow. It should not be assumed that all topographic names were quaintly meaningful in this way, however. Certainly such Celtic names as Creedy, Nymet and Yeo must already have seemed as arbitrary as their Anglo-Saxon counterparts now often appear to us.

Perhaps as early, but certainly by some date in the ninth century, there developed another kind of charter – the king's writ – an official letter authenticated by the royal seal. Those that survive, from the reign of Æthelred onwards, are invariably brief and written in a simple epistolatory style, if in some cases, like that from Edward the Confessor confirming privileges at Staines (p. 43), such phrases as:

on wæterum ond on werum . . . be strande ne be lande

have all the sound of traditional mnemonic phraseology such as might have derived from customary law. But it is interesting to recognize the emergence of an official civil service vernacular in England anticipating the rest of Europe by centuries. Less formal letters – especially those between laymen, the great majority of which could have seemed of only immediate and local interest to both the sender and the recipient – had little chance of survival. The fragment of a letter to 'Brother Edward' (p. 43) seems to have been preserved only because it was incorporated into notes on the biblical injunctions concerning abstention from blood. And probably even this was the work of an ecclesiastic, bearing signs in one passage of the high style of the Benedictine preacher.

But while it might be mistaken to suppose that even in the recital of land-boundaries we have the authentic voice of the Saxon peasant, there is no doubt but that as time went on it was not only clerks who would need to read and write. From the ninth century at least, we find the vernacular used for a wide variety of documents recording lawsuits, wills, sales, donations, guild regulations, the manumission of slaves and so forth. Most were brief enough. But we are fortunate in possessing the fairly extensive memoranda of a late Anglo-Saxon reeve, regarding his functions in employment, the compulsive listings of which offer an intimate insight into the neurotic concerns of overworked estate management (p. 30). Noted down in a not unattractive style, these memoranda employ vocabulary which although then of the most common, everyday sort, now conjures up a graphic picture of the rural scene by its very obscurity. Perhaps here if anywhere, with a man who feels he cannot afford to forget anything: 'not even a mousetrap or, what is still more trivial, a hasp-peg', we have the voice of the sheep-fold and of the threshing-floor. But however informative, the insights such documents provide are usually quite incidental to their original utilitarian purpose. It is incidental to the record of an exchange of lands between Bishop Æthelwold and a certain Wulfstan Uccea that we are given the unique sight of a tenth-century Northamptonshire witch dragged from her home to be drowned at London Bridge (p. 35). And although not without a certain confidence, and even on occasions an admittedly high style, such documents are quite without literary pretensions of any kind.

But in a society where every evening will have called for entertainments of the kind witnessed by Bede in the introduction to his story of Cædmon, the cultivation of a story-telling art must have flourished, both in verse and prose forms of delivery. And there would be told not only fictional tales of dragon-slayings and the eye-witness accounts of foreign travellers, but also matters of past and recent history. We know that Edward the Confessor made a habit of relating to his household once every Easter the story of Olaf Tryggvason, partly reading it aloud and partly extempore. The kind of stories that might be told by first-hand witnesses are exemplified by the anecdotes told about Guthlac by Wilfrid and Cissa to Felix (cf. p. 94). And although these stories were related too soon after the event for many of the usual narrative accretions to have occurred around the life of the saint, Felix already knows of certain miracles believed to have attended Guthlac's birth. We have a particularly well-documented account of how the story of the death of St Edmund was handed down by word of mouth (p. 158); when Abbo was first persuaded to write the story down, it was already some 120 years and four generations after the event. By this time legends were already beginning to gather around the figure of Edmund in East Anglia; as customary with saints, stories arose about his birth and childhood. His dealings with the sons of Ragnar Lothbrok were elaborated and we learn how the Vikings placed their confidence less in force of arms than in Ubba's devilish arts: he is lifted up so as to put the 'evil eye' on the English armies.

It must have been from a body of oral traditions such as these, then current in the north, that Bede took some of the most vivid stories he tells. His account of Edwin's conversion, for instance: the persuasive arguments of an anonymous councillor, to whom is attributed one of the most arresting similes of early times – that of the sparrow flying through the firelit hall in mid-winter; the dramatic picture of the cynical pagan high-priest Coifi riding on the forbidden stallion to desecrate his own temple, while the onlookers stand back in amazement – this is great narrative literature by any standard, and almost certainly derived from oral sources. But in fact many of the best-known stories from the Anglo-Saxon period have survived only because they were written down by post-Conquest historians, writing in Latin, some of whom specifically acknowledge oral sources. We know the story of King Alfred's burning of the cakes only from the Annals of St Neots, of Cnut and the waves from Henry of Huntingdon, of Lady Godiva's ride through Coventry only through Roger of Wendover. The tales of Offa of Angeln and his queen, merely hinted at in *Beowulf*, survived to be told at length, elaborated and paralleled with other stories told about the later Offa of Mercia, only by an anonymous twelfth-century monk of St Albans. Middle English romances like *King Horn* and *Havelok the Dane* are certainly using Anglo-Saxon story materials.

One such story seems to have been preserved in a relatively pristine form. While many of the entries in *The Anglo-Saxon Chronicle* that deal with events prior to the Conversion must inevitably depend on oral transmission at some stage, most are simple accounts of battles and genealogies which have all the mnemonic allusiveness of the most ancient poetic records, *Widsith* and *Deor*. But in the account of the blood-feud between Cynewulf and Cyneheard incorporated in the annal for 755 we have what is in effect a completely developed 'short story'. The author describes a chain of violent events, politically motivated, the first and last acts of which are separated by a period of thirty years, but which can be linked by a clear understanding of the motives involved. The dramatic possibilities of the material: both physical – the stealthy approach and encirclement of the sleeping king, his violent death and the woman's screams – as well as mental – the conflict of loyalties between relatives and friends – are all utilized to portray a vivid and moving picture of the problems that might confront the heroic *comitatus* in the middle years of the eighth century, which compares interestingly with some of the more 'literary' poetic uses of the same theme. But here the author is clearly not concerned with mere historical rapportage; his theme is the triumph of loyalty under trial in heroic society, with a full understanding of the tragic moral and social implications of his subject. He employs a compelling variation of narrative, direct and reported speech, so that the reader's interest is never allowed to flag. At the same time there remain signs of its oral transmission: the constant opening of sentences with 'And . . .' and an infuriating lack of precision about pronouns which leads to some confusion as to the identity of the protagonists.

Parallel with both this 'oral' tradition and with the voice of documentary record, there is some evidence for the development of an alternative and more 'literary' prose tradition, albeit perhaps limited in both range and quantity. While the early medieval Church naturally regarded Latin as the lingua franca of scholarship, it was clear that in England the vernacular represented the only means of furthering its missionary aims. And in view of what we know of the general modus operandi of the early Anglo-Saxon Church, we might have assumed that some translation from Latin into English would have been undertaken relatively early. Writing to Egbert of York towards the end of his life in 734, Bede tells how he has often supplied translations of such things as the Apostles' Creed and the Lord's Prayer to monks ignorant of Latin. And Bede's pupil Cuthbert gives a moving picture of the great scholar on his death-bed, dictating with his dying breath the last words of a translation of St John's Gospel. Probably Bede was not alone. We know also that from the early eighth century there had arisen the custom of adding interlinear English glosses to the Psalter and Canticles and perhaps to other service books also, furnishing what was in effect a continuous if literal translation. These were merely the forerunners of the fine idiomatic Gospel translations of later Anglo-Saxon times. But how soon such books, let alone such desiderata as a vernacular martyrology, homiliary, computus or penitential, could have been supplied for the benefit of the lower clergy is uncertain.

One genre which certainly flourished early in the period was that of the saint's life. Already by the time of Bede there were extant in Northumbria anonymous Latin lives of Gregory, Cuthbert and Ceolfrith as well as a southern Life of St Æthelburh of Barking. The anniversaries of the saints will have been occasions for commemorative sermons, which if addressed to the laity must inevitably have been in the vernacular, although it remains uncertain when they may first have been thought worthwhile writing down. There is good evidence for an eighth- or ninth-century Mercian school of English verse hagiography witnessed by the two *Guthlac* poems, *Andreas* and the Cynewulfian poems *Elene*, *Juliana* and *The Fates of the Apostles*. The Mercian monk Felix seems to have written his Latin *Life of Guthlac* by the middle of the eighth century and no doubt simple vernacular prose versions soon followed. Hagiography is a notoriously conventional kind of writing. But, bared of Felix's extravagant Latin, the Old English *Life of Guthlac* presents a not unattractive, and often humorous, account of both the domestic circumstances and the mental conflicts endured by a moody young nobleman converted to the contemplative life of an eighth-century hermit.

Such saints' lives as this would have supplied plentiful material for popular sermons. And no doubt it was this tradition which gave rise to the so-called Blickling homilies, a Mercian collection of sermons copied down at one stage during the second half of the tenth century but apparently deriving from some previous date, and offering sermons and saints' stories in a style very different from that favoured by the scholarly revival of the tenth-century Benedictine Renaissance. The author, or authors, of the Blickling homilies display neither Ælfric's learning nor his theological sophistication, retailing legends without any apparent awareness of their religious significance. They draw extensively on such apocryphal sources as the Gospel of Nicodemus, the dramatic content of which was to exercise a continuous appeal for audiences throughout the Middle Ages, to supply vivid and sensational pictures of Hell and the Last Days. Characteristically they offer a superabundance of exciting visual imagery within a very short space. The narrative quality itself is often clumsy; one only need compare Ælfric's re-telling of the homilist's lost bull story which prefaces the Michaelmas sermon, done with far greater clarity in fewer sentences. But on the other hand, few of Ælfric's sermons are as totally effective as some of the Blickling homilies, overpowering in the sheer awfulness of their imagery and exhortations. And this is achieved without any of the Benedictine preacher's usual rhetorical devices. The Blickling homilies employ what is in many respects a very much plainer style, even if often more overtly poetic in its use of metaphor: Christ is the 'golden blossom', and Mary's womb, Christ's bower, is 'adorned with lilies and roses'.

But whatever the standing of English literature by the time of King Alfred, it seems clear that the Golden Age of Latin learning had long passed. If the picture Alfred paints in the preface to his translation of *The Pastoral Care* of the decay of learning at the beginning of his reign (p. 60) is a little exaggerated for the sake of polemic, the achievements of the age of Bede and Alcuin must certainly have seemed splendid looking back over a generation of destructive warfare. But equally, it would be wrong to attribute too much to the influence of the Viking irruptions, however destructive they may have been locally. It is sobering to realize that it was precisely during England's period of greatest political debility and military disasters, the reign of Æthelred and the institution of Danegeld, that the great cultural reflorescence of the Benedictine Renaissance took place; whereas the body of extant literature we can ascribe to the period of peace and prosperity under Edward the Confessor is very slight indeed. However, it was the belief that it was the failure of his people to maintain the educational ideals of Bede and Alcuin – which was at least the indirect cause of the divine retribution he thought lay behind the Viking ravages – which led Alfred to embark on a decisive and well-documented step in the history of English prose. If social and political order was dependent on the existence of a sound educational system, the king would himself, together with the assistance of a pleiad of English and foreign scholars gathered round him for the purpose, embark on a programme of translations which would make accessible 'those books most necessary for men to know', by the contemplation of which his countrymen might come to understand both their present position and the means of national recovery.

The programme of books on which Alfred chose to centre his scheme is less idiosyncratic than might at first appear; his choice is dictated by a clear educational rationale. It would contain both moral and social philosophy, national and world history. Each book had a clear didactic theme, either implicit or explicit. In Boethius's *Consolation of Philosophy*, for instance, Alfred could inform with specifically Christian values the reflections of a Roman nobleman awaiting violent death after a sudden reversal of fortune. It is interesting to find that at the very end of the Anglo-Saxon period all these books, either in the original Latin or in English translation, were thought necessary by Leofric for his new cathedral library at Exeter. Of course, not all these 'Alfredian' translations were the work of King Alfred himself. It was Wærferth of Worcester, for example, who translated the collection of legends about early Italian saints which we know as *The Dialogues of Gregory the Great*. And although Ælfric certainly believed the translation of Bede's *History* to have been by Alfred, traces of Anglian dialect in the oldest manuscripts suggest that this was in fact the work of one or other of the king's four Mercian collaborators.

Even those translations for which we know Alfred to have been responsible differ greatly in their style. His first known work, his rendering of Gregory's *Pastoral Care*, is a relatively close translation from the original, 'sometimes word for word, sometimes in paraphrase'. But his approach to the works of Boethius and Orosius, on the other hand, is very different. By judicious editing out of unnecessary material and the expansion of unfamiliar or interesting points with supplementary notes and illustrations, many apparently drawn from his experience as a soldier and man of affairs, Alfred presents us with what are virtually new books, or at least re-interpretations of the old as seen through the eyes of a ninth-century Germanic king. Some of the most substantial and useful supplementary material Alfred incorporates, lies in the accounts he was able to provide of voyages into the Scandinavian hinterland, as told him by two seamen, Ohthere and Wulfstan, visiting his court (p. 62). Describing lengthy voyages of discovery undertaken respectively to the Arctic north and deep into the Baltic, the tales they tell of these remote lands and of the strange tribes that inhabit them – the only non-Indo-European races of the north, the Lapps of the White Sea and the Ests living around the mouth of the Vistula – must have seemed particularly exotic at this time. If Alfred's preface to *The Pastoral Care* seems rather heavy with over-subordination, later in such extended original sequences as these Alfred shows himself master of an easy independent style. The travellers' tales especially are told in fluent and uncomplex prose, occasionally slipping into the immediacy of direct speech to supply a shrewd picture of these curious if cautious and practical seafarers.

The preface to Alfred's last known work, the *Soliloquies of St Augustine* (p. 67), offers the picture of a man looking back over his life's writings, anxious that others should sustain the programme he had begun. The extended collection and constructional metaphor he employs is a singularly vivid and apt description of his works, a vigorous defence of his editorial choice in selecting and re-arranging his materials in the way he thinks best to supply any deficiencies he may find. Of course Alfred's scheme was essentially for works of translation, rather than for original literary compositions. But it was not an unremarkable venture on which to have embarked at a relatively advanced age and amidst the multifarious anxieties and duties of a still precarious reign. In an apologia for what was perhaps his most complex work, the translation of Boethius, he implores subsequent scholars simply to pray for him and not to blame him if they feel that they could have done better, 'for according to the measure of his understanding and according to his leisure, every man must say what he says and do what he does'. Even in times less distraught, few can fail to sympathize with such a plea.

After two hundred years Ælfric, one of the great luminaries of Benedictine letters, can look back sadly and claim that there were no adequate translations but those King Alfred had left. The tenth-century monastic revival had led to a great restoration of learning, art and literature, in which fine manuscripts especially would be produced in large numbers. But in the lay field there was still an enormous body of ignorance which those like Ælfric were concerned to redeem. He has 'seen and heard much error in many English books which, in their innocence, unlearned men have considered great wisdom'. And so it is that, like Alfred before him, Ælfric undertakes a programme of writings which has both moral as well as educational intentions, the more pressing 'especially at the present time, which is the end of the world'. Born some time about the middle of the tenth century, Ælfric was the product of Æthelwold's reformed school at Winchester. From an early age he seems to have gained a reputation for scholarship, and was soon lionized by prominent laymen. In 989, shortly after the death of his revered master, Ælfric was sent to Ealdorman Æthelweard's new foundation at Cerne Abbas in Dorset. And there in seclusion he was able to complete the great bulk of his very prolific writings. In something over a hundred sermons, eighty of which were issued in the two volumes of so-called Catholic Homilies, Ælfric makes accessible a considerable body of orthodox theology as well as a fairly comprehensive survey of Christian world history from Creation to the Last Judgement. Typical are methodical expositions of Scripture, as exemplified in that on the Epiphany

(p. 136), using three- or four-fold exegesis in the Augustinian manner. In others, such as his sermon on The Sacrifice on Easter Day, he embarks on closely ordered arguments dealing with more difficult matters such as the nature of the Eucharist (p. 149). Ælfric's constant reference to the Church fathers whom he cites as authorities testifies to his concern for orthodoxy; and he would certainly have been appalled by the controversy which was to surround his teachings in a later age. The sermon was perhaps the most considerable literary reflex of the Benedictine Renaissance. If it is not a genre the twentieth century finds immediately attractive, we must admit that few modern sermons are as inherently compulsive. Ælfric's work was certainly popular among his contemporaries; his sermon on The Greater Litany, for example (p. 143), survives in no less than sixteen copies. He displays a fine common sense, eschewing in one breath apocrypha, astrological nonsense and social snobbery. He wears his learning lightly and there is the occasional sympathetic insight into the mind of a scholar who is well aware that his scholarship may not be to all tastes, as when towards the end of the second volume of homilies he remarks: 'We dare not lengthen this book much more, lest it be out of moderation and stir up men's antipathy because of its size.'

Ælfric's sermons had included several accounts of the lives and passions of those saints 'whose festivals were observed by the English'. He was to compose a further volume of the lives of those saints 'whom the monks, but not the laity, honour by special services'. Addressed to Æthelweard, 'for the strengthening of your faith', this volume was perhaps intended for private reading. Certainly the lives are more varied in length than the sermons, less regular, and with few direct addresses to the listener, such as indicate the preacher's voice. He refers to them as 'translations', but in fact he adapts his originals freely 'in case the fastidious should be bored by their being told in our language at as great a length as in Latin', remarking that 'brevity does not always mar discourse, but often makes it more beautiful'. His sources are varied but monastic concern for chastity naturally favoured the example of virgin saints in particular. Stories like that of Agatha (p. 164) could furnish a compelling, if highly conventionalized, demonstration of devotion under persecution, involving the drama of theological debate between the saint and her persecutors, the sensation of a series of lurid tortures leading to her eventual death, and posthumous miracles which might attest to the martyr's sanctity. But following the tradition of native hagiography it was possible to demonstrate that men inspired by the grace of God were not only to be found in the past and distant Mediterranean. The English nation could also boast saints, like the Christian warrior King Edmund, whom we are shown confronting the forces of Viking paganism (p. 158). Like Alfred, Ælfric was concerned with the moral revival of his nation at a time of foreign invasion. Of his translations of such biblical stories as those of Esther or Judith he remarks that he provides them 'as an example for you, that you also may defend your country with weapons against an invading army'.

In addition to homilies, saints' lives, and several idiomatic bible translations, epitomes and commentaries, Ælfric was responsible for such works as a treatise on ecclesiastical astronomy and chronology, written to enable clergy to understand the complicated calculations by which the date of Easter and other festivals was ascertained, a number of pastoral letters written for the use of Wulfsige of Sherborne and Wulfstan of York, which reveal him as an authority on canonical and liturgical matters, and, 'since grammar is the key that unlocks the meaning of those books', the first Latin grammar in any vernacular, and valuable for its incidental treatment of English. But of all his prodigious output, Ælfric is now perhaps best known for one of his most modest works: the slight but charming Latin colloquy, a sustained conversation-piece with all the pithiness and humour of some of the exchanges of real life. Although the substance of the dialogue is realistic enough, its Old English form is not, inasmuch as, being a mechanical gloss of the Latin original, it cannot reproduce the cadences of everyday speech. But Ælfric's is by far the most readable of all the monastic colloquies that survive, not simply an excuse for drilling syntax and vocabulary, but literature in its own right offering a complete panorama of late Anglo-Saxon life to illustrate the general literary theme of the usefulness to society of all sorts and conditions of men, and their ultimate dependence on the ploughman, one of the stable figures of English literature.

In his original writings, however, Ælfric shows himself one of the great stylists of Old English prose, capable of clarity, balance and a carefully controlled variety of syntactic patterns certainly not available to all writers. He claims in the homilies to be 'avoiding garrulous verbosity and strange expressions, seeking rather with pure and plain words, to be of use to my audience by simple speech'. This is a typical medieval disclaimer. In fact his 'plain style' is achieved through a sophisticated refinement and elaboration of the natural cadences of spoken English, regularly and systematically exploited. For the *Lives of the Saints* he was to develop a more mannered 'high style' of rhythmic prose, in which in addition to the usual patterning devices of repetition, parallelism, assonance and syntactical balance, he redoubles the sense of unity and coherence by employing a regular sequence of alliterative units, breaking the sense into short phrases and giving a total effect very similar to that of Old English alliterative verse.

All Ælfric's major work seems to have been completed during the fifteen years after he first went down to Cerne Abbas. In 1005 he was asked to go as abbot to the new foundation of his wealthy friend Æthelmær at Eynsham in Oxfordshire. He apparently maintained his old contacts; we hear of him lending a quantity of books to the Oxfordshire thegn Wulfgeat, or rebuking his host Sigeweard for having pressed him to drink too much on his last visit to East Heolon. But administrative and pastoral duties now seem to have proved too great for the scholar of Cerne Abbas; and apart from a few occasional pieces and some revision of his earlier works, Ælfric seems to have written no more.

Sustained composition was no doubt a luxury in which only the leisured could indulge. It is not without significance that one of the pastoral letters Ælfric had been commissioned to write in earlier times had been for Wulfstan of York. Like Ælfric, Wulfstan was a product of the Benedictine Renaissance. But what we can glimpse of him through his writings reveals a very different and in many ways a more attractive and sympathetic personality than that of the retiring scholar. Circumstances had thrust Wulfstan into the centre of the stage at a singularly disquieting time, when England was once more cowed by Viking attacks, when the exaction of Danegeld was habitual and the nation exiled their king. Bishop of London from 996 and Archbishop of York from 1002, Wulfstan is concerned almost solely with current issues. A preacher of undoubted eloquence, the *Liber Eliensis* describes him as 'the most learned of councillors, in whom spoke the very wisdom of God'. Rather than indulge in scriptural commentaries or lives of saints, Wulfstan addressed himself directly to the people, attacking the abuses of his age, what he took to be the inevitable moral degeneration of the Last Days. In the year Æthelred was finally driven into exile, he preaches his 'Sermon to the English at the time of the greatest Danish persecution' (p. 178), exhorting, wheedling, using both irony and sarcasm as well as direct threats, with a vehemence which is still imposing after almost a thousand years. Using a balanced patterning and system of repetitions no less sophisticated, if less mannered, than that of Ælfric, Wulfstan's forcefulness is marked most obviously by direct appeals to his audience, such as:

> Leofan men . . . utan don swa us þearf is . . .

a plentiful use of intensifiers, like:

> georne, mid ealle, ealles to swyðe, oft and gelome,

and sentences often beginning with conjunctions which insistently press the sense on to its conclusion: 'What else are all these calamities but the wrath of God on the people!' But although best known for his impassioned style, Wulfstan was also capable of a plainer kind of expository prose, like that in which he reworked Ælfric's sermon on false gods (p. 184), a calm and reasoned dismissal of pagan follies which clearly represent no direct threat to the Church. He is much more concerned with the abuse of the Church by Christian folk, and with such degenerate social habits as those which so upset the author of the anonymous letter to Brother Edward (p. 43). As legislator and canonist, Wulfstan was concerned with moral regeneration in the affairs of both Church and State. In many of the archbishop's sermons we can recognize substantial verbal parallels with some of the laws of Æthelred and Cnut, which we know Wulfstan to have been responsible for drafting (pp. 8, 178). But by far his most important work in this area was to be the so-called *Institutes of Polity*, the most considered Anglo-Saxon legal tract and the earliest vernacular example of the well-defined medieval genre of 'estates literature', the first English document to deal directly with political theory (p. 187). Beginning with a consideration of Christian kingship, going on to set out the duties of each of the governing classes of Anglo-Saxon society, and concluding with reflections on the whole duty of man, its treatment of the relationship between Church and State represents the culmination of implications already present four centuries earlier in the oldest Kentish laws.

It is not insignificant that at the end of his life Wulfstan should have chosen to compose this essay in the Latin Königspiegel tradition in his native tongue. It is clear that by the end of the Anglo-Saxon period there was no genre of literature to which the vernacular was considered inappropriate. It was used not merely for legal documents, which English tradition had long demanded should be in English prose, and for all matters of civil record and daily commerce; it was equally at home in the church, used amidst an enormous number of homilies and sermons, for prayers and liturgies, penitential and martyrological tracts, pastoral letters and even canon law; there were fine idiomatic translations of the gospels and other books of the Bible. And if some scholars like Ælfric were always a little hesitant about embarking on subjects they felt to be the province of scholars alone, and therefore best treated in Latin, the lingua franca of scholarship, others were not. Byrhtferth of Ramsey felt able to compose his elaborate mathematical treatise on the reckoning of time in alternate paragraphs of the highly ornate Latin characteristic of the period, and an idiomatic and confident vernacular prose (p. 265). And it seems taken for granted that botanical and medical text-books, even when dealing with such abstruse matters as the development of the human foetus (p. 263), should be issued in a simple English, eschewing all rhetoric in order to convey facts and instructions economically and with accuracy. But by the side of such pragmatic works, there had developed a taste for tales of oriental wonder. In the Old English *Apollonius of Tyre*, we have not only the first love story in English, but the beginning of a romance genre full of sentimentality, artificiality and exciting incident of the kind which was to become familiar in later medieval times (p. 234). The existence of an extended work of fiction, apparently written purely for pleasure, which uses a highly contrived plot set in an exotic Byzantine world where startling coincidences could and did occur, helps to put the strong Germanic theme of *Beowulf*, the only other sustained narrative fiction in Old English, into perspective.

There is no reason why the remarkable variety of English prose extant on the eve of the Conquest should not have survived the Norman invasion. In the south of England the high quality annals of the Anglo-Saxon Chronicles were maintained unbroken; and at Peterborough certainly continued into the second half of the twelfth century to provide some of the most graphic insights that we possess into the condition of England during the Anarchy.

When in the opening years of the twelfth century the English resistance-fighter Leofric the Deacon wrote a memoir of his friend Hereward the Wake, and the Life of Wulfstan II came to be composed by his one-time chaplain Colman, they both found it natural to do so in English, although we know of them both now only in Latin translations. The works of Alfred, Ælfric and Wulfstan continued to be copied, and therefore presumably in demand, throughout the twelfth century; and indeed the only copies we possess of such works as *The Soliloquies of St Augustine* or the Kentish Laws, we owe to interest taken in them during Norman times. And there can be demonstrated a continuous development of the Old English homiletic and hagiographic traditions to blossom in the literary excellence of Middle English tracts of the *Sawles Ward* and *Ancrene Wisse* type, and the so-called 'Katherine Group' of saints' lives.

Abbreviations

EEMF.   Early English Manuscripts in Facsimile.
EETS.   Early English Text Society.
MGH.   *Monumenta Germaniae Historica.*
PL.   *Patrologia Latina*, ed. J.-P. Migne.

Except where otherwise specified, biblical references are to the Vulgate text.

SELECT BIBLIOGRAPHY

A GENERAL WORKS

ALEXANDER, M. *Old English Literature* (London, 1983).

BATELEY, J. 'The nature of Old English prose', in *The Cambridge Companion to Old English Literature*, ed. M. Godden and M. Lapidge (Cambridge, 1991), 71–87.

CLAYTON, M. 'Homiliaries and Preaching in Anglo-Saxon England', *Peritia*, 4 (1985), 207–42.

GATCH, M. M. *Loyalties and Traditions* (New York, 1971).

—— *Preaching and Theology in Anglo-Saxon England: Ælfric and Wulfstan* (Toronto, 1977).

GORDON, I. A. *The Movement of English Prose* (London, 1966).

GREENFIELD, S. B. and CALDER, D. *A New Critical History of Old English Literature* (New York, 1986).

KER, N. R. *Catalogue of Manuscripts containing Anglo-Saxon* (Oxford, 1990).

LAPIDGE, M. 'The saintly life in Anglo-Saxon England', in *The Cambridge Companion to Old English Literature*, ed. M. Godden and M. Lapidge (Cambridge, 1991), 243–63.

STANLEY, E. G. (ed.) *Continuations and Beginnings* (London, 1966).

SZARMACH, P. E. (ed.) *Studies in Earlier Old English Prose* (Albany, New York, 1986).

SZARMACH, P. E. and HUPPÉ, B. F. (eds.) *The Old English Homily and Its Backgrounds* (Albany, New York, 1978).

WILSON, R. M. *The Lost Literature of Medieval England* (London, 1952).

WRENN, C. L. *A Study of Old English Literature* (London, 1967).

B SPECIFIC STUDIES

Editions and some other works are mentioned in the head-note to each piece.

BAKER, P. S. 'Byrhtferth's Enchiridion and the computus in Oxford, St John's College 17', *Anglo-Saxon England*, 10 (1981), 123–42.

BARLEY, N. F. 'The Letter to Brother Edward', *Neuphilologische Mitteilungen*, 79 (1978), 23–4.

BETHURUM, D. 'Stylistic features of the Old English laws', *Modern Language Review*, 27 (1932), 263–79.

—— 'The form of Ælfric's Lives of Saints', *Studies in Philology*, 29 (1932), 515–33.

BROWN, W. H. 'Method and style in the Old English Pastoral Care', *Journal of English and Germanic Philology*, 68 (1969), 666–84.

CAMERON, M. L. 'Bald's Leechbook: its sources and their use in its compilation', *Anglo-Saxon England*, 12 (1983), 153–82.

—— 'Bald's Leechbook and cultural interactions in Anglo-Saxon England', *Anglo-Saxon England*, 19 (1990), 5–12.

DALBEY, M. A. 'Hortatory tone in the Blickling Homilies', *Neuphilologische Mitteilungen*, 70 (1969), 641–58.

—— 'Patterns of preaching in the Blickling Easter homily', *American Benedictine Review*, 24 (1973), 478–92.

DEEGAN, M. and SCRAGG, D. (eds.) *Medicine in Early Medieval England* (Manchester, 1987).

DONNER, M. 'Prudery in Old English fiction', *Comitatus*, 3 (1972), 91–6.

EKBLOM, R. 'Alfred the Great as geographer', *Studia Neophilologica*, 14 (1941–2), 115–44.

FARRAR, R. S. 'Structure and function in representative Old English saints' lives', *Neophilologus*, 57 (1973), 83–93.

FELL, C. E. 'Some implications of the Boniface correspondence', in *New Readings on Women in Old English Literature*, ed. H. Damico and A. H. Olsen (Bloomington, Indiana, 1990), 29–43.

FOWLER, R. 'Some stylistic features of the Sermo Lupi', *Journal of English and Germanic Philology*, 65 (1966), 1–18.

FRANTZEN, A. J. *King Alfred* (Boston, 1986).

GARMONSWAY, G. N. (ed. and transl.) *The Anglo-Saxon Chronicle* (London, 1953).

—— 'The development of the colloquy', in *The Anglo-Saxons*, ed. P. Clemoes (London, 1959), 248–61.

GEROULD, G. H. 'Abbot Ælfric's rhythmic prose', *Modern Philology*, 22 (1925), 353–66.

GOEPP, P. H. 'The narrative material of Apollonius of Tyre', *English Literary History*, 5 (1938), 150–72.

GRUNDY, L. *Books and Grace: Ælfric's Theology*, London Medieval Studies, 6, 1991.

HART, C. 'Byrhtferth and his Manual', *Medium Ævum*, 41 (1973), 95–109.

HURT, J. *Ælfric* (New York, 1972).

KNOWLES, D. (introd.) *Bede's Ecclesiastical History of the English Nation* (London, 1954).

KOBAYASHI, E. 'On the "lost" portions in the Old English Apollonius of Tyre', in *Explorations in Linguistics*, ed. G. Bedell *et al.* (Tokyo, 1979), 244–50.

KOTZOR, G. 'Anglo-Saxon martyrologists at work: narrative pattern and prose style in Bede and the *Old English Martyrology*', *Leeds Studies in English*, NS 16 (1985), 152–73.

KUBOUCHI, T. 'A note on prose rhythm in Wulfstan's De Falsis Deis', *Poetica*, 15–16 (1983), 57–106.

KUHN, S. M. 'Was Ælfric a poet?', *Philological Quarterly*, 52 (1973), 643–62.

LEINBAUGH, T. H. 'The sources for Ælfric's Easter sermon: the history of the controversy and a new source', *Notes and Queries*, 231 (1986), 294–311.

MALONE, K. 'King Alfred's north: a study in medieval geography', *Speculum*, 5 (1930), 139–67.

MCINTOSH, A. 'Wulfstan's prose', *Proceedings of the British Academy*, 35 (1949), 109–42.

MIDDLETON, A. 'Ælfric's answerable style: the rhetoric of the alliterative prose', *Studies in Medieval Culture*, 4 (1973), 83–91.

MOLONEY, B. 'Another look at Ælfric's use of discourse in some saints' lives', *English Studies*, 63 (1982), 13–19.

OGAWA, H. 'Stylistic features of Old English Apollonius of Tyre', *Poetica*, 34 (1991), 57–74.

ORTON, P. 'King Alfred's prose Preface to the Old English Pastoral Care, LL. 30–41', *Peritia*, 2 (1983), 140–8.

OWEN, G. R. 'Wynflæd's wardrobe', *Anglo-Saxon England*, 8 (1979), 195–222.

PAYNE, F. A. *King Alfred and Boethius* (Madison, 1969).

POTTER, S. 'The Old English Pastoral Care', *Transactions of the Philological Society* (1947), 114–25.

—— 'King Alfred's last preface', *Philologica; the Malone Anniversary Studies* (Baltimore, 1949), 25–30.

—— 'Commentary on King Alfred's Orosius', *Anglia*, 71 (1953), 385–437.

RIEDINGER, A. R. 'The Englishing of Arcestrate: woman in Apollonius of Tyre', in *New Readings on Women in Old English Literature*, ed. H. Damico and A. H. Olsen (Bloomington, Indiana, 1990), 292–306.

SISAM, K. 'An early fragment of the Old English Martyrology', *Review of English Studies*, NS 4 (1953), 209–20.

SZARMACH, P. E. 'The meaning of Alfred's Preface to the Pastoral Care', *Mediaevalia*, 6 (1980), 57–86.

WATERHOUSE, R. 'Ælfric's use of discourse in some saints' lives', *Anglo-Saxon England*, 5 (1976), 83–103.

—— 'Modes of address in Ælfric's Lives of Saints homilies', *Studia Neophilologica*, 54 (1982), 3–24.

WHITELOCK, D. 'Archbishop Wulfstan, homilist and statesman', *Transactions of the Royal Historical Society*, 4th Series, 24 (1942), 25–45.

Anglo-Saxon Prose

LEGAL PROSE

THE LAWS OF WIHTRÆD, 695

Wihtræd came to the throne of Kent in 690 after a period of anarchy, and died in 725. This code was issued early in his reign, and at a time when heathenism was still considered a menace.

The most complete collection of Anglo-Saxon laws, and the sole copy of the laws of the Kentish kings, is that contained in the first part of the Textus Roffensis, a twelfth-century Rochester MS. almost certainly compiled at the time of Bishop Ernulf, 1115–24. The second part consists of a Rochester Cathedral cartulary. There is a complete facsimile edition by P. Sawyer, *Textus Roffensis*, EEMF. VII, XI, Copenhagen, 1957–62.

The text of Wihtræd's code is found on ff. 5–6ᵛ of the Textus Roffensis. It is edited by F. Liebermann, *Die Gesetze der Angelsachsen*, Leipzig, 1903, I, pp. 12–14, and by F. L. Attenborough, *The Laws of the Earliest English Kings*, Cambridge, 1922, pp. 24–31.

These are the decrees of Wihtræd, King of the people of Kent.

During the rule of Wihtræd, the most gracious King of the people of Kent, in the fifth year of his reign, the ninth indiction, the sixth day of Rugern,[1] there was gathered together in the place which is called Berghamstyde[2] a deliberative assembly of notable men. Berhtwald, Archbishop of Britain, was there, and the aforenamed king; there was also present the Bishop of Rochester (the one who was called Gefmund); and every order of the Church of the nation declared itself in agreement with the loyal people. There, with the consent of all, the notable men devised these decrees and added them to the legal customs of the people of Kent, as it tells and declares hereafter:

1. The Church shall have freedom from taxation; and they are to pray for the king, and honour him of their own free will, without compulsion.

2. [Violation of] the Church's protection is to be fifty shillings, like the king's.

3. Men living in an illicit union are to turn to a righteous life

---

[1] Literally 'Rye-harvest'; presumably therefore August.
[2] Probably Bearsted near Maidstone.

with repentance of sins, or to be excluded from the fellowship of the Church.

4. Foreigners, if they will not regularize their marriages, are to depart from the land with their possessions and with their sins; our own men in the nation are to forfeit the fellowship of the Church, without suffering confiscation of property.

5. If, after this assembly, it happens that a noble-born man enter into an illicit union contrary to the command of the king and the bishop and the decree of books,[1] he is to compensate his lord a hundred shillings, according to ancient law. If it be a common man, he is to compensate fifty shillings; and both are to forsake that union, with repentance.

6. If a priest allow an illicit union, or neglect the baptism of a sick man, or be so drunk that he cannot, he is to cease his ministration pending the bishop's judgement.

7. If a tonsured man under no authority goes looking for hospitality, they are to give it to him once; and it is not to happen that they entertain him longer, unless he has permission.

8. If anyone grant his man freedom at the altar, he is to have the rights of a freeman of the people; the freedom-giver is to have his inheritance and wergild[2] and guardianship of his family, wherever he may be, even across the frontier.

9. If a servant, contrary to his lord's command, perform servile work between sunset on Saturday evening and sunset on Sunday evening, he is to compensate his lord eighty sceattas.[3]

10. If a servant ride on his own business on that day, he is to compensate his lord six [sceattas], or be flogged.

11. If, however, a freeman [work] during the forbidden time, he is to forfeit his healsfang;[4] and the man who detects it is to have half the fine and [the profit of] that work.

12. If a husband sacrifice to devils without his wife's knowledge, he is to forfeit all his property or his healsfang. If they both sacrifice to devils, they are to forfeit healsfang and all their property.

13. If a slave sacrifice to devils, he is to compensate six shillings or be flogged.

---

[1] Presumably ecclesiastical canons.
[2] Literally 'man-price', the monetary value set on a man according to his rank, and used as a yard-stick for assessing either fines or compensation.
[3] An early coin valued at one twentieth of a shilling.
[4] Literally 'an embrace', a technical term apparently applied to a proportion of the wergild.

14. If anyone give his household meat during a fast, he is to redeem both freeman and slave with healsfang.

15. If a slave eat it of his own accord, [he is to compensate] six shillings or be flogged.

16. A bishop's word and the king's is to be incontrovertible without an oath.

17. The head of a monastery is to clear himself with a priest's exculpation.

18. A priest is to purge himself by his own asseveration, in his holy vestments before the altar saying thus: *Veritatem dico in Christo, non mentior.*[1] A deacon is to purge himself similarly.

19. A cleric is to purge himself with three of his equals, his hand alone on the altar; the others are to stand by to discharge an oath.

20. A stranger is to purge himself at the altar with his own oath; similarly, a king's thegn.

21. A common man [is to purge] himself at the altar with three of his equals; and the oath of all of these is to be incontrovertible. Then the Church's right of exculpation is:

22. If anyone accuse a bishop's servant or a king's, he is to clear himself by the hand of the reeve: the reeve is either to purge him or give him up to be flogged.

23. If anyone accuse a bond-servant of the Church in their midst, his lord, if he be a communicant, is to clear him by his oath alone; if he is not a communicant, he is to have a second good compurgator in the oath,[2] or pay, or give him up to be flogged.

24. If a layman's servant accuse the servant of a cleric, or a cleric's servant accuse the servant of a layman, his lord is to clear him by his oath alone.

25. If anyone slay a man in the act of thieving, he is to lie without wergild.

26. If anyone catch a freeman in possession of the goods, then the king is to decide one of three things: either he is to be killed, or sold overseas, or redeemed with his wergild. He who catches and secures him is to have half; if he is killed they are to give him seventy shillings.

27. If a slave steal and they ransom him, [it is to be for] seventy

---

[1] 'I speak the truth in Christ, I do not lie.'

[2] The following compurgation formula is found, together with other forms of oaths, on f. 38ᵛ of the Textus Roffensis (printed by Liebermann, p. 398): 'In the name of Almighty God, I stand here thus as a true witness to X, unbidden and unbought; thus I saw with my eyes and heard with my ears, that which I say with him.'

shillings, whatever the king wish; if they kill him, they are to pay half to the owner.

28. If a traveller from afar or a foreigner leave the road, and he then neither shouts nor blows a horn, he is to be regarded as a thief, to be either killed or ransomed.

AN ANGLO-DANISH PEACE-TREATY, 878

After Guthrum's defeat by Alfred at Edington in 878, it was clear that the great Danish invasion of the mid-ninth century had reached stalemate. The country was partitioned, oaths and hostages were exchanged, and Guthrum's army retired into the north and east part of England, subsequently known as Danelaw.

The terms of the Anglo-Danish peace-treaty then drawn up are found in Corpus Christi College, Cambridge, MS. 383, an important eleventh- or twelfth-century collection of laws and other documents related for the most part to those of the Textus Roffensis (see p. 3), and probably itself from St Paul's Cathedral library. Two versions of the treaty are found, a shorter and a longer, occupying pp. 6 and 83–4 respectively, in the same twelfth-century hand. Both versions are printed by F. Liebermann, pp. 126–8, and the longer only, by Attenborough, pp. 98–100 (see p. 3).

This is the peace which King Alfred and King Guthrum and the councillors of all the English race and all the nation which is in East Anglia have all agreed upon and confirmed with oaths, for themselves and for their subjects, for those both born and unborn, who care for God's favour and ours.

1. First concerning our boundaries: up the Thames, and then up the Lea, and along the Lea to its source, then in a straight line to Bedford, then up the Ouse to Watling Street.

2. Then this. If a man be slain, we will reckon English and Danish at an equal value: at eight half-marks[1] of refined gold, except for the peasant who occupies rented land, and their freedmen; those are also valued equally: both at two hundred shillings.

3. And if anyone accuse a king's thegn of manslaughter, if he dare clear himself by oath, he is to do it with twelve king's thegns; if anyone accuse a man who is less powerful than a king's thegn, he is to clear himself by oath with eleven of his equals and with one king's thegn – and thus in every case which involves more than four mancuses[2] – and if he dare not, he is to pay a three-fold compensation, whatever it is valued at.

[1] A Scandinavian measure of weight.
[2] A gold coin equal to thirty pence.

4. And that each man is to know his guarantor [when buying] men, and horses and oxen.

5. And on the day when the oaths were sworn we all said that neither slave nor freemen might go without permission into the Viking host, any more than any of theirs to us. If, however, it happen that from necessity any of them wish to trade with us or we with them, in cattle and in goods, it is to be allowed, on condition that hostages shall be given as a pledge of peace and as evidence that one may know that no deceit is intended.[1]

TRIAL BY ORDEAL

Under certain circumstances an accused man might be required to undergo a ritual ordeal as a test of guilt or innocence. Three basic forms of the ordeal seem to have been known to the Anglo-Saxons. The accused might be cast into water to see whether he floated or sank, or he might be given bread or cheese to swallow to see whether or not he choked with guilt, or he might be required to lift a stone or iron ball out of boiling water.

The following formula is found in the Textus Roffensis f. 32, and is printed by Liebermann, pp. 386–7, and Attenborough, pp. 170–2 (see p. 3).

Decree Concerning Hot Iron and Water

1. And of the ordeal, we charge by the commands of God and of the archbishop and all the bishops, that no man come into the church after they carry in the fire with which they must heat the ordeal, except for the priest and he who must undergo it. And from the stake to the mark shall be measured nine feet, by the feet of the man who undergoes it. And if it be by water, they are to heat it until it becomes hot enough to boil, whether the vessel be iron or bronze, lead or clay.

2. And if the accusation be 'single', the hand is to be plunged in up to the wrist to reach the stone, and if it be three-fold, up to the elbow.

3. And when the ordeal be ready, then two men from either side are to go in, and they are to be agreed that it be as hot as we said earlier.

4. And an equal number of men from either side are to go in and stand down the church on both sides of the ordeal; and all those are to be fasting and abstaining from their wives at night; and the

---

[1] Literally, 'know that one has a clean back'.

priest is to sprinkle holy water over them all – and each of them is to taste the holy water – and to give them all the book to kiss, and the sign of Christ's cross. And no one is to continue making up the fire after they begin the consecration; but the iron is to lie upon the embers until the last collect; then they are to lay it upon the post, and no other words are to be spoken inside, except that they are earnestly to pray Almighty God that he make the whole truth plain.

5. And he is to undergo it, and they are to seal up the hand; and after the third day they are to look and see whether it be corrupt or clean within the seal.

6. And the ordeal is to be invalid for him who breaks these rules, and he is to pay the king a hundred-and-twenty shillings as a fine.

THE LAWS OF ÆTHELRED, 1008

This was the fifth code issued by Æthelred and the first in which the hand of the statesman Archbishop Wulfstan is unmistakably present. The Latin paraphrase of a second, rather longer recension, perhaps drawn up for his northern province, but usually recognized as a separate, sixth code, specifically acknowledges Wulfstan's part in its compilation.

Two copies of this code are found in Wulfstan's own hand-book, British Library MS. Cotton Nero A 1, ff. 89–92ᵛ and 116ᵛ–19ᵛ (see p. 178); and there is a further copy in Corpus Christi College, Cambridge, MS. 201B, pp. 48–52, which contains homilies, laws and other matters of interest to Wulfstan, as well as the Old English Apollonius of Tyre (see p. 234).

The text is edited by Liebermann (see p. 3), pp. 236–47, and A. J. Robertson, *The Laws of the Kings of England from Edmund to Henry I*, Cambridge, 1925, pp. 78–90.

In nomine domini, anno dominicae incarnationis mviii.[1] This is the decree which the King of the English and both ecclesiastical and lay councillors have devised and decreed.

1. First then this: that we should all love and honour one God and earnestly hold to one Christian faith and completely cast out every heathen practice; and we have all confirmed both with word and with pledge that we will hold to one Christian faith under one royal authority. And it is the decree of our lord and his councillors that just laws be raised up and every injustice zealously be suppressed, and that every man be allowed the benefit of law, and that peace and friendship be justly maintained in this land in the sight of God and the world.

2. And it is the decree of our lord and his councillors that

---

[1] In the name of the Lord, from the year of the Lord's birth 1008.

Christian men and the uncondemned are not to be sold out of the land, especially not into the heathen nation. But care is diligently to be taken that those souls which God bought with his own life be not destroyed.

3. And it is the decree of our lord and his councillors that Christian men be not condemned to death for all too small offences. But on the contrary, merciful punishments are to be decreed for the benefit of the people, and God's handiwork and his own purchase which he dearly bought be not destroyed for small offences.

4. And it is the decree of our lord and his councillors that men of every order are each earnestly to submit to that duty which befits them, in the sight of God and the world. And especially God's servants – bishops and abbots, monks and women in orders, priests and nuns – are to submit to duty and live according to rule and to intercede diligently for all Christian people.

5. And it is the decree of our lord and his councillors that every monk who is out of a monastery and not observing a rule, is to do what is needful for him: willingly submit to a monastery with all humility, and cease from misdeeds and atone very diligently for what he has violated; he is to consider the word and pledge which he gave to God.

6. And the monk who has no monastery is to come to the bishop of the region and pledge himself to God and to men that thenceforth he will at least observe three things, that is, his chastity, and monastic dress, and the service of his Lord, as well as ever he can. And if he carry out that then he will be entitled to the greater consideration, wherever he dwell.

7. And canons, where there is property so that they can have a refectory and dormitory, are to maintain their minster with justice and chastity, as their rule directs; otherwise it is right that he who will not do so should forfeit the property.

8. And we entreat and admonish all priests to defend themselves against the wrath of God.

9. They know full well that they may not lawfully have sexual intercourse with a woman. But he who will abstain from this and maintain chastity, may have the favour of God, and in addition, as a worldly honour, be entitled to a thegn's wergild and a thegn's privileges both in life and in the grave. And he who will not do what befits his order, may impair his dignity in the sight of both God and the world.

10. And also every Christian man is diligently to avoid unlawful intercourse and justly keep the divine laws. And every church is to be under the protection of God and of the king and of all Christian people. And henceforth no man is to bring a church under subjection, or make a church the subject of illegal trade, or expel a minister of the church without the bishop's consent.

11. And God's dues are to be diligently paid every year. That is: plough-alms fifteen days after Easter, and the tithe of young live-stock by Pentecost, and of the fruits of the earth by All Saints Day, and 'Rome-money'[1] by St Peter's Day and lighting-dues three times a year.

12. And it is best that payment for the soul always be paid at the open grave. And if any body be buried elsewhere outside of the parish, payment for the soul is nevertheless to be paid to the minster to which it belongs. And all God's dues are to be diligently furthered, as is necessary. And festivals and fasts are to be properly observed.

13. The Sunday festival is to be diligently observed, as befits it. And markets and public meetings are to be willingly abstained from on that holy day.

14. And all St Mary's festivals are to be diligently honoured, first with a fast and afterwards with a feast. And at the festival of each apostle there is to be fasting and feasting, except that at the festival of Philip and James we enjoin no fast, because of the Easter feast.

15. Otherwise, other feasts and fasts are to be diligently kept, just as those kept them who kept them best.

16. And the councillors have determined that St Edward's[2] Day shall be celebrated throughout England on the 18th of March, (17) and a fast every Friday, unless it be a festival.

18. And ordeals and oaths[3] are forbidden on festivals and legal Ember days and from the Advent of the Lord until the octave of Epiphany and from Septuagesima until fifteen days after Easter.

19. And at those holy seasons, as it is right, there is to be peace and unity among all Christian men, and every dissension is to be set aside.

20. And if anyone owe someone else a debt or compensation in respect of worldly matters, he is diligently to pay it before or after.

---

[1] The tax of 'Peter's pence', cf. p. 27.
[2] See p. 180ff.
[3] Cf. p. 7.

21. And every widow who conducts herself correctly is to be under the protection of God and of the king. And each is to remain without a husband for twelve months; afterwards she herself is to choose what she will.

22. And every Christian man is to do what is needful for him: diligently take heed of his Christian faith, and frequently attend confession, and make known his sins unhesitatingly and atone earnestly, as he is directed. And also everyone is to prepare himself for attending Eucharist, often and frequently, and order words and actions aright, and carefully keep oath and pledge.

23. And every injustice is to be diligently cast out from this land, so far as it can be done.

24. And deceitful actions and hateful abuses are to be severely shunned, that is: false weights and wrong measures and lying testimonies and shameful frauds, (25) and dreadful perjuries, and devilish acts of murder and of manslaughter, of stealing and of robbery, of avarice and of greed, of over-eating and of over-drinking, of deceits and various breaches of law, of injuries to clergy and of adultery, and of many kinds of misdeeds.

26. But henceforth God's law is to be earnestly loved in word and deed; then God will at once become gracious to this nation. And one is to be diligent about improvement of the peace and improvement of the coinage everywhere in the land, and about the repair of fortresses in every region, and about military service also, according to what is decreed, whenever there be need, (27) and about the provision of ships, as zealously as possible, so that each may be equipped immediately after Easter every year.

28. And if anyone without permission desert an army in which the king himself is, it is at peril to himself and all his possessions; and he who otherwise deserts the army is to forfeit a hundred-and-twenty shillings.

29. And if any excommunicated man – unless it be one seeking protection – remain anywhere in the neighbourhood of the king before he has earnestly submitted to divine penance, then it is at peril to himself and all his property.

30. And if anyone plot against the king's life, he is to forfeit his life; and if he wish to clear himself by oath, he is to do it at [the value of] the king's wergild, or with the three-fold ordeal[1] in English law.

[1] See p. 7.

31. And if anyone commit ambush or open resistance anywhere against the law of Christ or the king, he is to pay wergild, or fine, or compensation, depending on what the need be. And if he illegally resist with assault, and so bring it about that he is killed, he is to lie without compensation to any of his friends.

32. And henceforth forever the injustices which before this were too widely habitual, are to cease.

33. And every injustice is to be diligently suppressed. Because it is only by suppressing wrong and loving righteousness that there will be any improvement in the land, in the sight of God and the world.

34. We must all love and honour one God, and completely cast out every heathen practice.

35. And let us loyally hold to one royal lord, and all defend life and land together as well as ever we can, and from our inmost heart beseech Almighty God for help.

DOCUMENTARY PROSE

THE BURGHAL HIDAGE

The so-called 'Burghal Hidage' enumerates a ring of forts defending Wessex at the opening of the tenth century. The list begins on the Kent/Sussex border then traverses the coastal counties as far as Devon, returning with a more northerly sequence along the Severn estuary and the line of the Thames. Responsibility for the physical maintenance and manning of each fort was distributed among the surrounding villages, calculated in proportion to the number of hides each contained. A further paragraph describes the basis of assessment by which the walls were maintained and defended. This memorandum was apparently drawn up after 914 when the fortress was built at Buckingham, but before Edward the Elder assumed full control of Mercia in 919.

Our text was originally contained in a collection of legal and historical documents compiled at Winchester from the mid-tenth to early eleventh century: British Library MS. Cotton Otho B XI. This MS. was almost totally destroyed by fire in 1731 – during which the folio containing the Burghal Hidage was irretrievably lost. But the text survives in a transcript made by Laurence Nowell in 1562: British Library Additional MS. 43703, ff. 255–6. It is edited by R. Flower, *London Medieval Studies*, 1 (1937), 60–4, and by A. J. Robertson, *Anglo-Saxon Charters*, Cambridge, 1939, pp. 246–9; see also D. Hill, 'The Burghal Hidage: The Establishment of a Text', *Medieval Archaeology*, 13 (1969), 84–92. The first section is also found in a number of thirteenth- and fourteenth-century copies, adding statistics for forts in Worcestershire, Warwickshire and Essex, by way of an appendix.

Three hundred hides[1] belong to Eorpeburnan[2] – and 24 hides; to Hastings belong 5 hundred hides; and to Lewes belong twelve hundred hides; and to Burpham belong seven hundred hides and 20 hides; to Chichester belong 15 hundred hides; then belong to Portchester 5 hundred hides; and one-and-a-half hundred hides belong to Southampton; and to Winchester belong twenty-four hundred hides; and to Wilton belong fourteen hundred hides; and to Chisbury belong 5 hundred hides; and to Twyneham belong 5 hundred hides less 30 hides; and to Wareham belong 16 hundred hides; and to Bredy belong eight hundred hides less forty hides; and to Exeter belong four and 30 hides and 7 hundred hides; and to Halwell belong three hundred hides; and to Lydford belong one-and-a-half hundred hides less 10 hides; and to Pilton belong

---

[1] *Hide*: originally as much land as would support one family.
[2] Unidentified, but possibly Castle Toll, Newenden, Kent.

four hundred hides less 40 hides; and to Watchet belong 5 hundred hides and 13 hides; and to Axbridge belong four hundred hides; and to Lyng belong 100 hides; and to Langport belong 6 hundred hides; and to Bath belong ten hundred hides; and twelve hundred hides belong to Malmesbury; and to Cricklade belong 14 hundred hides; and 15 hundred hides to Oxford; and to Wallingford belong 24 hundred hides; and 16 hundred hides belong to Buckingham; and to Sashes[1] belong 10 hundred hides; and 6 hundred hides belong to Eashing; and to Southwark belong eighteen hundred hides.

For one acre's-breadth[2] of wall-maintenance and guarding it, requires 16 hides. If each hide is represented by one man, you can allocate four men to each rod. Then for twenty rods there are required eighty hides in wall-maintenance; and by the same reckoning as I have reckoned above, a furlong requires one-and-a-half hundred hides and 10 hides. For two furlongs 20 hides and three hundred hides serve; then for three furlongs eighty hides and 400 hides are required; for 4 furlongs 40 hides and 6 hundred hides; for five furlongs' circuit eight hundred hides are required in wall-maintenance; for six furlongs requires sixty hides and nine hundred hides; for 7 furlongs, 20 hides and 11 hundred hides; for eight furlongs' circuit, eighty hides in wall-maintenance and 12 hundred hides; for nine furlongs, 40 hides and 14 hundred hides; for 10 furlongs requires 16 hundred hides; for 11 furlongs requires 60 hides and 17 hundred hides; for 12 furlongs' circuit requires 20 hides and nineteen hundred hides in wall-maintenance. If the circuit is greater, you can easily work out the additional amount from this table, since one furlong always requires sixty men and 100; then each rod is allocated four men.

GRANT OF LAND AT CREDITON, 739

This land charter is item 1 in the Crawford Collection of documents, Bodleian MS. Eng. hist. a.2. It conveys land at Crediton, Devon from Æthelheard King of the West Saxons to Forthhere Bishop of Sherborne, for the purposes of founding a monastery there. The charter is dated 10 April 739, but survives only in an eleventh-century copy. A tenth-century copy of the boundaries alone is number 2 of the Crawford Collection. The boundary description is lengthy, an unusual feature for such an early document, and may have been elaborated at an intervening stage. As customary with this type of document, the first and last paragraphs are in Latin.

1 An island in the Thames at Cookham, Berkshire.
2 The 'breadth' of an acre is four rods (poles or perches), i.e. one chain.

The text is edited by A. S. Napier and W. H. Stevenson, *The Crawford Collection of Early Charters and Documents*, Oxford, 1895, pp. 1–3, and by W. de G. Birch, *Cartularium Saxonicum*, London, 1885–99, III, pp. 666–8.

+ *In the name of the Lord God, Jesus Christ the Saviour. According to the Apostle, all things that are seen are transitory and those that are not seen are eternal.*[1] *Therefore perpetual and lasting things ought to be purchased with things earthly and perishable, God granting his support. Wherefore I, King Æthelheard, have taken care to bestow for ever on our bishop, Forthhere, some land for the construction of a monastery, that is, twenty hides in the place which is called Creedy, with all the privileges existing in it; and I have confirmed this gift before appropriate witnesses, so that no one may violate what has been enacted before such distinguished councillors without danger to his soul.*

Now these are the lands. First from the Creedy bridge to the highway, along the highway to the plough ford on the Exe, then along the Exe until the grassy islets, from the grassy islets onto the boundary ridge, from the boundary ridge to Luha's tree, from Luha's tree to the enclosure gate, from the enclosure gate to Dodda's ridge, from Dodda's ridge to Grendel's pit, from Grendel's pit to the ivy grove, from the ivy grove to the ford at Woodcock hollow, from the ford at Woodcock hollow to 'Fernbury', from 'Fernbury' to the Eagle ridge, from Eagle ridge to the ford in the wooded hollow, from the wooded hollow to Tettanburn, from Tettanburn upstream until the Lily brook, from the Lily brook to the middle ridge, from the middle ridge to the ford on the highway, from the ford on the highway to Cyrtlan gate, from Cyrtlan gate to the crab-apple, from the crab-apple to the green road, from the green road to the wolf-trap, from the wolf-trap upstream to where the water-course divides, then up the middle of the ridge, along the ridge until the path, from the path straight as a shaft to the alder, south over to the precipice, from the precipice to the head of Birch hollow, from the head of Birch hollow to Hana's ford, thence to the broad ash, from the broad ash to the head of Fox hollow, thence to the stone ford on the Yeo, from the stone ford to the alder-copse, from the alder copse to the land-slip, thence to the green hill, from the green hill to the highway, to the kite's post, thence to Beornwine's tree, thence to the billy-goat's ford, from the billy-goat's ford to Brunwold's tree,

[1] 2 Corinthians, IV 18.

thence to Ash hollow, then to the brook, along the stream to the Teign, upstream on the Teign to the road ford, thence to Franca's hollow, from Franca's hollow to the head of Dirtcombe, thence to the deer pool, from the deer pool to the long stone, thence to the head of Hurra's hollow, from the head of Hurra's hollow to the rushy ford on the Nymet, thence to the higher hill, from the higher hill to the wren's stronghold, thence to Cydda's ford, from Cydda's ford to Cæfca's grove, thence to Cain's acre, from Cain's acre to the head of Wolf hollow, thence to the stone mound, from the stone mound to the cress pool, from the cress pool to the fuel ford, thence to the dyke's gate, from the dyke's gate to Unna's mound, thence to the Pig hollow, from Pig hollow to Egesa's tree. On the Nymet until the Dalch, upstream until the willow slade, from the willow slade to eight oaks, thence to Hawk hollow, from Hawk hollow to the enclosure gate, thence out on the precipice, thence to Beonna's ford on the Creedy, thence upstream until Hawk hollow, thence to the enclosure gate, thence to the old highway until the East Creedy, then along the stream to Creedy bridge.

And to this land I will add this freedom, and establish firmly that it is to be immune and eternally secure from all monetary requirements and all royal matters and secular works, except only for military matters. Whosoever augments it, may his benefits be increased, and whosoever diminishes or alters it, may his joy be turned to sorrow, and may he suffer hell-torments for ever. This grant was made in the year of the incarnation of our Lord Jesus Christ 739, the seventh indiction, on the 10th of April.

+ Sign of the hand of King Æthelheard. + Sign of the hand of Cuthred.[1] + Sign of the hand of Frithogyth.[2] + I Daniel, bishop,[3] have signed canonically. + I Forthhere, bishop, have agreed and signed. + Sign of the hand of Ealdorman Herefrith. + Sign of the hand of Abbot Dudda. + Sign of the hand of Ealdorman Ecgfrith. + Sign of the hand of Ealdorman Puttoc.

RECORDS OF TIDENHAM MANOR, GLOUCESTERSHIRE

Tidenham was a large and valuable estate occupying the tongue of land between the River

---

[1] Probably Æthelheard's successor, who came to the throne about 740.
[2] Æthelheard's queen.
[3] Bishop of Winchester 705–44.

Wye and the Severn Estuary. Across the Wye lay Wales. The estate was traversed by the Roman road from Gloucester to Caerleon, and Offa's Dyke began here. Belonging originally to the bishops of Llandaff and then the kings of Wessex, in 956 Tidenham was granted by King Eadwig to Bath Abbey which in turn, some time between 1061 and 1065, leased it to Archbishop Stigand.

The sole copy of the relevant documentation is found in a late twelfth-century cartulary of the Abbey of Bath: Corpus Christi College, Cambridge, MS. 111, pp. 57–8, 73–5. It is edited by W. Hunt, *Two Chartularies of the Priory of St Peter At Bath*, [London] 1893, pp. 5–6, 18–19, and W. de G. Birch, *Cartularium Saxicum*, London, 1885–99, III, pp. 100–3. In the following translation, place-names are kept as close as possible to the original source, thus: Street rather than Stroat, King's-farm rather than Sedbury. See also generally F. Seebohm, *The English Village Community*, London, 1883, pp. 148–59.

Grant by King Eadwig to Bath Abbey, 956

An elaborate Latin preamble, drawn up in the first year of King Eadwig's reign, transfers this land to the monastery of St Peter in Bath, 'where there are pleasant baths emanating from the warm springs there'. It is to include rights over: fields, pastures, meadows, woods and fisheries, and be free from all secular obligations, save for the universal requirements (*trimoda necessitas*) of military service, bridge- and fortress-construction.[1] There follows an impressive anathema – invoking eternal hell-fire and devils with iron goads – against those who seek to divert the terms of this grant. Then, in English, come the boundaries of the estate itself:

These are the land-boundaries at Tidenham. From Wye-mouth to the yew-tree's headland,[2] from the yew-tree's headland onto the stone row, from the stone row onto the shining corner, from the shining corner onto the yew-wood, from the yew-wood onto the broad marsh, from the broad marsh onto the double ford, from the double ford onto the east island creek out into the Severn.

The document is then affirmed by Eadwig and his brother Eadgar, Archbishop Oda, and an impressive list of no less than nine bishops, six *duces* and fourteen *ministri*.

Description of the Estate

In Tidenham there are 30 hides: 9 of demesne land, and 21 hides of tenanted land. At Street there are 12 hides – 27 rods of rent-land, and on the Severn 30 basket-weirs.[3] At Middle-farm 5 hides

---

[1] Cf. the estate memorandum, below, p. 26.
[2] 'Headland' here in the sense of a spit of land around which water flows.
[3] A fish-trap constructed out of creels on a wooden framework.

– 13 rods of rent-land, 14 basket-weirs on the Severn, and 2 grid-weirs[1] on the Wye. At King's-farm are 5 hides – 13 rods of rent-land, and 1 hide above 'The Dyke' that is now also rent-land; and that outside the enclosure is still partly demesne land. Part of it is appointed for rent to the Welsh boatmen. At King's-farm, on the Severn 21 basket-weirs, and on the Wye 12. At Bishop's-farm are 3 hides, and 15 basket-weirs on the Wye. In Llan Cewydd[2] are 3 hides and 2 grid-weirs on the Wye, and 9 basket-weirs.

Throughout all that estate the due per rod is 12 pence and 4 'alms-pence'. At each weir which is within the 30 hides every alternate fish belongs to the landlord, and each rare fish which is of value – sturgeon and porpoise, river- or sea-fish; and nobody is to sell any fish for money when the lord is on the estate before telling him about it.

From Tidenham much levied-work is due. The geneat[3] must work either on the estate or off the estate, whichever you bid, and ride, and perform carrying services, and supply cartage, drive herds and do many other things. The gebur[4] must perform his duties: he must plough half an acre as week-work, and himself fetch the seed from the lord's barn – a whole one for church-dues from his own barn however.[5] For weir-construction 40 larger or one fother of [small] poles, or build 8 yokes for 3 tides,[6] 15 poles for field-fencing, or ditch 5, fence and ditch 1 rod of the fort-enclosure, reap an acre-and-a-half, mow half, [and] work at other works, always in proportion to the work. Supply: 6 pence after Easter, half a sester[7] of honey; at Lammas 6 sesters of malt; at Martinmas a ball of good net-yarn. On the same estate it stands that he who has 7 pigs shall supply 3, and thereafter always the tenth – and even so a mast-levy when there is mast.

Lease to Archbishop Stigand, 1061–5

Here it is declared in this document that Abbot Ælfwig and all the fellowship at Bath have leased 30 hides of land at Tidenham to Archbishop Stigand for his lifetime, for 10 marks of gold and for 20 pounds of silver; and after his day it shall revert to the holy

[1] A fence-like contrivance for catching salmon.
[2] A Welsh place-name: 'St Cewydd's Church', presently Landcaut.
[3] For this class see 'Duties and Perquisites', below, p. 27.
[4] The lowest rank of freeman, see 'Duties and Perquisites', below, pp. 27–8.
[5] I.e. a whole acre, and with seed from his own barn.
[6] I.e. spring, middle and neap tides.
[7] A measure of uncertain quantity; perhaps twelve bushels or two gallons.

minster, with its produce and its people, as fully and as completely as it then is – and in addition 1 mark of gold, and 6 porpoises, and 30 thousand herrings each year.

As witness to this: King Edward, and the Lady Eadgyth, and Archbishop Ealdred, and Bishop Hereman, and Bishop Gisa, and Earl Harold, and Earl Tostig, and Abbot Æthelnoth, and Abbot Æthelwig, and Abbot Æthelsige, and Abbot Ordric, and Esgar the Staller,[1] and Ralph the Staller, and Bondig the Staller, and many other good men whose names are not written here.

And if any man be so bold as to want to alter this, be he anathematized by Christ and by Saint Mary and by Saint Peter the holy apostle, and by all Christ's saints, for ever in eternity, unless he afterwards very rapidly make reparation for it.

TWO EXETER DONATIONS

In about 932 Athelstan founded at Exeter a monastery, dedicated to St Mary and St Peter. He endowed it munificently, and most notably gave a collection of some twelve dozen holy relics including those of Christ and the Apostles as well as those of local saints like Sidwell and Petroc. He expelled those Britons who remained in the city and rebuilt its walls. Subsequently Athelstan's foundation acquired cathedral status when in 1050 the see of Crediton was transferred to Exeter for greater safety, Bishop Leofric installing canons in place of the monks. By this time the foundation had become impoverished, and when Leofric died in 1072, he bequeathed to the cathedral a long list of estates and personal property including several books which may still be identified.

Records of both donations are found in a preliminary quire added to the front of one of the books Leofric gave to the cathedral, a tenth-century French copy of the Gospels: Bodleian Library MS. Auct. D.2.16. The records occupy ff. 8–14 and 1–2 respectively. Two further copies of the Leofric bequest were made in two other of Leofric's books: the copy of the Gospels that contains the apocryphal Gospel of Nicodemus (see p. 207), and the Exeter Book of Old English verse.

Both texts were printed in W. Dugdale, *Monasticon Anglicanum*, London, 1817–30, II, pp. 527–9. There is a critical edition of the former by M. Förster, *Zur Geschichte des Reliquienkultus in Altengland*, Munich, 1943, pp. 63–114, and of the latter by A. J. Robertson, *Anglo-Saxon Charters*, Cambridge, 1939, pp. 226–30, and together with a facsimile in *The Exeter Book of Old English Poetry*, ed. R. W. Chambers *et al.*, Exeter, 1933.

I The Athelstan Donation

Here in this document is described the collection of holy relics which Athelstan, the celebrated king, gave to the monastery of St Mary and St Peter at Exeter, to the praise of God, for the redemption of his soul and all those who seek out and honour the holy place for eternal salvation.

---

[1] A Scandinavian term for a post apparently equivalent to Marshal or Constable.

Assuredly the same King Athelstan, when he came to the kingdom after his father Edward – and by the grace of God ruled all of England singly, which prior to him many kings had shared between them – on one occasion came here to Exeter,[1] so it was said of old in the sayings of the most righteous men. And he began to debate and take council as to how he might best promote, from his royal treasury, the praise of God and his own and his nation's eternal profit.

Almighty God, who is ever a help and assistance to all those who intend well, sent to the good king the idea that with transitory treasures he should obtain imperishable treasures. So he sent overseas loyal and discriminating men. And they went to lands as distant as they could travel, and with those treasures acquired the most precious treasures that might ever be acquired on earth, which was the greatest collection of relics gathered together from every place far and wide. And they brought them to the aforesaid king; and for that the king with great joy thanked God.

Then he commanded that here in Exeter, where God had previously sent him the edifying idea, they should build a monastery to the honour of God and of the heavenly queen St Mary, Christ's mother, and of St Peter the chief Apostle, whom the same king had chosen as his patron. And he gave to the place twenty-six manors, and he bestowed the third part of the aforesaid relics on the place for the eternal redemption of his soul, and as a help to all those who with faith seek out and honour the holy place in which the collection of relics is.

Now we wish to tell you, without any deception, what the collection of relics is, which is here in this holy minster, and forthwith set out the inscriptions which make clear without any doubt what each one of those relics is.

First, from the same precious wood of the holy cross on which Christ suffered and thereon redeemed us all from the power of the Devil. From the Lord's sepulchre. From the garment which our Lord himself wore when he was here in the world among men. From the manger in which our Lord lay when he was born of St Mary. From the Jordan in which our Lord was baptized. From the spear with which our Lord's holy side was opened on the cross. From the table on which the Saviour refreshed himself with his

[1] The occasion of an important assembly held probably near the middle of Athelstan's reign, 924–39. A law code issued at the time says that it was held over Christmas.

twelve Apostles. From Mount Sinai, upon which God appeared to the holy Moses and there revealed to him the old law. From the thorn bush which miraculously burned and yet was unharmed by every burning, when God himself spoke with the holy Moses from the same thorn. From the mountain upon which our Lord fasted. From the candle which the angel of God kindled with heavenly light at our Lord's sepulchre on Easter Eve. From the altar which our Lord himself consecrated. From the place where our Lord was conceived. From Mount Olivet, upon which the Saviour prayed to his heavenly Father on bended knees prior to his passion; and afterwards he ascended into heaven from that same mountain. From the garment of the heavenly lady St Mary. From the head-dress of the same mother of God, and from her hair. From a certain holy place which the archangel Michael revealed on earth.[1] From the body of St John the Baptist and from his dress. From the beard of St Peter the Apostle. From St Peter's hair. From St Peter's garment. From the neckbone of St Paul the Apostle, and from his clothes. From the staff of St Andrew the Apostle. From the clothes of St John the Apostle and Evangelist, who was so loved by our Lord that at his meal he leaned upon his breast. And when he suffered for us on the cross, then he committed his dear mother St Mary to that same John, his beloved, so that he should take care of her.

Here also is part of that heavenly food which was found in the tomb of John the Apostle. From the head of St Bartholomew the Apostle. From relics of St James the Apostle. From the head of St Stephen the first of Christ's martyrs, and from his holy blood, and from the stone with which he was stoned to death. From the martyr St Olympanus, who was kinsman of the Apostle Peter. From the relics of the noble martyr St Lawrence, and from the coals with which for Christ's name he was roasted.[2] From the deacon and martyr St Vincent. From the bones of Christ's illustrious champion and martyr St George. Several bones of the martyr St Sebastian. From relics of the two brothers and martyrs Tiburtius and Valerian. From the pope and martyr St Urban. From the bishop and martyr St Apollinaris. From bones of the martyr St Candidus. From relics of the martyr St Maurice. From the martyr St Quintinus. From the martyrs Lucian and Maximian. From St Quirinus, martyr. From the pope and martyr St

[1] See p. 129.
[2] See p. 163.

Cornelius. From St Marcellus. From St Peter the martyr. From St Julian the martyr. From relics of the celebrated deacon and martyr St Cyriacus. From relics of the martyr Chrysanthus and the virgin Daria.[1] From the martyr St Gervase. From the martyr St Christopher.[2] From the body of the martyr St Conan. From the martyr St Vitus. From the precious martyrs Crispin and Crispianus. From relics of the martyr St Nicasius. From relics of St Juvenalis, and from his arm. From the martyr St Tiburtius. From the blood of the martyr St Vivian. From the martyr Euresius. From bones of the martyr St Benignus. From the noble martyr St Pancras. From St Desiderius the martyr. From the martyr St Justus and from St Laudus. From the pope St Felix. From bones of the martyr St Caesarius and from his clothes. From the martyr St Eustace. From relics of St Edward the King, who was slain, guiltless; but Christ afterwards honoured him with many signs.[3]

Also here there are relics of many martyrs who for Christ's name were martyred in Jerusalem. From St Vitalis the un-vanquished martyr, who for Christ's name was thus buried alive in the ground and there crushed to death with earth and stones. But now he lives with bliss in the heavenly firmament and benevolently intercedes with Christ for all those who here in the earth with faith call on him. Here also is the tooth of the blessed martyr St Maurice who suffered for Christ's name under the Emperor Maximian. And six thousand and sixty-six martyrs suffered with him in addition, who attained the crown of martyrdom entirely through his exhortation.

These moreover are the relics of the holy confessors, that is 'acknowledgers' of Christ, who renounced this treacherous world and with austere conduct merited the heavenly kingdom. First, from the relics of the celebrated bishop St Martin, who here in life, among many other signs, raised up three men to life from death with his prayers. From the celebrated pope St Silvester. From St Gregory. From the noble teacher St Jerome, who among many other books which he composed, nobly translated from Hebrew and Greek into Latin the great Bible in which there are seventy-two books. From relics of St Augustine, the wise and learned bishop, who composed a thousand books in praise of Christ and for the eternal profit of all Christ's congregation. From the

[1] See pp. 85–6.
[2] See pp. 79–80.
[3] See p. 180.

apostolic St Germanus, who in this country and in other countries also on all sides wrought many miracles through God. From St Basilius' tooth and from his pastoral staff. From the body of the bishop St Evurtius, to whom when he performed the mass there appeared *dextera Dei*, that is the right hand of God, and blessed the offering with a heavenly blessing. From relics of St Audoen. From bones of the bishop St Maurilius. From the bishop St Gall. From the bishop St Lupus. From the holy abbot St Benedict. From relics of the precious bishop St Remigius who converted all the Frankish kingdom to the faith of Christ; and from his cope and from his tunic and from his hair-shirt that he wore. From the body of the holy bishop St Anianus. From the body of St Maximin, confessor. From relics of the bishop St Wulfram. From St Crispus. From relics of the venerable and the favoured bishop St Nicholas, who through the power of God makes known many good things everywhere on sea and on land to those who with faith inwardly call on him in God's name. From bones of St Petroc, and from his hair and from his clothes. From the abbot St Winwaloc. From the bishop St Winard. From St Winnoc. From St Wigenoc. From the hair of the bishop St Tuda. From relics of the illustrious bishop St Odo. From the arm of the bishop St Juvenal. From the arm of the bishop St Donatus. From the arm of St Hipolytus, Christ's confessor. From the head of St Conogan and from his arm. From relics of St Designatus. Rib of St Avitus the bishop. From bones of the bishop St Melanius. From the body of the bishop St Withenoc. From relics of St Valerian. From St Tudwal. From the sepulchre of St Simeon. From the stone which St Silvanius three times carried to Rome. From clothes of St Salvinus. From St Maioc and St Ermelan. From the bishop St Liudger. From St Sigebrand. From the precious saint of Christ St Marcellus, and from St Vivian. From the holy abbot St Wulfmar. From relics of the holy deacon St Peter, who was pupil of St Gregory the noble pope who sent baptism here to this land and Christianity to us Englishmen.

Also here are relics of many holy women and of the holy virgins of Christ, who through the grace of God vanquished the ancient devil and all fleshly lusts, and, some through conduct of holy life, some through victorious martyrdom, are joined to Christ the heavenly bridegroom. First, from the finger-joint of St Mary Magdalen, who here in life washed our Lord's feet with her tears, whom our Lord greatly loved and honoured in that when he arose from death he wished to appear first to her. From St Elisabeth.

From relics of St Agatha,[1] some four of her teeth and from her holy veil. From the holy virgin St Juliana, who in the strife of her martyrdom was so greatly strengthened by divine grace that she bound and flogged the devil who came to her in prison. From the noble virgin St Cecilia. From St Agnes. From the virgin St Praxedis. From St Eugenia. Rib of the holy virgin St Felicula. From St Margaret. From St Lucia. From St Mamilla. From the holy queen St Baldhild. From St Leonilla. From the noble virgin St Gertrude. From relics of St Genevieve. From St Morwenna. From the holy servant of Christ St Ælfgifu, who would daily perform her confession before she went into church. From the gentle virgin St Sidwell who, guiltless, was slain by her father's mower; and afterwards Almighty God displayed many miracles at her tomb. From St Sigeburgh. From St Werburgh. Cheek-bone of the precious virgin St Bridget who in life here wrought many miracles through God and enlightened the hearts of many men through the example of her holy conduct.

II The Leofric Bequest

Here in this gospel book is described what Bishop Leofric has bestowed upon the minster of St Peter's at Exeter where his episcopal seat is. With the help of God and through his advocacy and through his treasure: he restored what was previously alienated, that is, first, the estate of Culmstock; and the estates at Branscombe and Salcombe; and the estate at St Mary Church; and the estates at Staverton and at Sparkwell; and the estate at Marshall; and Sidwell's plot; and the estate at Brightston; and the estate at Topsham, although Harold took it away illegally; and the estate at Stoke; and the estate at Sidbury; and the estates at Newton and at Norton; and the estate at Clyst that Wid had. Then these are the additional estates with which he has endowed the monastery from his own possessions, for the sake of his lords' souls and his own, for the maintenance of the servants of God who have to intercede for their souls, that is: first, the estates at Bampton and at Aston and at Chimney;[2] and the estates at Dawlish and at Holcombe and at Southwood. And when he took over the monastery he found no more estates belonging to it there

---

[1] See p. 164.
[2] These three estates are in Oxfordshire; all the remainder are in South Devon.

than an estate of two hides at Ide – and there was no more livestock on it than seven bullocks.

This then is the acknowledgement by which he has acknowledged God and St Peter in church treasures for the holy minster. That is, he has bestowed on it there: two episcopal crosses and two large decorated crosses, besides other small silver neck-crosses, and two large decorated gospel books, and three decorated reliquaries, and one decorated altar, and five silver chalices, and four corporals, and one silver tube, and five complete mass-vestments, and two dalmatics, and three epistle-vestments, and four sub-deacon's maniples, and three cantor's copes and three cantor's staffs, and five costly altar-cloths, and seven coverings, and two carpets, and three bear-skins, and seven seat-covers, and three dorsals, and two wall-hangings, and six mazers, and two decorated bowls, and four horns, and two large decorated candlesticks, and six smaller decorated candlesticks, and one silver censer with a silver incense-spoon, and eight cups, and two standards, and one banner, and six chests, and one military waggon, and one casket – and formerly there were only seven hanging-bells, and now there are sixteen hanging- and twelve hand-bells – and two complete missals, and one collectarium, and two epistle-books, and two complete choral books, and one nocturnale, and one *Ad te levavi*,[1] and one book of tropes, and two psalters, and a third psalter as they sing it at Rome, and two hymnals, and one valuable benedictional and three others, and one English gospel book,[2] and two summer lectionaries, and one winter lectionary, and the *Regula Canonicorum*, and a martyrology, and one book of canon law in Latin, and one penitential in English, and one complete homiliary for winter and summer, and Boethius' book in English,[3] and one large English book about various things composed in verse.[4] And when he took over the monastery he found no more books than one capitulary, and one worn-out nocturnale, and one epistle-book, and two very poor worn-out lectionaries, and one poor mass- vestment.

And he acquired many Latin books for the monastery, as follows: the *Liber Pastoralis*,[5] and the *Liber Dialogorum*, and the books of the four prophets, and Boethius' book *De Consola-*

---

[1] The opening words of the office for Advent Sunday.
[2] That containing the apocryphal Gospel of Nicodemus, see p. 207.
[3] See p. xvii; the Exeter copy has not survived.
[4] The Exeter Book.
[5] See p. 60.

tione, and the *Isagoge* of Porphyrius, and one *Passionalis*, and Prosper's book, and Prudentius' book *Psychomachia*, and Prudentius' *Liber Hymnorum*, and Prudentius' *Liber de Martyribus*, and the book of the prophet Ezekiel, and the *Song of Songs*, and the book of the prophet Isaiah separately, and Isidore's book *Etymologiae*, and the *Passiones Apostolorum*, and Bede's *Expositio super Evangelium Lucae*, and Bede's *Expositio super Apocalipsin*, and Bede's *Expositio super Septem Epistolas Canonicas*, and Isidore's book *De Novo et Veteri Testamento*, and Isidore's book *De Miraculis Christi*, and Orosius' book,[1] and the *Liber Machabeorum*, and Persius' book, and Sedulius' book, and Arator's book, and the *Diadema Monachorum*, and the glossaries of Statius, and the *Liber Officialis* of Amalarius.

And after his death he there bestows his chapel along with himself, in respect of all those things which he himself performed in God's service, on the condition that in their prayers and services the servants of God who are there continually commend his soul to Christ and to St Peter and to all the saints to whom the holy minster is consecrated, that his soul may be the more acceptable to God.

And may he who wishes to deprive God and St Peter of this gift and this grant be deprived of the kingdom of heaven, and be he eternally condemned to the torment of hell.

TWO ESTATE MEMORANDA

These two tracts, drawn up probably some time during the tenth or eleventh century, provide close insight into the management of an estate during the later Anglo-Saxon period. They occupy pp. 96–107 of the same collection of laws and other documents that contains the Alfred-Guthrum Peace Treaty (see p. 6). The texts are edited by Liebermann, pp. 444–55 (see p. 3).

I Duties and Perquisites

The thegn's law. The law of the thegn is that he be entitled to his chartered estates, and that he perform three things in respect of his land: military service and the repair of fortresses and work on bridges. Also on many estates further land-duties arise by order of the king, such as [servicing the] deer-fence at the king's residence, and equipping a guard-ship and guarding the coast, and attend-

1 See p. 62.

ance on his superior, and [supplying a] military guard, almsgiving and church dues, and many other different things.

The geneat's[1] duty. The geneat's duty varies, depending upon what is determined for the estate. In some he must pay ground rent and one store-pig a year, and ride, and carry and supply cartage, work and entertain his lord, reap and mow, cut deer-fences and maintain hides, build and fence fortifications, conduct strangers to the manor, pay church dues and alms, attend his superior, and guard the horses, carry messages far and near, wherever he is directed.

The cottager's duty. The cottager's duty depends upon what is determined for the estate. In some he must work for his lord each Monday throughout the year, or three days each week at harvest-time. He need not pay ground rent. He ought to have five acres; more, if it be the custom on the estate; and if it ever be less, it will be too little, because his labour must always be available. He is to pay his hearth-penny[2] on Ascension Day, just as every freeman ought, and serve on his lord's estate, if he is ordered, by guarding the coast, and [work] at the king's deer-fence, and at similar things according to what his rank is; and he is to pay his church dues at Martinmas.

The gebur's[3] duties. The gebur's duties vary; in some places they are heavy, in others moderate. On some estates it is such that he must perform such work as he is directed from two week-days each week for every week throughout the year, and three week-days at harvest-time, and three from Candlemas to Easter; if he performs cartage, he need not work while his horse is out. At Michaelmas he must pay ten pence tax, and at Martinmas twenty-three sesters of barley and two hens; at Easter one young sheep or twopence. And from Martinmas until Easter he must lie at his lord's fold as often as it is his turn. And from the time when they first plough until Martinmas he must plough one acre each week and prepare the seed in the lord's barn himself; also two acres for the asking, and two for pasture; if he need more grass, then he is to earn it as he is allowed. He is to plough his three acres as tribute-land and sow it from his own barn. And he is to pay his hearth-penny. And every two are to support one deer-hound. And each tenant is to give six loaves to the swine-herd when he drives

---

[1] Originally the 'companion' of heroic society; a tenant of some standing.
[2] The tax of 'Peter's pence', levied on every house.
[3] The lowest rank of free-man, roughly comparable with the later villein.

his herd to the mast-pasture. On the same estate where these arrangements exist they ought to give the tenant, for the occupation of the land: two oxen and one cow and six sheep and seven sown acres on his piece of land. He is to perform all the duties which appertain to him throughout the year. And they are to give him tools for his work and utensils for his house. When death befalls him, his lord is to take charge of what he leaves.

This estate-law exists on certain estates; at some places, as I have said, it is heavier, at some places also lighter; for all estate-customs are not alike. On some estates a tenant must pay tax in honey, on some tax in food, on some tax in ale. He who looks after the administration is to take care that he always knows what is the ancient arrangement on the estate, and what the custom of the people.

Concerning him who looks after the bees. If he maintain a swarm subject to tax, the beekeeper ought to pay what is arranged on the estate. With us it is arranged that he pay five sesters of honey as tax; on some estates a greater tax arrangement pertains. Also, at certain times, he must be ready for many kinds of work at his lord's pleasure, besides ploughing on request and reaping on request and mowing meadows. And if he is well provided with land, he must be supplied with a horse so that he may furnish the lord with a beast of burden or go out himself, whichever he is directed. And a man of such condition must do many things; I cannot recount them all now. When death befall him, the lord is to take charge of what he leaves, except for what should be free.

The taxable swineherd. The taxable swineherd ought to pay for his butchering, according to what is determined on the estate. On many estates it is the custom that he supply fifteen pigs for killing every year, ten old and five young – he is to have for himself whatever he rears beyond that; on many estates a greater swineherd's due pertains. Each swineherd is to take care that after the slaughter of his swine he prepare and singe them properly: then he will be fully entitled to the perquisites. He must also, as I said before about the bee-keeper, always be ready for every sort of work, and provided with a horse at the lord's need. After death, a slave swineherd and a slave bee-keeper are subject to one law.

Concerning the swineherd who goes with the property. The swineherd belonging to the property who keeps the estate herd ought to have a young pig to keep in a sty, and his perquisites when he has prepared the bacon, and the other rights which pertain to a slave.

Concerning men's provisions. One servant ought to have as provisions: twelve pounds of good corn and the carcasses of two sheep and one good cow for eating and the right of cutting wood according to the custom of the estate.

Concerning women's provisions. For a female slave: eight pounds of corn for food, one sheep or threepence for winter supplies, one sester of beans for Lenten supplies, whey in summer or one penny. All serfs ought to have Christmas supplies and Easter supplies, an acre for the plough and a 'handful of the harvest', in addition to their necessary rights.

Concerning retainers. A retainer ought to have what he might earn in twelve months from two acres, one sown and the other unsown; he is to sow the one himself; and he ought to have his food and shoes and gloves. If he can earn more, he is to keep the profit himself.

Concerning the sower. When he has properly sown every seed throughout the space of a year, a sower ought to have one basket-full of every kind of seed.

Concerning the oxherd. With his ealdorman's knowledge, the oxherd may pasture two or more oxen with the lord's herd on the common pasture – with that to earn shoes and gloves for himself. And his food-cow may go with the lord's oxen.

Concerning the cowherd. A cowherd ought to have an old cow's milk for seven days after she has newly calved, and the beestings of a young cow for a fortnight. And his food-cow is to go with the lord's cows.

Concerning the shepherd. The shepherd's right is that he have twelve nights' dung at Christmas, and one lamb from the year's young, and one bellwether's fleece, and the milk of his flock for seven days after the equinox, and a bowl-full of whey or buttermilk all summer.

Concerning the goatherd. A goatherd ought to have the milk of his herd after Martinmas, and before that his share of whey and one year-old kid, if he takes good care of his herd.

Concerning the cheese-maker. To the cheese-maker pertain a hundred cheeses, and that she make butter for the lord's table from the wrung-out whey; and let her have all the buttermilk except for the herdsman's share.

Concerning the granary-keeper. The granary-keeper ought to

have the corn spilt at the barn door at harvest-time, if his ealdorman allow him it, and he deserve it with faithfulness.

Concerning the beadle. Because of his office, the beadle ought to be more free from work than other men, since he must always be ready. Also he ought to have some small piece of land for his labour.

Concerning the forester. The forester ought to have every tree brought down by the wind.

It is appropriate that they reward the hayward's labour from those parts which lie near the pasture; because if he has previously neglected it, he can expect [to be blamed for damage to sown fields].[1] And if he is granted such a piece of land, by common law it must be nearest the pasture; because if out of laziness he neglect his lord's, his own will not be well protected, if it be provided thus. Then if he properly guards all he must look after, he will be fully entitled to a good reward.

As I said before, estate laws are various. Nor do we apply these regulations, which we have previously spoken about, in all districts. But we tell what the custom is where it is known to us. If we learn better, we will readily delight in and maintain it, according to the custom of the people among whom we then live. Wherefore one must learn the laws in the district lovingly, if one does not wish to lose good opinion on the estate. There are many common rights; in some districts there are due: winter supplies, Easter supplies, a harvest-feast for reaping, a drinking-feast for ploughing, a reward for mowing, a meal at the haystack, a log from the waggon at wood-carrying, a rick-cup at corn-carrying, and many things which I cannot recount. However, this is a memorandum of men's provisions, and all that I have previously related.

II The Discriminating Reeve

The discriminating reeve must know both the lord's rights respecting the estate and the rights of the people according to how councillors of olden days have decided it – and the season for every occupation which appertains to the manor, because on many estates the occupation comes earlier than on others: both an

---

[1] Presumably as a result of dissatisfied straying animals. The defective text is restored from a contemporary Latin translation.

earlier time for ploughing and an earlier mowing, and so also both
winter hill-pasturing and every other kind of occupation.

He who looks after the administration is to take care that he
protect and promote everything according to what is best for it;
and also according as he is able, as the weather directs him. He
must prudently consider and diligently look into all those matters
which may be to the lord's advantage.

If he wants to begin well, he may not be lax nor too over-
bearing; but he ought to know both the lesser and the greater,
both the more and the less important of what appertains to the
manor, both in the manor and on the down, both in the woods
and in the water, both in field and in fold, both indoors and
out. Because I tell the truth: should he be disdainful or negligent
to undertake and attend to what appertains to cow-shed or
to threshing-floor, it will soon be apparent in what appertains
to them in the barn.

But I advise that he do as I said previously: take care of both the
more important matters and the less, so that neither go wrong if
he can help it, not grain nor sheaf, not meat nor lard, not cheese
nor rennet, nor any of those things that can ever be profitable. A
good reeve must look after his lord's affairs thus, do what he will
with his own. The more diligent he is the more he will be valued, if
he conducts himself in common with the wise.

He must always stimulate his servants with admonition as to
what the lord requires, and also reward them according to what
they merit. He should never allow his servants to over-rule him,
but he is to command each one with the authority of the lord
according to the rights of the people: it is better for him to be
forever out of office than in, if those whom he should govern can
govern him; it is not prudent for a lord to allow that.

He can always find something in which he can be useful, and
make those useful things which will help him. However, it is most
necessary that he discover how he may promote the well-being of
the soil by cultivation, when it be time.

In May and June and July in summer one may: harrow, carry
out manure, procure sheep-hurdles, shear sheep, build, repair,
construct in timber, cut wood, weed, make folds, construct a fish-
weir and mill; at harvest time reap, in August and September and
October: mow, cut wood, gather in many crops, thatch, cover
over and clean out folds, make ready cow-sheds and also pig-sties
before too severe a winter come to the manor, and in addition

diligently promote the well-being of the soil; in winter, plough, and in hard frosts: cleave timber, establish an orchard, and perform many indoor jobs, thresh, chop wood, make cattle-stalls and pig-sties, build a stove at the threshing-floor – for an oven and kiln, and many things requisite to the manor – and a hen-roost also; in spring, plough and graft, sow beans, plant out a vineyard, dig ditches, cut a deer-fence, and soon after that, if the weather be fine, plant madder, sow flax, and woad-seed as well, plant out herbs, and many things; I cannot recount all that a good reeve must see to.

He can always find something to repair on the manor – he need never be idle when he is in it: put the house in good order, set to rights and make it clean, and fence drains, repair breaches in the dykes, make good the fences, root out weeds, make walk-ways between the houses, make tables and benches, provide horse-stalls, maintain the flooring, or such things as may be profitable.

He must provide many tools for the manor, and keep many implements for the buildings: axe, adze, bill, awl, plane, saw, spoke-shave, tie hook, auger, mattock, crow-bar, share, coulter; and also goad-iron, scythe, sickle, hoe, spade, shovel, woad-trowel, barrow, broom, mallet, rake, fork, ladder, curry-comb and shears, fire-tongs, steelyard; and many cloth-working tools: flax-lines, spindle, reel, yarn-winder, stoddle, beams, press, comb, card, weft, woof, wool-comb, roller, slay, crank, shuttle, seam-pegs, shears, needle, beater.

And if he has skilled workmen he must assist them with tools: miller, shoe-maker, lead-founder, and other workers – each occu-pation will itself show what pertains to it; there is no man that can enumerate all the tools which one must have.

One must have: waggon covers, ploughing gear, harrowing tackle and many things which I cannot now name, as well as: a measure, awl, threshing-floor flail, and many utensils: cauldron, leaden vessel, kettle, ladle, pans, pots, fire-dog, dishes, skillets, tubs, buckets, churn, cheese-vat, bags, punnets, bushels, sieves, seed-basket, riddle, hair-sieve, sieve-rack, fans, troughs, ash-wood pails, hives, honey-bins, beer-barrels, bath-tub, dishes, flasks, bowls, basins, cups, strainers, candlesticks, salt-cellar, spoon-case, pepper-horn, chests, coffers, yeast-boxes, seats, stools, chairs, bowls, lamp, lantern, leather bottles, resin-box, comb, cattle-bin, manger, fire-screen, meal-store, eel-tank, oven-rake, dung-shovel.

It is difficult to tell all that he who looks after the administration must think of. He must neglect nothing that might ever prove useful: not even a mousetrap therefore, or what is still more trivial, a hasp-peg. Many things are necessary for the faithful reeve of a household and a frugal governor of men. I have set out what I know; let him who is better informed explain it more fully.

REGULATIONS OF THE CAMBRIDGE THEGNS' GUILD

In a number of places we hear of the existence of various social groupings with mutual interests: clubs or associations who needed to regularize their proceedings. At Cambridge, men of thegnly status linking together in a guild for mutual benefit, arrived at a code of behaviour to govern guildhall meetings and cover certain arrangements in the case of death of one of their members, or to maintain a feud. Often having some religious basis, such associations typically entered their records into space left in a church book.

This text was written in the late tenth century on a blank leaf (now detached) of an eighth-century gospel-book which once belonged to the Abbey of Ely: British Library MS. Cotton Tiberius B V, f. 74. The text was edited by G. Hickes, *Linguarum Veterum Septentrionalium Thesaurus Grammatico-Criticus et Archaeologicus*, Oxford, 1703–5, IV, pp. 20–1, and by B. Thorpe, *Diplomatarium Anglicum Ævi Saxonici*, London, 1865, pp. 610–13.

Here in this document is the declaration of the agreement which this association has agreed in the Thegns' Guild in Cambridge. That is, then:

First, that each should give the others an oath of true loyalty – on holy relics – in respect of God and of the world; and all the association would always support him who had most right.

If any guild-member pass away, all the guild-membership is to bring him to where he wanted; and he who does not come for that [is to pay] the guild a sester of honey; and the guild-membership is to provide half the feast for him who has passed away; and each shall contribute two pence for the alms-giving; and from that they are to bring the appropriate amount to St Audrey.[1] And then, if any guild-member be in need of his association's help, and it is made known to the reeve of the nearest guild-member (unless the guild-member himself be near), and the reeve neglects it, he is to pay one pound. If the lord neglects it, he is to pay one pound, unless he be about [his] lord's necessary business or a sick-bed.

And if anyone slay a guild-member, there is to be nothing other than eight pounds in compensation. If the slayer sneers at

---

[1] I.e. Ely Cathedral, resting-place of the seventh-century abbess St Æthelthrytha; see also pp. 82–3.

compensation, all the guild-membership is to avenge the guild-member – and all are to bear [the feud]. If then someone avenges him, all are to bear it alike.

And if any guild-member should slay any man, and does it as a compelled-avenger and in compensation for the insult to him, and the slain man be worth twelve-hundred,[1] each guild-member should assist with half-a-mark for assistance; if the slain man be a ceorl, two oras;[2] if he be servile,[3] one ora.

However, if the guild-member slay anyone in folly and in error, he himself should bear responsibility for what he has done. And if a guild-member slay a guild-member through his own folly, he himself is to bear responsibility towards the relatives for what he violated, and buy back his guild-membership with eight pounds – or forfeit association and friendship for ever. And if a guild-member eat or drink with the one who slew his fellow-guild-member (unless it be in the presence of king, or diocesan bishop, or ealdorman), he should pay one pound – unless he, with two of his bench-fellows, can deny that he knew him.

If any guild-member malign another, he is to pay a sester of honey, unless he clear himself with two of his bench-fellows. If a retainer draw a weapon, the lord is to pay one pound; and the lord is to get from him what he can, and all the guild-membership is to assist him in recovering his money. And if a retainer wound another, the lord is to avenge it, and all the guild-membership together; so that, resort to whatever he may resort, he shall not have life.

And if a retainer sit within the partition, he is to pay a sester of honey; and if anyone has someone sitting at his feet, he is to do the same.

And if any guild-member pass away or fall sick outside the area, his fellow guild-members are to fetch him, and bring him, dead or living, to where he wants, under the same penalty as has been stated if he pass away at home and a guild-member not attend the body. And the guild-member who does not attend his morning-discussion[4] is to pay his sester of honey.

---

[1] I.e. 1,200 shillings, the wergild of a thegn.
[2] A unit of currency (but not a coin) introduced by the Danes and worth sixteen pence or one eighth of a mark.
[3] Literally, 'if he be Welsh'.
[4] A business-meeting held the morning after a guild-feast.

A WITCH DROWNED

This exchange of lands between Æthelwold, Bishop of Winchester 963–84, and a certain Wulfstan Uccea can be dated some time between 963 and 975. The record survived copied into a twelfth-century Peterborough cartulary: Society of Antiquaries of London MS. 60, ff. 54ᵛ–5. The text is printed by W. de G. Birch, *Cartularium Saxonicum*, London, 1885–99, III, pp. 372–3, and A. J. Robertson, *Anglo-Saxon Charters*, Cambridge, 1939, p. 68.

It is declared here in this document that Bishop Æthelwold and Wulfstan Uccea have exchanged estates with the cognisance of King Edgar and of his councillors. The bishop gave Wulfstan the estate at Washington[1] and Wulfstan gave him the estate at Yaxley[2] and at Ailsworth.[3] Then the bishop gave the estate at Yaxley to Thorney[4] and that at Ailsworth to Peterborough. And the estate at Ailsworth had been forfeited by a widow and her son because they drove an iron pin into Wulfstan's father, Ælfsige; and it was discovered, and they took the deadly thing from her closet. Then they seized the woman and drowned her at London Bridge; and her son got away and became an outlaw. And the estate went into the hands of the king, and the king then granted it to Ælfsige; and afterwards his son, Wulfstan Uccea, gave it to Bishop Æthelwold, just as it says above.

[1] Sussex.
[2] Huntingdonshire.
[3] Northamptonshire.
[4] Thorney Abbey, Cambridgeshire.

LETTERS

Vernacular letters of a domestic kind rarely if ever survive – but note the tone of that addressed to Brother Edward (below, p. 43). On the other hand, Latin correspondence was voluminous in certain ecclesiastical circles. Occasionally taking the form of significant official memoranda, this could acquire historiographic status (e.g. the exchanges between Pope Gregory and the missionary Augustine as cited by Bede, *Ecclesiastical History*, I, *passim*). Where translated, as in the case of Wynfrith's reporting on a monk's out-of-the-body experience, it was clearly because the theme was of general interest. More often than not, however, it will have been with particular institutional purposes in mind: copied on – perhaps even fictionalized – with some ulterior motive – as with the 'Letter from Edwin to Ælfsige' (below, p. 44) which was presumably intended to lend authority to the custom described. But the later Anglo-Saxon royal secretariat certainly recognized the need for an official writ to be despatched in English, cf. p. 43.

WYNFRITH TO EADBURGA, 716–17

Wynfrith, better known under his later adopted name of Boniface, was educated in monasteries at Exeter and Nursling, and later worked in the north German mission-field, where in 755 he was eventually slain by a pagan Frisian war-band – and promptly recognized as a saint in his homeland. During his years abroad he maintained a regular correspondence, in Latin (E. Dümmler, ed., *S. Bonifatii et Lulli Epistolae, MGH, Epistolae*, III, vi, Berlin, 1892) with friends at home – sending presents such as hunting-birds and weapons to Æthelbald of Mercia.[1] He wrote frequently to English nuns of his acquaintance, who would send him gifts of clothing or books in exchange for small luxuries such as pepper, spices, incense or wine. He enjoyed especially good relations with members of the community at Minster-in-Thanet and its abbess Eadburga (familiarly 'Bugga'), a West Saxon princess, successor of St Mildred at Minster,[2] 'dearest of all her sex' – whom he asks for a special copy of the Epistles of St Peter to be written in gold lettering so as to impress his 'carnally minded' audience, and to whom he relays advice to delay visiting Rome until the Saracen threat be passed. This particular letter (Dümmler, pp. 252–7) was written in response to her request for a reliable account of an 'out-of-the-body' experience reported by a monk from Much Wenlock; and it is not until he has been able to interview the monk personally that he replies.

The theme was a popular one at this date (cf. below, pp. 73, 86, 97, 135). The English text – more a reworking than a translation – survives in an early eleventh-century miscellany, probably from Worcester, including, appropriately, a version of Wærferth's translation of Gregory's *Dialogues*, homilies, fragments of lives of the fathers, etc.: British Library MS. Cotton Otho C 1, Vol. 2, ff. 143ᵛ–6. The text was edited by K. Sisam, *Modern Language Review*, 18 (1923), 253–72. The English version omits the opening and concluding formulae, and changes from third to first person narrative and back again without warning.

---

[1] Cf. The Life of Guthlac, below, pp. 107–8.
[2] Cf. 'Trouble at Sandwich', below, p. 205.

To the blessed virgin, so very loved, Lady Eadburga, praise-worthy for her long perseverance in the observance of the monastic life, Wynfrith, one of the least in Christ Jesus, sends most affectionate greeting. You have asked me, dearest sister, to describe to you in writing the marvellous visions of the man who recently died and came to life again in the convent of the Abbess Milburga,[1] as they were revealed to him and were related to me by the venerable Abbess Hildelida.[2] And now, thanks be to Almighty God, I am able to fulfil your wish more completely and more accurately because I myself recently spoke with the aforesaid resurrected brother when he returned to this country from overseas.

Here it says in this book that Dom Wynfrith first sent this letter to this country, concerning a certain priest who had passed away for a time and then returned to his body again. He said that he came to this country and that he spoke with the priest. And he then told me the wonderful sight which he saw when he was out of the body, and he told me this entirely in his own words.

He said that, a toll having been taken, his body had become sick, and was suddenly deprived of spirit. And it seemed to him that it was like when a man has open eyes covered over with a thick garment; and then suddenly the covering was taken away, and then was revealed to his sight all the things which he never saw before, nor were disclosed; and everything that he saw was completely strange to him. And then eventually all the dark covering was thrown from off his eyes: then it seemed to him that all this middle-earth were gathered before his bodily sight; and he surveyed all peoples and all parts of the earth, and waters of the sea, in a single view. And it seemed to him then that angels who were such as if they were burning, then led him out of the body, and he might not look on them for anything, because of the great brightness with which they were surrounded; and they sang with very pleasant and very harmonious voices, and they said: *Domine, ne in ira tua arguas me, neque in furore tuo corripias me,* that is, 'Lord, rebuke us not in thy wrath, neither chasten us in thy hot displeasure.'[3] And he said that they raised him up into the air; and he then saw fire burning, encircling around all this

---

[1] I.e. Much Wenlock, Shropshire; like Whitby and its continental prototypes, a double monastery for both sexes, ruled by an abbess.

[2] A constant correspondent of Wynfrith, the now very elderly Abbess of Barking, Essex, to whom Aldhelm dedicated his *De Virginitate*.

[3] Psalm XXXVII 2.

middle-earth, and the flame was blasting forth with very immense greatness. And it was very terrible ascending; 'and when I surveyed it, all this middle-earth and all its works looked like nothing other than a ball of thread. And I saw that that fire would blast over the whole middle-earth if the angel had not set Christ's cross-symbol against the fire, and thus stayed it. And the flame prevailed in a great part. And I was quite intolerably hurt in my eyes from the terror of the great burning; and most of all, my sight was stinted because of the brightness of the shining spirits. And then in the bright sight an angel touched my head, and through that I was kept safe and sound from the danger of those flames.'

And he said that, in the time he was out of his body, there was gathered thither so great a host of souls passing forth, as he did not imagine that all human kind were so countless a host as that was. And he said also that there was a great host of cursed spirits, and also those bright angels who were speaking there: they had a great dispute with the cursed spirits about the faithful souls who were going out from the body: and the devils were accusing the souls, and they were heaping the weight of their sins on them; the angels were excusing and lightening their sins.

And the man said that he himself heard all his wickedness and his own sins which he had committed from his youth, or that he committed in carelessness, his sins that he had not wished to confess, and that he committed in forgetfulness, or that he did not entirely know involved sin. And each of those sins called out in its own voice against him, and they grievously rebuked him; and every one of those sins which he committed in his youth, in its own person was brought forth in their midst; and they were speaking thus. One said: 'I am your covetousness by which you illicitly coveted against God's commandment.' One said: 'I am the vain boasting, which you boastfully raised up among men.' One said: 'I am the lying with which you sinned when you were lying.' One said: 'I am the frivolous word which you spoke idly.' One said: 'I am the sight through which you transgressed.' One said: 'I am the shamelessness and disobedience with which you were disobedient to your spiritual superiors.' One said: 'I am the torpor and laziness with which you were careless in devotion to holy writ.' One said: 'I am the wandering thought and frivolous amusement with which you endanger other men's lives and lose your own life, and I busied you overmuch in church and out of church.' One said: 'I am the sloth with which you were affected so that you rose late to confess God.' One said: 'I am the frivolity . . .' And they said a lot of things like this to him. And all that he had committed in his living days of his life, which he neglected to confess, and many sins there which he never imagined involved sin, cried out very terribly against him; and the cursed spirits were in chorus with all those sins; and they were accusing him very bitterly, and they were telling all the places and all the times in which those crimes were done. And he saw there also a certain one of those men whom earlier while he was living he wounded; and the man was still alive – but he was led thither as witness of his evil; and the wound was open and the blood was flowing, and it was calling out in its own voice, and expressing opprobrium, and he drew attention to the blood's flux very cruelly, and he imputed and heaped a great multitude of sins on him. And the ancient enemies affirmed and declared that he was in their power and their portion.

'Then the few strengths which I, wretched, unworthily and imperfectly practised, excused me. One said: "I am the fasting with which he cleansed his body against evil desires." One said: "I am the pure prayer that he poured out in the Lord's sight." One said: "I am the service to the weak, which he kindly performed for the sick." One said: "I am the psalmody which he performed for God in recompense for his frivolous words." ' And thus each of those strengths called out for him and was excusing him against his sins. And the angelic spirits also were magnifying these, 'and they then affirmed those strengths which were defending me; and my strengths seemed much greater than ever I imagined that I could have performed by my own strength'.

And he said also that he saw fiery pits in the nether regions of the middle-earth, and they were blasting upwards very terribly; and in among the fiery flames he saw flying wretched spirits, which were in the likeness of dark birds; and they were weeping and teeth-gnashing and bewailing with human voice their own fear and that present torment; and for a little time they sat on the edges of the pits, and afterwards they always fell wailing into the pits. Then one of the holy angels said to him: 'This little rest signifies that the Almighty Lord will grant these souls coolness and rest after the coming Doomsday.'

And under those pits, in the nether hell, the man heard a very terrible groaning and very great lament of those wailing souls. Then one of the angels said to him: 'This groaning and this lament which you hear here in this nether hell, those are the souls to whom the kind mercy of God will never come; but they must suffer the eternal flame.'

And he also saw there in a certain place a very wonderful beauty, and there rejoiced a host of very beautiful souls; then they invited him to come into their bliss, if he were allowed. There came thence a very great sound, and he was in a very great sweetness: this, then, was the breath of those blessed souls. This place was, then, the famous Paradise, as the angels told him that it was.

And he saw there a fiery river, which was filled with boiling torment,[1] and it was all burning on the inside, and it was a wonderful terror; and there was a log over the river like a bridge. Then the holy souls hastened to that bridge from the meeting they were at, and they were eager that they should cross over the river. Then some of them crossed very resolutely over the bridge. And some of them were slipping off the log, so that they fell into the torturing river. Some fell in a foot's depth; some with the whole body; some up to the knees; some up to the middle; some up to the heels. And yet, after it came up out of the river of pitch, each one of those souls was brighter than it was before. Then an angel spoke to him about those falling souls: 'These are the souls who, after the journey hither required a certain gracious cleansing, and God's compassion, that they be worthy to be brought to him.'

And he said that there he saw shining walls, which were of great brightness and of wonderful length and of immeasurable height. Then said the holy angels: 'This is the holy and the splendid city of Jerusalem, in which the blessed souls and the holy spirits are forever joyful.' And then those souls who came over the river, which I told about before, then hastened with all might towards these walls. He then said that they were very brightly shining, and he said that because of this great brightness his eyes were hurt so that he couldn't look at anything in the brightness.

He said also that there had come to the meeting the soul of a certain man who had died while serving as abbot, and it was very comely to see. Then the devils seized the soul and they said that it was for their portion and in their power. Then one of the holy angels answered them and said: 'I will now quickly show you, you wretched spirits, that this soul will not be in your power.' Then, when this was said, there suddenly came there a very great throng

---

[1] Properly 'pitch'.

of shining souls, and they were speaking thus: 'This abbot was our superior, and he won us all for God with his teaching, and by this merit he will be redeemed, and he will not be in your power.' Then the angels fought with the devils, and the angels prevailed over the devils so that they saved the soul from the power of the wicked spirits. Then the holy angel rebuked the devil and said: 'Now you know that you took this soul without justice; now depart, you wretched spirits, now into that eternal fire.' And when the angel had said this, then the wicked devil raised up a quite immeasurable wailing, and they cast themselves with deadly flight into the burning pits. And after a little while they came into that meeting again, and they disputed about the merits of men's souls.

And they disputed also about the deserts of those men who live differently in this life. And he said also, in the time that he was out of the body, that he could survey those men who were contaminated with sins, and also those who were serving God through much holiness and through piety had favour with Almighty God. And he saw that the men of God were continually shielded by the angels, and the angels were joined to them with friendship and with love. And he said about those men who were filled with evil sins, that devils were continually joined to them. And he said when a man sinned, either in word or in deed, that the devils constantly told that to the worst devils, and that they brought it into their midst with laughter. And he said that when a man transgressed, the devils brought each sin separately to the other devils to witness; and he said that immediately the Devil taught the man the sins, he immediately informed the devils.

And he said that he saw here in the world a girl grinding at a mill. Then, lying by her, she saw another girl's spindle, very beautifully carved, with a lovely fleece. Then she stole it. Then the devils were immediately filled with quite immeasurable glee; and there five of the worst devils immediately ran and reported the theft as a crime to the meeting of other devils; and they denounced the theft as a crime, and said that that girl was guilty. And he also said that he saw there the soul of a certain old priest in great sorrow, who had died a little earlier, and whom he served when he lay in his fatal illness; 'and then, when he was expiring he asked me to ask his brother to free for him a certain handmaiden that they both had in common'; then he promised him it. But because of his covetousness, his own brother[1] disregarded the request and

---

[1] Literally, 'his body's brother'.

would not fulfil it. Then his soul was in the deepest lamentation, and was accusing the faithless brother, and grievously rebuked him.

> At this point the English version omits a paragraph alluding to the outcome of crimes committed by the then still living King Ceolred of the Mercians.

And then, when all was said and surveyed thus, the blessed angels ordered that his soul return again to his body without delay. And he then informed believing men about all that was there revealed to him; and those who mocked it, them he refused to tell. And he explained her sin to a certain woman; she was dwelling in a distant country, and he informed her how, if she herself wished, she might deserve that Almighty God were merciful to her. And he explained all this spiritual vision to a certain mass-priest. This mass-priest's name was Bogia; and he instructed him to inform men about the vision. And he informed the priest that, for love of God, he was formerly for many years girdled with an iron girdle, and nobody knew anything about it.

And he said that when he had to return to his body, in all the vision, he had seen no other creature he despised so very much as his own body, nor nothing seemed so hateful nor so contemptible; and he never smelt a fouler stench as it then seemed to him that the body smelled, except for the devils and the burning fire which he saw there. And it was then commanded him that he return to his body at daybreak – and previously he had gone out of his body at first cock-crow.

> The Latin text goes on to say that after his return, tumours and blood in his eyes prevented him seeing for a week. He said that he had seen many other things that he had now forgotten. Indeed, they said subsequently his memory was less good than before. Wynfrith finishes:

> *At your earnest request I have written these things as he told them to me in the presence of three pious and most venerable brethren, who may be taken as trustworthy witnesses to my writing.* [Finally, in poetic rhythm:] *Farewell; may you live as a virgin the true angelic life, and with good repute reign eternally in heaven with Christ.*

A LETTER TO BROTHER EDWARD

This fragmentary letter was added to comments on the biblical injunctions concerning abstention from blood (Genesis IX, Leviticus XVII) included in a twelfth-century collection of Ælfrician writings from Worcester: Bodleian MS. Hatton 115, ff. 60ᵛ–1. The text was printed by F. Kluge, *Englische Studien*, 8 (1885), 62.

Now that you have asked me this, I tell you also, brother Edward, that you do wrong to forsake the English customs which your fathers followed and to love the customs of heathen men who begrudge you life, and by such evil customs thereby make it clear that you despise your race and your forefathers, when to their shame you dress in the Danish fashion with bared necks and blinded eyes. I say no more about that shameful manner of dress except what books tell us, that he is accursed who follows the customs of heathen men in his life and thereby dishonours his own race.

I also ask you brother, since you are more often among women in the countryside than I am, that you should say something to them – if you can say it to them for embarrassment, however; it embarrasses me greatly to say it to you. I have often heard it said, and it is deplorably true, that at their feasts these country women will often drink, and even eat, in privies; and it is a disgraceful act and great folly and ignominious disgrace that anyone should ever be so ill-mannered that he fill the mouth with food above and at the other end pass the excrement from him, and so imbibe both the ale and the stench that he might satisfy his wicked gluttony thus in particular. I cannot for embarrassment talk about the shameful deed as disgustingly as it is disgusting, that anyone should eat in a privy; but it is never necessary for any virtuous man.

A WRIT OF EDWARD THE CONFESSOR

This confirmation of privileges may have been issued by Edward shortly before his death in the opening days of 1066. It survives in a late eleventh-century copy still preserved among the muniments of Westminster Abbey (no. XVI). The text is edited by F. E. Harmer, *Anglo-Saxon Writs*, Manchester, 1952, pp. 362–3.

King Edward sends friendly greetings to Bishop William and Earl Harold and Esgar the Staller and to all my thegns and my loyal friends in Middlesex. I declare to you that I will and I grant that St Peter and the brethren at Westminster shall have for their maintenance the manor of Staines with the Staines estates within London, and with it jurisdiction over thirty-five hides, with all the associated lands that I have given to the holy place for the redemption of my soul; and everything lawfully appertaining thereto, in church and in mill, in woods and in fields, in pasture and in heath, in meadows and in eyots, in waters and in weirs, and in all things as fully and as completely as they were assigned to the jurisdiction of Staines in olden times, or I myself ever held them. And again, I grant them similarly that they have with it [rights of]: authority and jurisdiction, toll and tax, thief-taking and sanctuary, breach of the peace and forcible entry, obstruction and false declaration, and all other rights in all matters that shall arise there, during festivals and out of festivals, within the borough and outside the borough, on the street and off the street. Wherefore I will not for any reason permit anyone to withdraw or alienate my gift and my alms by so much as an acre of land, insofar as it appertained to the manor in any man's life-time, or anyone to have any authority there in any matter or at any time, by strand or by land, except the abbot and the brethren for the needs of the monastery. And I will and strongly adjure that this protection for the holy place remain firm and steadfast for ever in perpetuity. Amen. God keep you all.

EDWIN TO ÆLFSIGE, 1032

The monk Edwin, school-master at a Winchester monastery, apparently intends to tell his bishop about a vision he has had of St Cuthbert, and his subsequent journey to the saint's shrine, despite his abbot's prohibition. He then goes on to describe how he was reconciled to his abbot through the mediation of a neighbouring monastery. The two monasteries concerned were: Old Minster and New Minster, i.e. the seventh-century cathedral foundation at Winchester, now called the 'Old Monastery' to distinguish it from a second monastic foundation ('New Monastery'), built in the same enclosure alongside the old cathedral, and consecrated in 903. At first, relations between the two institutions were uneasy until peace was established by Bishop Frithestan. This concordant was later re-made by the sainted Bishop Æthelwold, who at his accession in 963 replaced the secular canon-priests of the cathedral by Benedictine monks. Edwin's letter outlines the terms of this ratification and the circumstances in which it took place. It was doubtless this that would make such a document important to Winchester authorities; independent copies were preserved in the archives of both institutions: added in an apparently late twelfth-century hand to a blank leaf in the Liber Vitae of New Minster, British Library MS. Stowe 944, ff. 40–40ᵛ, and about the same date added to the early twelfth-century Cartulary of St Swithun's (the former Old Minster): British Library Additional MS. 15350, ff. 116ᵛ–17.

The text was edited by W. de G. Birch, *Liber Vitae: Register and Martyrology of New Minster and Hyde Abbey*, Winchester, 1892, pp. 96–100, and by F. E. Harmer, *Anglo-Saxon Writs*, Manchester, 1952, pp. 401–2.

I Edwin, monk, master of the children at New Minster, greet you well, Bishop Ælfsige.[1] I inform you, lord, that three years ago now, I lay in my 'porticus'[2] about noon-tide, and there the holy Cuthbert[3] openly appeared to me. I was very glad about this. I went to my abbot Ælfwine[4] and asked him that I might journey north to the saint and visit him. But my abbot Ælfwine refused me this and further forbade it. I then took my own counsel, and hied me thither north. And there Bishop Æthelwine[5] received me with honour. And God and the saint granted me that I wash him with my hands, and comb his head with a comb, and cut his hair with scissors, and clothe him all with new clothing, and take his old garments off him. Some I left there, and some I have here.[6] Now lord, I recollected that I didn't have my abbot's permission, and so I returned home, and I came into Old Minster and sought Christ and St Peter and St Swithun, and would have you, but you weren't at home. But I found Leofwine the dean and all the brethren, and they received me honourably and gladly, and interceded for me with my abbot, and he received me gladly, praise be to God!

Now I will inform you lord Bishop Ælfsige, how this concordat was first established between Old Minster and New Minster, just as I myself heard [it] when I was young. Our lord St Æthelwold[7] lay sick, and the holy Dunstan[8] came from Canterbury to visit him; and our superior, Abbot Æthelgar,[9] went there, and monks with him – that was: Boia the old, and Dean Ælfric, and Ælfnoth the painter, and Ælfwine who is now abbot. And there came

[1] Ælfsige II, Bishop of Winchester, 1012–32.

[2] Literally 'porch', apparently an ante-chamber to the church, posssibly where school-lessons were conducted.

[3] Seventh-century hermit and Bishop of Lindisfarne, 685–7 (see Calendar, below, p. 84), the most popular saint in England prior to Becket's assassination; his relics by this time were at Durham Cathedral.

[4] Incumbent 1030–57.

[5] The name of a later Bishop of Durham, 1056–71; at this date it should have been Edmund, consecrated at Winchester in 1020.

[6] A few pages on in the New Minster manuscript their relic-list included pieces 'from the beard of St Cuthbert and of his clothing'.

[7] Bishop of Winchester 963–84, and a major figure in the monastic revival.

[8] Leader of the Benedictine revival, Abbot of Glastonbury 945, Bishop of Worcester 957, of London 959 and Archbishop of Canterbury 960–88.

[9] Subsequently Bishop of Selsey 980–8, and Archbishop of Canterbury 988–90.

monks from Old Minster, that was: Ealdwig, and Wulfstan the precentor,[1] and Dean Godwine and many others with them. Then the old monk Boia got up and went on his knees before St Æthelwold and asked him that he would fix good conventions between the two minsters in the monks' days, just as Bishop Frithestan[2] had fixed in the days of the priests: that was, that the two communities were to be wholly one in all divine worship; and that was, if any priest passed away in either place they should all come together and bury the body and perform all the services that belong to God; and on the day of the consecration of the church which is in Old Minster, the priests from New Minster should come to Old Minster and be there at evensong and at matins and at mass and at dinner; and the priests from Old Minster should come to New Minster on the Feast of St Judoc[3] in just the same way. And if there were misconduct by any priest in either minster, he should not go anywhere but seek out his neighbours and they intercede for him. Then when St Æthelwold heard this, he resolved that it should be thus now in his time and in that of the monks, and pronounced God's curse on all those who should ever rescind this; and as a token that it should be guaranteed gave two brown[4] mass-copes, one to Old Minster and the other to New Minster.

[1] Pupil and biographer of Æthelwold, poet and author of a treatise *De Tonorum Harmonia*.

[2] Bishop of Winchester 909–32.

[3] A seventh-century Breton saint whose relics were translated to New Minster on the occasion of its consecration in 903. His feast-day was 13 December.

[4] Or if gold- or silver-embroidered, possibly, 'shining'.

WILLS

Some fifty or so Anglo-Saxon wills exist, providing sometimes graphic evidence for the personal wishes of the testator respecting the disposal of particular pieces of property. Occasionally, as with Ætheling Æthelstan's (below, pp. 56–9), the will originated in written form, but normally the written document was merely the adventitious record of an attested oral declaration. Although often witnessed by an impressive number of individuals, these did not add their signatures in the modern sense, since the scribe wrote their names uniformly; probably the cross in front of each name was touched in token. A single sheet of parchment would normally suffice; only rarely are there 'chirographic' copies – i.e. formal duplicates in which a line of large letters (typically CYROGRAPH) separating the two were cut horizontally in half, so that only when both were present was authenticity proven (cf. again Ætheling Æthelstan's). Most wills survive only in late copies made by monastic scribes, where their foundation was a significant beneficiary of lands or the like. Several women's wills exist (e.g. Wynflæd's, below, p. 51). But, rather surprisingly, the wills of only two Anglo-Saxon kings survive: one that of Eadred, died 955 (ed. W. de G. Birch, *Cartularium Saxonicum*, London, 1885–93, III, pp. 74–6), the other that of King Alfred.

THE WILL OF KING ALFRED, C. 885

Alfred reigned from 871 to 899. This will, his second, was not made until he had five children. It is unlikely that he would have made a legacy to Bishop Wærferth of Worcester, before he became the king's literary helper in the mid-880s (see below, p. 60); the terminus ante-quem must be 888, when Archbishop Æthelberht died. The text survives only in later copies. In 1031 the scribe Ælsinus incorporated one in the Liber Vitae of New Minster, British Library MS. Stowe 944, ff. 29ᵛ–33. And another, accompanied by translations into Latin and Middle English, was added to the fourteenth-century Liber Abbatiae of Hyde Abbey, Shirburn Castle MS. ff. 8ᵛ–10.

There are editions by E. Edwards, *Liber Monasterii de Hyda*, Rolls Series XLV, London, 1866, pp. 52–75, W. de G. Birch, *Liber Vitae: Register and Martyrology of New Minster and Hyde Abbey*, Winchester, 1892, pp. 74–80, and by F. E. Harmer, *Select English Historical Documents of the ninth and tenth Centuries*, Cambridge, 1914, pp. 15–19. The Stowe MS. was reproduced by W. B. Sanders, *Facsimiles of Anglo-Saxon Manuscripts*, Southampton, 1878–84, III, xxii.

It starts with a justificatory preamble:

I King Alfred, with God's grace and with the advice of Archbishop Æthelred[1] and witness of all the councillors of the West Saxons, deliberated about the need of my soul and about my inheritance which God and my ancestors gave to me, and about that

[1] Archbishop of Canterbury 870–88.

inheritance which my father King Æthelwulf bequeathed to us three brothers, Æthelbald, Æthelred and me, and such that whichever of us lived longest, he should succeed to all. But it happened that Æthelbald passed away; and we two – Æthelred [and I] – with the witness of all the councillors of the West Saxons, entrusted our share to our relative King Æthelbert, on condition that he restore it as completely to our possession as it was when we entrusted it to him. And he then did so, both that inheritance and what he had gained by use of what we had in common, and what he himself acquired.

When it so happened that Æthelred succeeded, then I asked him in front of all our councillors that we two might divide that inheritance and he give me my share. Then he told me that he could not easily divide it, because he had very often tried it before; and he said that after his day he would grant to no man rather than me what he enjoyed of what we had in common, and acquired. And I was then well satisfied with that. But it happened that we were all troubled by the heathen people.[1] Then we two spoke about our children, that they would have need of certain property, whatever might happen to the two of us in those troubles. Then, when we were at an assembly at Swinbeorg[2] we two declared in witness of the councillors of the West Saxons that whichever of us two live longer, that he grant to the other's children the lands which we two ourselves obtained and those lands which King Æthelwulf gave us while Æthelwold was living, except for those he had bequeathed to us three brothers. And both of us gave the other his pledge, that whichever of us two lived longer, that he should succeed both to land and to treasures and to all his possessions, except for the part which each of us had bequeathed his children.

But it happened that King Æthelred passed away. Nobody told me then of any will nor any testimony that it was any other than as we two had earlier declared before witness. Then, when we now heard many disputes about the inheritance, I now brought King Æthelwulf's will to our assembly at Langanden, and they read it in front of all the councillors of the West Saxons. Then, when it was read, I asked them all for my sake – and offered them my pledge that I would never estrange anyone because they spoke what [they

---

[1] The Danes, with whom Alfred would eventually sign a peace-treaty, see above, p. 6.
[2] The exact location of named places has been the subject of considerable, and often inconclusive, investigation.

thought] was right – and that none of them should hesitate either for love of me or for fear of me to pronounce the common law, lest any man say that I wrongly condemned my child relations, either older or younger. And then they all pronounced rightly and declared that they could not think of any righter right or could hear one in the will. 'Now that all that is in it has come into your hand, then you bequeath it and grant it into the hands of relative or stranger, whichever be preferable to you.' And they all gave me their pledge and set their hand [to it] that during their life nobody should ever change it in any other way except just as I myself declare it on the last day.

* * *

I Alfred, King of the West Saxons, with God's grace and with this witness, declare what I want respecting my inheritance after my day. First, I grant my older son Edward[1] the estate at Stratton in Trigg-shire, and Hartland, and all the conveyanced land which Leofheah holds, and the estate at Carhampton, and at Kilton, and at Burnham, and at Wedmore – and I am desirous of the community at Cheddar that they choose him on the terms which we have earlier declared – with the estate at Chewton and what belongs thereto. And I grant him the estate at Cannington, and at Bedwyn, and at Pewsey, and at Hurstbourne, and at Sutton, and at Leatherhead, and at Carshalton.

And all the conveyanced land which I have in Kent, and at the lower Hurstbourne, and at Chiseldon, they should give to Winchester[2] on the terms which my father declared earlier – and my private property at the lower Hurstbourne which I entrusted to Ecgwulf.

And to my younger son:[3] the estate at Arreton, and that at Dene and that at Meon, and at Amesbury, and at Deone, and at Sturminster, and at Yeovil, and at Crewkerne, and at Whitchurch, and at Axmouth, and at Branscombe, and at Cullompton, and at Tiverton, and at Milbourne, and at Exminster, and at Sutheswyrthe, and at Lifton – and the estates which belong thereto, that is, all that I have among the Cornish except for Trigg-shire.

And to my oldest daughter:[4] the manor at Wellow; and to the

---

[1] Edward the Elder, who succeeded hs father as king, 899–924.
[2] Winchester Cathedral foundation, later the 'Old Minster', see above, p. 44.
[3] Æthelweard, little known to history, died 922.
[4] Alfred's three daughters were respectively: Æthelflæd, wife of Æthelred II of Mercia; Æthelgifu, Abbess of Shaftesbury (see below, p. 52), and Ælfthryth, wife of Baldwin II, Count of Flanders.

middlemost: at Kingsclere and at Candover; and to the youngest:
the manor at Welig, and at Ashton and at Chippenham.

And to my brother's son Æthelhelm: the manor at Alding-
bourne, and at Compton, and at Crondall, and at Beeding, and
at Beddingham, and at Burnham, and at Thunderfield, and at
Eashing. And to my brother's son Æthelwold: the residence at
Godalming, and at Guildford, and at Steyning. And to my relative
Osferth: the manor at Beckley, and at Rotherfield, and at
Ditchling, and at Sutton, and at Lyminster, and at Angmering,
and at Felpham – and the estates which belong thereto. And to
Ealhswith:[1] the manor at Lambourn, and at Wantage and at
Edington.

And to my two sons a thousand pounds: five-hundred pounds
each. And to my oldest daughter, and the middlemost and the
youngest, and Ealhswith, to the four of them, four-hundred
pounds: a hundred pounds each. And to each of my ealdormen a
hundred mancuses; and Æthelhelm, and Æthelwold, and Osferth
likewise. And to Ealdorman Æthelred[2] a sword worth a hundred
mancuses. And to the men who follow me, to whom I gave money
now at Easter-time, you are to give them two-hundred pounds
and they are to share it between them: to each as much as will fall
to him according to the manner in which I just now shared it out.

And to the Archbishop 100 mancuses – and to Bishop Esne,[3] and
Bishop Wærferth, and that at Sherborne.[4] Moreover, let them
distribute for me and for my father and for the friends for whom
he interceded and I intercede, two-hundred pounds: fifty to mass-
priests over all my kingdom, fifty to poor servants of God, fifty to
the poor needy, fifty to the church in which I am at rest.[5]

And I don't know for certain whether there is as much money,
nor do I know if there is more, but I imagine so. If it be more, it is
to be in common to all those to whom I have bequeathed money;
and it is my wish that my ealdormen and my thegnly men are all
included, and it be distributed thus.

When previously I had written in another manner about my
inheritance, then I had property and more relatives, and had
entrusted the documents to many men – and written with these

---

[1] Alfred's queen.
[2] Married to Alfred's oldest daughter; although described here as Ealdorman, recognized
as King of Mercia from about 879.
[3] Unidentified, but possibly a Somerset-based suffragan.
[4] Then Wulfsige, but from *circa* 890 Alfred's friend and biographer Asser, cf. p. 62 below.
[5] Winchester Cathedral.

same witnesses. So I have now burnt all the old ones which I could discover. If any of them be found, nothing stands in that, because I now want, with God's help, that it should be thus.

And I want those men who have those estates to fulfil the directions which stand in my father's will, the very best they can. And if I have any unpaid debt to anyone, I want my relatives to pay it for certain. And I want the men to whom I have bequeathed my conveyanced land not to give it away from my family after their day, but I want, after their day, that it go to my closest, unless any of them have children; then I prefer that it go to the one begotten on the 'weaponed' side, as long as there be any worthy of it. My grandfather[1] had bequeathed his estate to the spear-side, not the spindle-side. So if I gave anyone in the female line what he acquired, then my relatives are to buy it back if they want to have it while living; if it be otherwise, let it go after their day, just as we have declared earlier. Therefore I declare that they are to pay for it, because they succeed to what is mine, which I may give to the female-line as well as the weaponed-line whichever I want.

And I pray in the name of God and of his saints that none of my relatives nor heirs disrupt any life-choice of those for whom I paid; and the councillors of the West Saxons pronounced it right that I might leave them either free or servile, whichever I want; but for love of God and for my soul's need, I want them to be entitled to their freedom and their choice. And, in the name of the living God, I command that no one trouble them – not with demands of money nor with anything, so that they cannot choose just such a master as they want. And I want them to give to the community at Damerham their title-deeds and their freedom to choose whichever control they prefer – for me and for Ælflæd[2] and for the friends for whom she interceded and I intercede. And for my soul's need, they should also seek out from livestock whatever may be, and also as it be suitable, and as you wish to allow me.

THE WILL OF WYNFLÆD, C. 950

Wynflæd was clearly associated with a religious community of some kind, perhaps as a lay member, possibly even lay-abbess. She was certainly wealthy, and may even have been related to the royal house (cf. H. P. R. Finberg, *The Early Charters of Wessex*, Leicester, 1964, p. 44);

[1] Ecgberht, King of the West Saxons, 802–39.
[2] Unidentified but perhaps a short form for Æthelflæd, Alfred's oldest daughter, see above, p. 49.

the two nunneries she mentions (Wilton, Wilts. and Shaftesbury, Dorset) are both Alfredian foundations. She may well have been that *religiose sancte conversacionis monialis femine Wenflede* to whom King Edmund gave two Dorset estates in 942 (Finberg, pp. 168–9). Her will survives only in a single incomplete and mutilated sheet of parchment: British Library, Harley Charter, VIII, 38 – perhaps a contemporary copy, since much inserted and corrected; several words are no longer legible and at least two are inexplicable. Wynflæd's will is unusually long, and exceptionally detailed.

The text is edited by J. M. Kemble, *Codex Diplomaticus Aevi Saxonici*, London, 1839–48, VI, pp. 130–4, and by D. Whitelock, *Anglo-Saxon Wills*, Cambridge, 1930, pp. 10–15. The MS. is reproduced by E. A. Bond, *Facsimiles of Ancient Charters in the British Museum*, London, 1873–8, III, no. 38.

+ Wynflæd declares what she wants in respèct of what she has, after her day.

She bequeaths to the church her offertory-[. . .], and her better offertory-cloth and her cross; and to the community refectory two silver cups; and as her 'soul-dues' a mancus of gold to each servant of God, and besides that one mancus to Ceolthryth, and Othelbriht, and Elsa, and Æthel[. . .]th; and one pound to the community at Wilton and one mancus to Fugel. And she bequeaths her daughter Æthelflæd her engraved ring and her cloak-pin, and the estate at Ebbesborne and the deeds in perpetual inheritance to dispose of as she pleases; and she [grants] her the men and the cattle and all that is there, except for what they shall give for her soul, both in men and in cattle. And at Charlton also, she grants her the men and the cattle, except for the freedmen, and that they find from the cattle at Charlton [half]-a-pound's-worth as 'soul-dues' to Milborne; and half-a-pound's-worth as 'soul-dues' from Chinnock to Yeovil. And Eadmær the estate at Coleshill and at Inglesham; and she also grants him, during his day, the estate at Faccombe, [which] was her 'morning-gift'; and after his day, if Æthelflæd lives longer than him, then she is to succeed to the estate at Faccombe, and after her day it will revert to Eadwold's hands. And if God wills that Eadwold be grown up enough in his father's day that he can hold estates, then I ask Eadmær that he give over one or other of the two estates, either at Coleshill or Adderbury – and after his day both.

And at Inglesham she wants them to find half-a-pound's-worth as 'soul-dues' to Wantage for her; and at Coleshill; and to find from the cattle 60 penceworth to Shrivenham, 60 to Coleshill, 60 to Childrey.

And they are to free Wulfwaru, to follow whom she pleases; [and . . .]ttryth also; and they are to free Wulfflæd on condition that she follow Æthelflæd and Eadgifu. And she bequeaths to Eadgifu one weaving-woman and one seamstress, the one called Eadgifu the other called Æthelgifu. And they are to free Gerburg and Miscin[1] and Hi[. . .] and the daughter of Burhulf at Chinnock, and Ælfsige and his wife and his older daughter, and Ceolstan's wife. And at Charlton, they are to free Pifus and Edwin [. . .] and [. . .]'s wife. And at Faccombe they are to free Eadhelm, and Man, and Johanna, and Sprow and his wife, and Enefæt, and Gersand, and Snell. And at Coleshill they are to free Æthelgyth, and Bica's wife, and Æffa, and Beda, and Gurhan's wife; and they are to free Wulfwaru's sister, Brihtsige's wife, and [. . .] the wright, and Ælfswith's daughter Wulfgyth. And if there be any penally enslaved person besides these whom she enslaved, she trusts to her children that they will release them for her soul['s sake].

And to Ælfwold her two aurochs horns, and a horse and her red tent. She bequeaths to Eadmær one cup closed with a lid – another to Æthelflæd, and asks that between them they find her two very beautiful drinking-cups for the refectory, or supplement her own ornamented cups [. . .] to the value of one pound. Then she would that they put into each cup half a pound of pennies, and they give back Eadwold his own 2 silver cups. And she bequeaths to him her gold-ornamented wooden cup so that he enlarge his bracelet with the gold, or that they change it for 16 mancuses of red, red gold – as much as has been put on it. And she bequeaths to him two chests, and in them bedding – all that goes with one bed.

And Eadmær is to restore to Eadwold as much cattle and as many men as he earlier bespoke him at Avon – and afterwards, he to his father as he wishes. And about the estate at Chinnock – after her day the community at Shaftesbury is to own it; and she owns the cattle and the men; then she grants to the community the geburs[2] who dwell on the rented land. And she grants to her son's daughter Eadgifu the slave-men, and the cattle except for the 'soul-due' which they must give to Yeovil; and she wants them to allow to stand on the estate 6 oxen and 4 cows with four calves. And of the slave-men at Chinnock she bequeaths to Eadwold: Eadstan's son Ceolstan, and Æffa's son, and Burhwyn, Martin, and Hisfig;

---

[1] Some of Wynflæd's slaves bear unusual names, possibly by-names, or familiar names of some kind.

[2] For the gebur, see Duties and Perquisites, above pp. 27–8.

and against that she bequeaths to Eadgifu: Ælfsige the cook, and Burga's daughter Ælfwaru, and Herestan and his wife, and Ecghelm and his wife and their child, and Cynestan, and Wynsige, and Brihtric's son, and Edwin, and Bunele's son, and Ælfhere's daughter.

And to Ealhelm's daughter Æthelflæd she bequeaths: Ælfhere's daughter (the maid), and her embroidered dress, and another of linen – or some linen cloth. And to Eadgifu two chests and in them her best bed-hanging and linen covering and all the bedding that goes with it; [. . .] and her best dark tunic, and her better cloak, and her two spotted wooden cups, and her old filigreed pin which is worth 6 mancuses. And let them give her 4 mancuses from her [. . .], and a long hall-hanging and a second short one, and three seat-covers. And she grants Ceolthryth whichever she prefers of her black tunics, and her best holy veil and her best fillet.

And to Æthelflæd the White her *cincdaðenan*[1] dress, and coif and fillet; and afterwards Æthelflæd is to look out from her nun's clothing what best she can for Wulfflæd and Æthelgifu, and supplement it with gold so that they both have 60 pennyworth at any rate; and for Ceolwyn and Eadburg it shall be 30 pennyworth. And there are two big chests, and a clothes-chest, and a little weaving-box, and also two old chests.

Then she grants Æthelflæd everything which is un-bequeathed in books and such small things, and she trusts that she will be mindful of her soul. And there are also wall-hangings, a certain one which would suit her – and the smallest she can give to her women. And she bequeaths to Cynelufu her share of the wild horses which are with Eadmær's. And she grants to Æthelflæd her *hyssa . . cuppe*[2] and the utensils and all the useful things that are inside, and also the homestead if the king grant it to her just as King Edward granted it to Brihtwyn her mother before. And Eadwold and his sister are to have her tame horses in common [. . .] over and above his own.

THE WILL OF BISHOP ÆLFWOLD OF CREDITON, *C.* 1000

In the early tenth century the diocese of Sherborne was divided and two new sees established, one at Wells and the other at Crediton, before removing to Exeter in 1050. The will of Ælfwold

---

[1] ? slashed to ease prostration.
[2] Read by Kemble, now illegible, and inexplicable.

III, Bishop of Crediton 998–1008, is preserved in a single contemporary copy: Bodleian Library, Oxford, MS. Eng. hist.a.2, xiii. The text is edited by A. S. Napier and W. H. Stevenson, *The Crawford Collection of Charters and Early Documents*, Oxford, 1895, pp. 23–4.

+ This is Bishop Ælfwold's will, that is, that he grants the estate at Sandford to the minster at Crediton as payment for his soul, with supplies and with men just as it stands, except for the penally enslaved men. And he grants one hide of it to Godric, and a plough-team of oxen. And he grants to his lord four horses, two saddled and two unsaddled, and four shields and four spears and two helmets and two mail-coats, and fifty mancuses of gold which Ælfnoth of Woodleigh owes him, and a sixty-four-oared ship – it is all ready except for the rowlocks; he would like to prepare it completely in a manner suitable for his lord, if God allows him. And to Ordwulf two books: Hrabanus and the Martyrology; and to the atheling[1] forty mancuses of gold and the wild cattle on the Ashburn estate, and two tents; and to the monk Ælfwold twenty mancuses of gold and a horse and a tent; and to the priest Brihtmær twenty mancuses of gold and a horse; and to his three kinsmen, Eadwold, Æthelnoth and Grimketel, to each of them twenty mancuses of gold and to each of them a horse; and to his kinsman Wulfgar two wall-hangings and two seat-coverings and three mail-coats; and to his brother-in-law Godric two mail-coats; and to the priest Edwin five mancuses of gold and his cope; and to his priest Leofsige the man whom he released to him earlier called Wunstan; and to Cenwold a helmet and mail-coat; and to Boia a horse; and to Mælpatrik five mancuses of gold; and to Leofwine Polga five mancuses of gold; and to the scribe Ælfgar a pound of pennies he lent to Tun and his sisters – they are to pay him. And to his sister Eadgifu a 'rubbing-cloth', and a dorsal and a seat-covering; and to the nurse Ælfflaed five mancuses of pennies; and to Leofwine Polga and Mælpatrik and Brihtsige, to each of the three of them a horse; and to each man of his household his mount which he had lent him; and to all his household servants five pounds to divide, to each according to his rank.

And to Crediton, three service-books: a missal, and a benedictional and an epistle-book, and a set of mass-vestments. And on every episcopal estate freedom to every man who was penally enslaved, or whom he had bought with his money. And to Wilton

---

[1] This might refer to either of Æthelred's sons, Athelstan or Alfred.

a chalice and paten of a hundred and twenty mancuses of gold – all but three mancuses. And to the chamberlain his bed-clothes.

And as witness to this are: Ælfgar's son Wulfgar, and Godric of Crediton, and the priest Edwin, and the monk Ælfwold and the priest Brihtmær.

THE WILL OF ÆTHELING ÆTHELSTAN, 1015

Ætheling (i.e. Prince)[1] Æthelstan was the son of King Æthelred by his first wife Ælfgifu; he was a frequent signatory to his father's charters from 997 to 1013, but seems to have died as a teenager in 1014–15. Several copies of this will were made, including two in near-contemporary hands: one a chirographic copy on a single sheet of vellum: British Library, Stowe Charter 37; and another on a single sheet in a near-contemporary hand, later endorsed with the date 1015: Canterbury Cathedral MS. AA.H. 68. Two further copies are found in the early twelfth-century Cartulary of St Swithun's (the former Old Minster), Winchester: British Library Additional MS. 15350, ff. 43ᵛ–4, 50.

The text is edited by J. M. Kemble, *Codex Diplomaticus Aevi Saxonici*, London, 1839–48, III, pp. 361–4, and by D. Whitelock, *Anglo-Saxon Wills*, Cambridge, 1930, pp. 56–62. The Canterbury and Stowe MSS. are reproduced by W. B. Sanders, *Facsimiles of Anglo-Saxon Manuscripts*, Southampton, 1878–84, I, xviii; III, xxxviii.

+ In the name of Almighty God. I Æthelstan the Ætheling declare in this document how I have granted my property and my possessions, to the glory of God, and for the redemption of my soul – and my father King Æthelred's, from whom I gained it.

That is: first that I grant that they free each penally enslaved man whom I acquired by sentence. And I grant 'in with me'[2] to Christ and St Peter, where I am to rest,[3] that estate at Adderbury which I bought from my father with two-hundred mancuses of gold by weight, and with 5 pounds of silver; and that estate at Marlow which I bought from my father with two-hundred-and-fifty mancuses of gold by weight; and that estate at Morden which my father let to me, I grant to that place for the souls of both of us (and I entreat him, for the love of God and of St Mary and of St Peter, that it may stand); and the sword with the silver hilt which Wulfric made, and the gold sword-belt and the bracelet which Wulfric made, and the drinking-horn which I earlier bought from the community at the Old Minster. And I want them to take that

[1] Cf. D. N. Dumville, *Anglo-Saxon England*, 8 (1979), 1–33.

[2] As 'soul-dues', a charitable payment to a religious community, cf. Wynflæd's will above, pp. 52–3; often, as here, for burial.

[3] I.e. Old Minster, the seventh-century cathedral foundation at Winchester, burial-place of the West Saxon kings.

money which Æthelwold's widow has to pay me, which I allotted
for her benefit, and deliver [it] to Bishop Ælfsige in the Old
Minster, for my soul – that is 12 pounds in amount. And I grant
to Christ Church in Canterbury the estate at Hollingbourne and
what belongs to it (except the one ploughland which I have
granted to Siferth); and the estate at Garrington. And I grant the
estate at Rotherfield to Nuns' Minster[1] for St Mary's sake; and a
silver basin of five pounds. And to New Minster[2] a silver cauldron
of five pounds, in the name of the Holy Trinity to whom the place
is dedicated. And I grant to Shaftesbury, to the Holy Cross and to
St Edward,[3] that 6 pounds I instructed my brother Edmund[4]
about.

And I grant to my father King Æthelred the estate at Chalton
(except for the eight hides which I have granted to my attendant
Ælmær), and the estate at Norton, and the estate at Mollington,
and the silver-hilted sword which Ulfketel owned, and the mail-
coat which is with Morcar,[5] and the horse which Thurbrand gave
me, and the white horse which Leofwine gave me.

And I grant to my brother Edmund the sword which King Offa
owned, and the sword with the engraved hilt, and one blade, and
one silver-coated blast-horn, and those estates which I acquired in
East Anglia, and the estate in the Peak valley; and from this
property I want them to pay each year one day's provisions to the
community in Ely on the Feast of St Audrey;[6] and give to the
monastery a hundred pence, and feed there on that day 100
needy; and may this charitable deed be enacted annually forever,
whoever might own the estates, for as long as Christendom stand.
And if they who have the estates do not want to perform these
charitable deeds, the property shall go to St Audrey's.

And I grant my brother Eadwig one silver-hilted sword. And I
grant Bishop Ælfsige the gold cross which is with Wynflæd's son

[1] A convent of St Mary, at Winchester, founded by King Alfred and Queen Ealhswith in the
later ninth century, brought into a single enclosure with Old and New Minsters in the mid-
tenth century.
[2] The second monastery at Winchester; see the Letter from Edwin to Ælfsige, above, p. 44.
[3] Edward the Martyr, Æthelred's half-brother (and thus Æthelstan's uncle), assassinated at
Corfe in 978, and interred at Shaftesbury in 980.
[4] I.e. Edmund Ironside, who succeeded Æthelred for a few months in 1016.
[5] A certain Morcar was murdered together with his brother Siferth, apparently by
Æthelred, in 1015, after which Edmund Ironside married Siferth's widow – making a bequest
to New Minster for Siferth's soul.
[6] I.e. 23 June: St Æthelthrytha, seventh-century abbess of Ely; see above, p. 33, and
Calendar below, pp. 82–3.

Eadric, and a black stallion. And I grant Ælfmær the estate at
Hambledon which he owned earlier – and I entreat my father for
God Almighty's sake, and mine, that he grant that which I have
granted him. And I grant Godwine, Wulfnoth's son, the estate at
Compton which his father owned earlier. And I grant Ælfswith my
foster-mother, for her great merits, the estate at Weston which I
bought from my father with two-hundred-and-fifty mancuses of
gold by weight. And I grant Ælfwine my mass-priest the estate at
Harleston and the patterned sword which Withar owned, and my
horse with my trappings. And I grant Ælfmær my dish-thegn
the eight hides at Catherington, and one pied stallion, and the
notched sword and my targe. And I grant Siferth the estate at
Hockliffe, and one sword and one horse and my curved shield.[1]
And I grant Æthelweard the Stammerer and Lyfing, the estate at
Tewin. And I grant Leofstan, brother of Leofwine Cwatt, the
estate property that I took from his brother. And I grant Leofmær
at Bygrave the estate which I earlier took from him. And I grant
Godwine the Slobberer the three hides at Lurgashall. And I grant
Eadric, Wynflæd's son, the sword on which the hand is marked.
And I grant Æthelwine my attendant the sword which earlier he
gave to me. And I grant Ælfnoth my sword-polisher the notched,
patterned sword, and my stag-huntsman the stud-herd which is
on Colungs' Ridge. And let them disburse from my gold to Ælfric
at Barton and Godwin the Slobberer as much as Edmund my
brother knows that I ought rightly to pay them.

Now, with all humility, in the name of Almighty God, I thank
my father for the answer which he sent me on the Friday after the
Feast of Midsummer,[2] by Ælfgar, Ælffa's son; which was, as he
told me in my father's words, that I might, by God's authorization
and by his, grant my property and my possessions as seemed to me
most advisable, both before God and before the world. And
witness to this answer are: my brother Edmund, and Bishop
Ælfsige, and Abbot Brihtmær[3] and Ælfmær, Ælfric's son.

Now, as my father's authorization stands in my will, I entreat
all the councillors, both ecclesiastical and lay, who may hear my
will read, that they be of assistance that my will may stand.

---

[1] The long kite-shaped shield held on the arm and covering the whole side, introduced
about this time for use on horseback, as distinct from the smaller, round, hand-held targe, used
on foot.
[2] See Calendar, below, p. 83.
[3] Abbot of New Minster, 1008–21.

I now declare that all those things which I have granted to God, to God's church and God's servants, are done for the soul of my dear father King Æthelred – and for mine – and of my grandmother Ælfthryth who raised me, and of all of those who assist me with these good things. And he who in any way changes this, will have to settle with Almighty God and with St Mary and with St Peter and with all those who praise God's name.

KING ALFRED

PREFACE TO ST GREGORY'S 'PASTORAL CARE'

One of the four great doctors of the Latin Church and Pope from 590 to 604, Gregory the Great was of particular interest to the English Church as the originator of the Augustinian mission. The *Cura Pastoralis* (PL., LXXVII 13–128) was probably his best-known work. For centuries considered a standard manual for clerics, it was recommended as indispensable reading by such authorities as Alcuin and Ælfric. Not unnaturally, it took first place in the programme of translations undertaken by Alfred during the later part of his reign (871–99) to counteract the cultural decline he describes in his preface. It was intended that a copy should be presented to each diocese in his kingdom. Alfred's preface takes the form of a letter addressed to each bishop.

Several MSS. of this work survive, but the most important is undoubtedly Bodleian MS. Hatton 20, the copy prepared probably under the direction of Alfred himself some time between 890 and 896 for presentation to Bishop Wærferth of Worcester, who was himself to translate Gregory's *Dialogues* for the king. There is a complete facsimile by N. R. Ker, *The Pastoral Care*, EEMF., VI, Copenhagen, 1956. The text was edited by Henry Sweet, *King Alfred's West Saxon Version of Gregory's Pastoral Care*, EETS., OS., XLV, L, London, 1871–2.

This Book is to go to Worcester

King Alfred sends greetings to Bishop Wærferth[1] with his loving and friendly words, and would declare to you that it has very often come to my mind what wise men there were formerly throughout the English people, both in sacred and in secular orders; and how there were happy times then throughout England; and how the kings who had rule over the people in those days were obedient to God and his messengers, and both maintained their peace and their morality and their authority at home, and also enlarged their territory abroad; and how they prospered both in warfare and in wisdom; and also how zealous the sacred orders were both about teaching and about learning and all the services which they had to perform for God; and how men from abroad came here to this land in search of knowledge and instruction, and how we should now have to get them from

[1] Bishop of Worcester 873–915.

abroad, if we were to have them. So complete was its decay among the English people that there were very few this side of the Humber who could comprehend their services in English, or even translate a letter from Latin into English; and I imagine that there were not many beyond the Humber. There were so few of them that I cannot even remember a single one south of the Thames when I succeeded to the kingdom. Thanks be to Almighty God that now we have any supply of teachers. And therefore I command you to do, as I believe you wish, that you disengage yourself as often as you can from the affairs of this world, so that you can apply the wisdom which God has given you wherever you are able to apply it. Think what punishments then came upon us in this world when we neither loved it ourselves nor allowed it to other men – we loved only to be called Christians, and very few loved the virtues.

When I remembered all this, then I also remembered how, before it was all ravaged and burnt, I had seen how the churches throughout all England stood filled with treasures and books, and there was also a great multitude of God's servants – they had very little benefit from those books, because they could not understand anything of them, since they were not written in their own language. As if they had said: 'Our forefathers who formerly held these places loved knowledge, and through it they acquired wealth and left it to us. One can see their footprints here still, but we cannot follow after them and therefore we have now lost both the wealth and the knowledge because we would not bend our mind to that course.' When I remembered all this, then I wondered greatly at those good wise men who formerly existed throughout the English people and had fully studied all those books, that they did not wish to translate any part of them into their own language. But then I immediately answered myself and said: 'They did not imagine that men should ever become so careless and learning so decayed; they refrained from it by intention and hoped that there would be the greater knowledge in this land the more languages we knew.'

Then I remembered how the law was first found in the Hebrew language, and afterwards, when the Greeks learned it, they translated it all into their own language, and all the other books as well. And afterwards in the same way the Romans, when they had learned them, they translated them all into their own language through learned interpreters. And all other Christian nations also translated some part of them into their own language. Therefore it seems better to me, if it seems so to you, that we also should translate certain books which are most necessary for all men to know, into the language that we can all understand, and also arrange it, as with God's help we very easily can if we have peace, so that all the youth of free men now among the English people, who have the means to be able to devote themselves to it, may be set to study for as long as they are of no other use, until the time they are able to read English writing well; afterwards one may teach further in the Latin language those whom one wishes to teach further and wishes to promote to holy orders.

Then when I remembered how the knowledge of Latin had previously decayed throughout the English people, and yet many could read English writing, I began amidst other various and manifold cares of this kingdom to translate into English the book which is called *Pastoralis* in Latin and 'Shepherd's Book' in English, sometimes word for word, sometimes in a paraphrase, as I learned it from my archbishop Plegmund,[1] and my bishop Asser,[2] and my priest Grimbold[3] and my priest John.[4] When I had learned it, I translated it into English as I understood it and as I could interpret it most intelligibly; and I will send one to every bishopric in my kingdom; and in each there will be a book-marker worth fifty mancuses.[5] And in the name of God I command that no one remove the book-marker from the book, nor the book from the minster; it is uncertain how long there may be such learned bishops, as now, thanks be to God, there are almost everywhere; therefore I desire that they should always lie at that place, unless the bishop want to have it with him, or it be anywhere on loan, or anyone be copying it.

TWO NORTHERN VOYAGES

Alfred was also responsible for a paraphrase of the early fifth-century *Historiae adversum paganos* by Paulus Orosius, a friend and associate of Augustine of Hippo (*PL.*, XXXI 663–1174). Written at the request of Augustine, this is an encyclopaedic history of the world from its Creation to the year 414, intended to demonstrate that those calamities which had recently

[1] Archbishop of Canterbury 890–914.
[2] Bishop of Sherborne *c.* 892–909.
[3] A Frankish monk from St Omer.
[4] A continental Saxon, made Abbot of Athelney by Alfred.
[5] It is tempting to regard the well-known gold, crystal and enamel Alfred jewel, found at Athelney in 1693, as the head of one of these objects. Was John also given a copy?

befallen the Roman Empire were not necessarily the consequence of Christianity. It begins with a brief geographical account of the world. Alfred was able to supplement Orosius' description of Europe with what appear to be verbatim reports of voyages to the White Sea and to the Baltic. As told by seamen called respectively Ohthere and Wulfstan, these reports exist in their own right as ninth-century travellers' tales.

For a thorough reconsideration of the question of authorship see E. M. Liggins and J. M. Bately, *Anglia*, 88 (1970), 289–322, 433–60.

One nearly contemporary copy of Alfred's Orosius survives: British Library MS. Additional 47967, an early tenth-century MS. probably written at Winchester. But the second quire, which contained all but a few lines of Alfred's travellers' tales, is missing. There is a facsimile edition of this manuscript, by Alistair Campbell, *The Tollemache Orosius*, EEMF., III, Copenhagen, 1953. A complete text is found occupying ff. 3–111ᵛ of an eleventh-century manuscript probably written at Abingdon: British Library MS. Cotton Tiberius B 1, which also includes the poetic *Menologium* and a collection of gnomic verses as well as the Abingdon version of the Anglo-Saxon Chronicle.

The text is well edited by Janet Bately, *The Old English Orosius*, EETS., SS., VI, London, 1980.

I Ohthere's Voyage to the White Sea

Ohthere told his lord, King Alfred, that he lived farthest to the north of all the Norwegians. He said that he lived by the western sea in the north part of the land. However, he said that the land extends very much further north; but it is all waste, except that Lapps camp in a few places here and there, hunting in winter and fishing in the sea in summer.

He said that on one occasion he wished to find out how far that land extended due north, or whether anyone lived north of the waste. Then he travelled close to the land, due north; he left the waste land on the starboard and the open sea on the port all the way for three days. Then he was as far north as the whale-hunters ever travel. Then he travelled still due north as far as he could sail for the next three days. Then the land turned due east – or the sea in on the land – he did not know which; he knew only that there he waited for a wind from the west and a little from the north, and then sailed east, close to the land, for as far as he could sail in four days. Then he had to wait there for a wind directly from the north, for at that point the land turned due south – or the sea in on the land – he did not know which. Then from there he sailed due south, close to the land, for as far as he could sail in five days. There a great river extended up into the land. Then they turned up into that river because they dare not sail beyond the river for fear of hostility, because on the other side of the river the land was all inhabited. Previously he had not met with any inhabited land since he left his own home. But to the starboard there was waste land all the way, except for fishers and fowlers and hunters – and they were all Lapps; and there was always open sea on his port. The Permians[1] had cultivated their land very well; but they dare not put in there. But the land of the Terfinns[2] was all waste, except where hunters or fishers or fowlers lived.

The Permians told him many stories both of their own land and of the lands which were round about them; but he did not know what the truth of it was, since he did not see it for himself. The Lapps and the Permians, it seemed to him, spoke almost the same language. He travelled there chiefly – in addition to observing the land – for the walruses, because they have very fine bone in their teeth (they brought some of those teeth to the king), and their hides are very good for ship's ropes. This whale is much smaller than other whales: it is no longer than seven ells long.[3] But the best whale-hunting is in his own land: those are forty-eight ells long, and the largest fifty ells long. He said that, as one of six, he slew sixty of those in two days.

He was a very wealthy man in that property in which their wealth consists, that is, in wild animals. When he visited the king he still had six hundred tame animals unbought. They call those 'reindeer'; of those, six were decoy reindeer; they are very valuable among the Lapps because with them they capture the wild reindeer. He was among the first men in the land. Nevertheless he had no more than twenty cattle, and twenty sheep and twenty swine, and the little that he ploughed, he ploughed with horses. But their income is chiefly in the tribute that the Lapps pay them. That tribute consists in animal skins and in bird feathers and whale-bone and in the ship's ropes which are made from the hide of whales and seals. Each one pays according to his rank. The noblest must pay fifteen marten skins, and five reindeer, and one bear skin, and ten ambers of feathers,[4] and a bear- or otter-skin coat, and two ship's ropes, both to be sixty ells long, one to be made of whale's hide, the other of seal's.

He said that the land of the Norwegians was very long and very narrow. All that they can either graze or plough lies by the sea; and even that is very rocky in some places; and to the east, and alongside the cultivated land, lie wild mountains. In those

---

[1] Probably the North Karelians, living in the south of the Kola peninsula.

[2] Lapps living in the east of the Kola peninsula.

[3] An ell is the distance measured from the elbow to the tip of the middle finger: about eighteen inches.

[4] An amber was a dry measure equal to four bushels.

mountains live Lapps. And the cultivated land is broadest to the south, and increasingly narrower the further north. To the south it may be sixty miles broad, or a little broader; and in the middle thirty or broader; and to the north, he said, where it was narrowest, it might be three miles broad to the mountains; and then the mountains in some places are as broad as one might cross in two weeks, and in some places as broad as one might cross in six days.

Then alongside that land to the south, on the other side of the mountains, is the land of the Swedes, extending northwards; and alongside that land to the north, the land of the Finns. Sometimes the Finns make war on the Norwegians across the mountains; sometimes the Norwegians on them. And there are very large freshwater lakes throughout the mountains; and the Finns carry their boats overland to the lakes, and make war on the Norwegians from there; they have very small and very light boats.

Ohthere said that the district in which he lived was called Halogaland.[1] He said that no one lived to the north of him. In the south of the land there is a trading-town which they call Sciringesheal.[2] He said that a man could sail there in a month, if he camped at night and had a favourable wind every day; and all the time he must sail close to the land. On the starboard is first Ireland,[3] and then the islands which are between Ireland and this country. Then this country continues until he comes to Sciringesheal, and Norway all the way on the port side. To the south of Sciringesheal a very great sea extends up into the land; it is broader than any man can see across. And Jutland is opposite on one side, and then Zealand. The sea extends many hundred miles up into the land.

And from Sciringesheal, he said that he sailed in five days to the trading-town which they call Hedeby;[4] this stands between the Wends[5] and the Saxons and the Angles, and belongs to the Danes. When he sailed there from Sciringesheal, then Denmark was to the port and open sea to the starboard for three days; and then for two days before he came to Hedeby there lay to his starboard:

[1/8] The present-day Nordland district of Norway.
[2] Identified as Kaupang in Vestfold, at the mouth of Oslofjord.
[3] The coast-wise sea voyage Ohthere describes is difficult to visualize. Perhaps he means Iceland.
[4] Old Schleswig in north Germany, destroyed c. 1050.
[5] Slavs living in Mecklenburg and Pomerania.

Jutland, and Zealand and many islands. The Angles dwelt in those lands before they came here to this country. And for those two days there lay to his port those islands which belong to Denmark.

II Wulfstan's Voyage to the Baltic

Wulfstan said that he travelled from Hedeby and that he was in Truso[1] within seven days and nights, since the ship was running under sail all the way. Wend-land was on his starboard, and to his port was Langeland and Laaland and Falster and Skane; and all these lands belong to Denmark. And then to our port was the land of the Burgundians,[2] and they have their own king. Then after the land of the Burgundians there were to our port those lands which are called, first: Blekinge, and Möre, and Öland and Gotland; and these lands belong to the Swedes. And Wend-land lay on our starboard all the way to the mouth of the Vistula. The Vistula is a very great river, and it separates Wit-land[3] and Wend-land; and Wit-land belongs to the Ests; and the Vistula flows out of Wend-land and flows into the Zalew Wislany;[4] and the Zalew Wislany is at least fifteen miles broad. Then the Elbing comes from the east into the Zalew Wislany from the lake on whose shore stands Truso, and there come out together into the Zalew Wislany: the Elbing from the east out of Estonia and the Vistula from the south out of Wend-land. And then the Vistula gives its name to the Elbing and flows west and north from that lake into the sea; therefore it is called the Vistula-mouth.

Estonia is very large, and there are many towns, and there is a king in every town. And there is very much honey and fishing; and the king and the richest men drink mare's milk, and the poor and the slaves drink mead. There is very great strife among them. And there is no ale brewed by the Ests, but there is sufficient mead.

And there is a custom among the Ests that, when a man is dead there, he lies inside with his relatives and friends, unburnt, for a month, or sometimes two; and the kings and the other high-ranking men so much longer, in proportion to the wealth they

---

[1] A lost town, perhaps Elblag on the Drausen Sea in north Poland.
[2] The island of Bornholm, from which the majority of the Burgundians had migrated in the third century, settling eventually in southern Gaul.
[3] What is now north-east Poland.
[4] An inland sea bordering the Gulf of Danzig. It forms the eastern mouth of the Vistula, now called the Nogat, which flows into this.

possess, so that it is sometimes half a year they remain unburnt and lie above ground in their houses. And all the time the body is inside, there must be drinking and sport until the day they burn him. Then on the same day they decide to carry him to the pyre, they divide up his property – what there remains after the drinking and the sports – into five or six, sometimes into more depending on what the amount of property is. Then they lay the largest share about one mile from the town, then the second, then the third until it is all laid down within the one mile; and the smallest share must be nearest to the town in which the dead man is lying. Then all the men who have the swiftest horses in the land must be assembled about five miles or six miles from the property. Then they all gallop towards the property; then the man who has the swiftest horse comes to the first and also the largest share, and so on one after another until it is all taken; and he who by galloping reaches the part nearest the town takes the smallest share. And then each rides on his way with the property, and may have it all. And therefore swift horses are very valuable there. And then when his treasure is thus all spent, they carry him out and burn him with his weapons and clothing. And they chiefly squander all his wealth with the long lying-in of the dead man, and with what they lay out along the routes, which the strangers gallop for and take. And it is a custom among the Ests that there men of every tribe must be burned; and if one finds there a single bone unburned, they must make great amends for it. And there is among the Ests a tribe that can produce cold; and dead men lie there so long without decay because they bring the cold upon them. And if one set down two vats full of ale or water, they will arrange for both to be frozen over, whether it be summer or winter.

PREFACE TO ST AUGUSTINE'S 'SOLILOQUIES'

The first chapter of this work is essentially a free rendering of the unfinished *Soliloquia* of Augustine, Bishop of Hippo in the province of Carthage, 354–430, and the foremost father of the Latin Church (*PL.*, XXXII 869–904). Cast in the form of a dialogue, its general theme is that of the immortality of the soul. Two further chapters, extending and illustrating the theme of the first, consist of an anthology of ideas culled from Boethius, Gregory, Jerome and other works by Augustine himself. No doubt this anthologizing is what underlies the collecting and constructional metaphor of Alfred's preface.

The sole surviving copy of this work occupies ff. 4–59ᵛ of a twelfth-century MS. now bound up with the *Beowulf* MS: British Library MS. Cotton Vitellius A XV. From the thirteenth *century this MS. belonged to the Augustinian priory at Southwick, Hampshire, and it was probably written for them.*

There are critical editions by W. Endter, König Alfreds des grossen Bearbeitung der Soliloquien des Augustins, Grein's Bibliothek der Angelsächsen Prosa, XI, Leipzig, 1922; and by Thomas A. Carnicelli, King Alfred's Version of St Augustine's Soliloquies, Harvard, 1969.

Then I gathered for myself staves and posts and tie-beams, and handles for each of the tools I knew how to use, and building-timbers and beams and as much as I could carry of the most beautiful woods for each of the structures I knew how to build. I did not come home with a single load without wishing to bring home the whole forest with me, if I could have carried it all away; in every tree I saw something that I needed at home. Wherefore I advise each of those who is able, and has many waggons, to direct himself to the same forest where I cut these posts; let him fetch more there for himself, and load his waggons with fair branches so that he can weave many a neat wall and construct many an excellent building, and build a fair town, and dwell therein in joy and ease both winter and summer, as I have not done so far. But he who taught me, to whom the forest was pleasing, may bring it about that I dwell in greater ease both in this transitory wayside habitation while I am in this world, and also in that eternal home which he has promised us through St Augustine and St Gregory and St Jerome, and through many other holy fathers; so I also believe that for the merits of them all, he will both make this road easier than it was hitherto, and also enlighten the eyes of my mind so that I can find out the straight road to the eternal home and to the eternal glory and to the eternal rest which is promised to us through those holy fathers. So be it.

It is no wonder, though, that one should labour for such material, both in the carrying and in the building; but every man, after he has built a cottage on land leased by his lord, with his help, likes to rest in it sometimes, and go hunting and fowling and fishing, and from that lease to provide for himself in every way, both on sea and on land, until the time when, through his lord's favour, he should merit chartered land and a perpetual inheritance. So may the rich benefactor, who rules both these transitory habitations and those eternal homes, bring it about. May he who created both and rules both grant that I may be fit for each: both to be useful here and especially to attain thither.

Augustine, Bishop of Carthage, made two books about his own meditations; those books are called *Soliloquia*, that is, concerning the deliberation and doubts of his mind – how his reason answered his mind when his mind was uncertain about anything, or it wished to know anything that it could not clearly understand before.

A CHURCH CALENDAR

Some twenty Anglo-Saxon Church calendars survive (cf. F. Wormald, *English Kalendars before A.D. 1100*, London, 1934), their differences of detail reflecting a diversity of local practices. The various festivals of the Church year: saint's-days and other liturgical events, were listed in simple chronological order, the name of the saint to be commemorated, many of them exceedingly obscure by modern standards, being entered against the day of their death – i.e. their 'birth' into new life. However, the text of which typical extracts are given here, supplied more information than could be found in a mere calendar of the catalogue type. Technically this is a 'martyrology', though embracing more than merely the martyrs of the Church. Internal evidence of dialect, and the kind of saints included, indicates that it was produced somewhere in Mercia – perhaps Lincolnshire – and probably in the ninth century. It includes well over two hundred entries in all, most of them narrative in character, albeit abbreviated and allusive. The author has an air of scholarly confidence, and could evidently draw on the resources of a very substantial library. He often began with Bede, but went on to consult Aldhelm, Jerome, Adamnan and a variety of other classical and patristic authorities.

No complete copy survives, but there are two large fragments from the late eleventh century: one, Corpus Christi College, Cambridge, MS. 196, pp. 1–110, very probably the remains of that bequeathed to Exeter Cathedral by Bishop Leofric in 1072 (see above, p. 25), more or less complete from 19 March to 21 December, and another, less complete, running from 31 December to 11 November, British Library MS. Cotton Julius A x, ff. 44–175. There are also odd leaves from two late ninth-century copies: British Library MSS. Additional 23211, f. 2, and 40165A, ff. 6–7, the latter reproduced in *The New Palaeographical Society Facsimiles* (1903–12), II, pl. 101.

The text was edited by G. Herzfeld, *An Old English Martyrology*, EETS., OS., CXVI, London, 1900, and more accurately by G. Kotzor, *Das altenglische Martyrologium*, Munich, 1981.

25 December: Christmas Day[1]

On the first day in the year, that is on the prime Yule-day, all Christian people celebrate Christ's birth. St Mary gave birth to him in the night in a hollow stone cave close to the city of Bethlehem; and immediately he was born, a heavenly light shone over all the land, and God's angel appeared to shepherds one mile east of the city, and told them that the saviour of all peoples was born, and the herdsmen heard a great singing of angels on earth. Then, when Christ was born, there had passed from the beginning of the world, five thousand years and one year off two hundred. In the year when he was born there were shown such signs to men as were not before nor never since. This year men saw three suns,

---

[1] No such headings are included in any of the MSS.

and another time three moons; and the Romans saw a fiery ball fall from heaven, and another time a golden ball. And this year they saw ears of wheat grow on trees; and in one country, when they broke their bread at dinner, then blood flowed from the bread, as it does from a man's body when he is wounded. And among the Egyptians this year many saw milk rain from heaven, and a lamb speak like a human being. And in Rome an ox spoke to the one ploughing, and it said: 'Why do you goad me! Good wheat will grow this year, but you won't be around then, nor eat it!' All this betokened that the pure virgin gave birth to a son, in that no man ever touched her but he who had a father in heaven without a mother, and had a mother on earth without a father. That bath in which St Mary bathed the child – through that many sick men were healed.

26 December: St Eugenia

On the first day is the festival of the noble virgin St Eugenia. It was in the days of the Emperor Commodus, and she loved Christ before she was baptized. She was the daughter of a very famous man who was called Philippus: he was the reeve of the famous town called Alexandria, and the whole nation of Egypt obeyed him. Then, when the girl was fifteen years old, her father wanted to give her to a certain nobleman as a bride. Then in the night she cut off her hair like men, and put on men's clothes and left her father's district with two attendants. Then she went into a monastery of men where no woman ever came before, and there she received baptism and waited on God, and served and lived with them, so that nobody could find out that she was a girl. And within three years she became the monastery's abbot; and she was so powerful with God that she gave blind men sight and healed the demon-possessed. And then, after many years, she was recognized by her father and brothers, whereupon she lived with virgins in their fashion. And after her father, she went with her mother to Rome, and there suffered martyrdom for Christ. There Necitius, the reeve of the city of Rome, insisted that she forsake Christ and believe in devil-worship. Then, when she refused that, he ordered a stone to be bound to her neck and flung into River Tiber. Then the stone broke asunder, and she floated away across the water to land. And then afterwards he ordered that they cast her into a burning oven – and it cooled immediately. Then he ordered that they put her in prison, and she was there ten nights and days without food. Then the Lord revealed himself to her on the very night of his birth and said to her: 'I will take you, Eugenia, and I am he whom you love; I ascended into heaven the same day on which I came to earth.' And the same day she sent forth her spirit to God; and her body rests near Rome on the road they call Latina.

JANUARY

On the eighth Yule-day is the beginning of the month which they call *Januarius*, that is in our language the Later Yule. That is the first month of the year with the Romans and with us. In that month are thirty-one days.

1 January: The Circumcision of Christ

On the first day of the month is the 'eighth day' of Christ and St Mary.[1] On that day Christ received the traditional circumcision and the traditional purification of the Jewish people, which was that they circumcised the male member of each boy-child on the eighth day after his birth; and to them the purification was as holy as baptism is to us. And Christ received the purification thus in order to signify to us that we should cut unclean thoughts from our hearts and licentious deeds from the body, if we want to have a life with God. And on the eighth day men gave Christ a name according to the traditional custom. The name was in Jewish *Jesus*, and in Greek *Sotor*, and in Latin *Salvator*, and in our language Saviour. The angel had told St Mary this name earlier, when she was pregnant.

6 January: The Epiphany[2]

On the sixth day of the month is the great and the famous day which the Greeks call *Epiphania*, and the people of Rome call it *Apparitia Domini*, that is in our language the Day of the Lord's Manifestation. On this day he made known by the four greatest marvels that he was true God. The first marvel was that three astronomers came from countries in the eastern parts to Christ

1 I.e. the eighth day of Christmas, the 'octave' of the Feast of the Nativity.
2 See also Ælfric's sermon on the Epiphany, below, p. 136.

when he was a child; and one brought him gold as a gift, in which was signified that he was true king; a second brought him incense, in which was signified that he was true God; the third brought him the herb myrrh, in which was signified that he was mortal man, and that through his death alone he freed all faithful men from eternal death. And on this same day Christ received baptism in the Jordan from John the Baptist, and he was thirty years of age, the Saviour, when he received the baptism. And on this day at a certain wedding Christ turned six vats full of water into the best wine; in each of these vats there might be two or three measures.[1] And on this same day Christ fed five thousand men from five loaves and from two fishes – also women and children, of whom there were countless – and of the broken loaves there was left twelve bins full.

9 January: St Pega

On the ninth day of the month is the passing of St Pega the holy virgin. She was sister of the hermit St Guthlac,[2] and after his passing, she put salt that he had previously blessed onto the eyes of a blind man, and he could immediately see.

16 January: St Fursey

On the same day [the sixteenth day of the month] is the passing of the mass-priest who was called St Fursey. He was born in the country of the Hibernians, that is, in the land of the Scots.[3] The spirit was led out of the body for a night, and he saw more dreadfulness and also gloriousness than he could tell men about. And the vision was so strong in his mind, that in the great chill of winter, when he thought or spoke about it, then he sweated all over; again, in the great heat of summer, when he remembered his journey, then he grew all pale and trembled. And then, when God's angels brought his spirit back to the body, then he looked on his own body just as if it were an unknown corpse, and he didn't want ever to return into the body, if he had not been compelled.[4]

This Fursey afterwards passed from the Scots into Britain; and

---

[1] The 'measure' here being equal to two 'ambers'.
[2] Cf. The Life of St Guthlac, below, pp. 110–13.
[3] Still at this date in Ireland.
[4] Cf. The Letter of Wynfrith, above, p. 42.

in the country of the East Angles he built the beautiful monastery that is called Burgh Castle. He did that in the days of King Sigeberht; and from there he went overseas into the country of Gaul to Clovis, King of the Franks, and there ended his days; and his body rests in the town of Péronne, and his merits were often clearly manifested there.

MARCH

In the third month in the year are thirty-one days, and the month is called in Latin *Martius* and in our language Rough-month.

2 March: St Chad

On the second day of the month is the passing of the bishop St Chad. And the miracles and life the scholar Bede wrote in his Books of the English People.[1] The archbishop[2] took this Chad from the northern frontier in the monastery of Lastingham, and sent him as bishop to the Mercians and Middle Angles and the people of Lindsey. And God's angels openly led him to heaven with delightful singing; and one of God's servants whose name was Owine, heard that; and the hermit St Egbert told Hygebald the abbot that the soul of the bishop Cedd came from heaven with a host of angels and fetched his brother's soul to heaven. The body of this bishop rests in the monastery at Lichfield.

7 March: SS Perpetua and Felicity

On the seventh day of this month is the commemoration of the holy women St Perpetua and St Felicity, whose bodies rest in Carthage, the great city in the country of Africa. When she was in her girlhood, Perpetua dreamed that she was in the shape of a man, and that she had sword in hand and that she strongly fought with it. That was all afterwards fulfilled in her martyrdom, when she overcame the devil and the heathen persecutors with manly determination.

Then there was the Christian woman Felicity, and she was with child when she was sent to prison for Christ. Then, when the persecutors wanted to leave her alone,[3] she wept and prayed God

1 *Historia Ecclesiastica Gentis Anglorum Libri*, IV 2–3 *et passim*.
2 Theodore, Archbishop of Canterbury, 668–90.
3 The execution of pregnant women being customarily postponed until after the birth.

to rid her of the child; and then that same night she gave birth to it, in the seventh month of the pregnancy; and she suffered martyrdom for Christ.

7 March: St Eosterwine

On the same day is the passing of the holy abbot who was called Eastorwine. He was here in Britain in St Peter's monastery at Wearmouth. That was a very noble man in the sight of the world, and much more noble in the sight of God. He was a thegn of King Ecgferth, but he gave up weapons and worldly ways and went into that monastery and was mass-priest and abbot there. And yet in the sight of God he was so humble that he held the plough and hammered iron and threshed corn and winnowed it, and milked ewes and led calves to the cows, and baked loaves and planted herbs. And he was then twenty-four years old. After twelve years of being in the monastery he forsook earthly limbs and sought the heavenly kingdom. And the day before the night he sent forth his spirit, he sat out in the sun and gave the kiss of peace to all the weeping and sorrowing brethren.

19 March: The Second Day of Creation

On the nineteenth day of the month is the second day of the world. On that day God created the firmament between heaven and earth, and between the two lakes – the upper and the lower. The upper lake is set there so that it cools the heat of the stars, lest it burn the creatures below too much. And the firmament surrounds everything, sea and earth, from outside, just as the shell surrounds the egg from outside, as scholars say.[1]

21 March: The Fourth Day of Creation

On the twenty-first day of the month is the fourth day of the world. On that day God set sun and moon in the firmament of heaven. The sun was then seven times brighter than it is now, and the moon then had the brightness that the sun has now. But then, when Adam and Eve sinned in Paradise, the stars diminished in their brightness, and they have not had anything but the seventh part of their light ever since. But on Judgement Day, when

[1] Cf. The Paris Psalter and the Metres of Boethius, ed. G. P. Krapp, New York, 1932, p. 182.

our Lord will renew all creatures, and all human kind rise up again and they will never sin any more, then the sun will shine seven times brighter than she now does, and she will never go to rest, and the moon will shine just like the sun now does, and he will never more diminish nor increase, but he will stand in his ordained place for ever, for as long as the stars here light this mortal world. Always when the moon goes after the sun, then his light increases; when he is in front of her then his light diminishes. And the nearer he is to the sun, the less his light is; and the further he is from her, the greater his light is – and yet he is always lit by the sun.

22 March: The Fifth Day of Creation

On the twenty-second day of the month is the fifth day of the world. On that day God created from water all kinds of swimming fish and flying birds. Naturalists say that the fish in the sea are of two-hundred-and-fifty-three kinds; and there is not anyone who knows how many kinds of birds there are over the earth. However, each bird lives in that out of which it was created: some always swim now on the salt waves from which they were created; and those that were created out of the fresh water live on pools and on rivers; and those which were made out of the dew of the grass sit in the fields and cannot swim; and those which were formed out of the drops from the trees live in the wood; and those which were made out of the water of the fen live in the fen.

23 March: The Sixth Day of Creation

On the twenty-third day of the month is the sixth day of the world. On that, Adam the first man was created, and Eve his wife was created out of his rib. They were so created that fire could not burn them, nor water drown, nor wild beast rend, nor thorn pierce; nor could they ever grow old or die – if they kept God's commandments. But when they did not keep to that, then they subjected themselves and all human kind to pain and old age, and to death. Adam lived here in exile nine-hundred-and-thirty years, and his bones are buried not far east of the town which is called Hebron; and his head is turned south and the feet north, and the grave is covered with dark and evil stones.

24 March: The Seventh Day of Creation

On the twenty-fourth day of the month is the seventh day of the world. On that day God rested from his work and hallowed it [the day].

25 March: Annunciation & Crucifixion

On the twenty-fifth day of the month the angel Gabriel first came to St Mary with God's message, and on that day in the city of Nazareth St Mary was made pregnant through the angel's word and through the hearing of her ears, like the trees when they blossom through the wind's breath. In the same place where her house was when the angel met her alone, Christian men built a large church. And then after thirty-two years and after three months, Christ was hanged on a cross on the same day; and immediately he was on the cross, then creation signified that he was true God: the sun darkened, and the day was turned into murky night from midday until three o'clock. Then, when he sent forth his spirit at three, the earth trembled, and stones burst, and stone walls collapsed; and the graves of dead men became open and many men saw the dead rise up from the graves and go through the holy town of Jerusalem until Christ rose again; then they departed with him, both with body and with soul, into eternal glory, so that we ourselves should undoubtingly believe, [and] that we should learn from that. The cross of Christ on which he was hung is in a church in the town of Constantinople, locked in a wooden chest; and when the chest is unlocked, there comes up a wonderful smell, and it is as pleasant as if all blossoms were collected there; and from the knots in the wood flows out a sweet-smelling moisture, which has the likeness of oil. If you give one small drop of this moisture to an infirm man, he is immediately better.

26 March: Christ's Descent into Hell[1]

On the twenty-sixth day of the month, Christ remained dead in his grave for us during the day, and his soul and his divinity together harrowed through the depths of hell and slew a host of devils with his divine sword and drove them into the depths of hell, and there bound them. There, all those men and women who

---

[1] Cf. The Gospel of Nicodemus, below, pp. 217–25.

had ever believed in him earlier, recognized him, and they rushed forth from the torments and bowed down at his feet, weeping, and said thus: 'Oh help us, Saviour, now you have come here. Though it be late, we always trusted in your coming; but now quench you these threats and breach these lamentations and make known your majesty in hell, as you did on earth where you redeemed living men by your cross; now save us dead [ones] by your death.' Adam and Eve also recognized him there, where they were suffocated by deep murk. Then, when they saw his bright light after that long age, there Eve implored him, for the sake of her kinship to St Mary, that he take pity on her. She said to him: 'Remember, my Lord, that she was bone of my bones and flesh of my flesh; therefore help me.' Then Christ released them both thence, and also sent before him countless blissful people when he wanted to journey again triumphant to the body.

27 March: Christ's Resurrection

On the twenty-seventh day of the month is the day on which our Lord arose from death; and after his arising, he showed himself to men ten times, as it is written in his gospel, and with his thegns ate broiled fish and honeycomb, and showed them the wounds in his hands and in his feet and the wounded side, so that they might the more truly understand that it was truly his own body that arose from death there.[1] The grave from which he arose is in Jerusalem; it is a circular building cut from a single stone, on which nine men may pray standing, and it is as high as a foot-and-a-half measure above a man's head; and the entrance is in the east, and on the right-hand side of the entrance, that is, on the northern side, is a stone bed seven feet long and three hands'-breadth higher than the floor of the building. On that bed rested the Lord's body, wound round in sheets, when he had died for us.

APRIL

When the Rough-month has passed, then the night is twelve hours long and the day the same. In the fourth month in the year there are thirty days; that month they call in Latin *Aprilis* and in our language Easter-month.

---

[1] Luke, XXIV 39–42.

3 April: SS Agape, Chionia & Irene

On the third day of the month is the commemoration of the holy virgins and blessed sisters St Agape and St Chionia and St Irene. These are very famous virgins in *De Virginitate*, that is, in the Book of Virgins.[1] In the days of the Emperor Diocletian these virgins suffered a famous martyrdom for Christ. The emperor gave them to his reeve, whose name was Dulcitius, in order that he should compel them to renounce Christ. Then as soon as he saw the virgins, he was stirred with shameful lust, and he went at night-time to the house where the virgins prayed to Christ, and he intended to debauch them. There were set there cooking-pots and pans, and through God's power he was deflected from the virgins and embraced the cooking-pots and kissed the pans, so that he was all black and sooty; and then, when he went out, his own men fled from him and thought that it was a *larva*, that is, a spectre. The retainer Sissinius ordered two of these virgins, Agape and Chionia, to be sent into the fire; and when the fire abated, the virgins had passed to Christ, and the bodies were so sound that neither their hair nor garments were burned.

11 April: St Guthlac[2]

On the eleventh day of the month is the passing of the hermit St Guthlac in Britain, whose body rests in the place which is called Croyland. His name is in Latin *Belli Munus*, and at his birth his holiness was immediately signified with heavenly signs. Men saw a beautiful hand come from heaven and mark the door of the house where he was born, and then return to heaven; and after he lived in a hermitage for about a year, he merited that an angel of God spoke to him every evening and again in the early morning, and told him heavenly mysteries.

28 April: St Christopher

On the same day [the twenty-eighth day of the month] is the passion of the great martyr St Christopher. In the days of the Emperor Decius he came into the city which is called Samos from the nation where men have dogs' heads[3] and from the land in which men devour each other. He had the head of a dog, and his

---

[1] By Aldhelm, ed. R. Ehwald, *MGH. Auct. Antiq.* XV 305–7, 443–7.
[2] See generally below, pp. 88–113.
[3] Cf. 'Wonders' below, pp. 228–9.

locks were immeasurably thick, and his eyes shone as bright as the morning-star, and his teeth were as sharp as a boar's tusks. He was faithful to God in his heart, but he could not speak like a man. Then, when he prayed God that he give him the speech of a man, there stood by him a certain man in a white garment and breathed into his mouth; then after that he could speak like a man. The emperor then sent two hundred soldiers to lead him to him. If he would not come to him, they were to slay him and bring him the head so that he could see what it was like. Then, when the soldiers came to him, they dared not approach him; but nevertheless he journeyed with them. Then, when he came to the emperor and he saw his appearance, he was so astonished that he fell off his throne. Then the emperor offered him gold and silver on condition that he turned from belief in Christ. Then, when he did not consent, he ordered him to be tortured with various torments. Then, when he could not overcome him with those, he ordered that they lead him out to beheading. Then Christopher prayed to the Lord, and prayed that God would never condemn in their sins any of those men who had any of his relics, nor that God's anger come upon them, nor that they have scarcity of wheat or other worldly goods. Then a voice came from heaven, and it said: 'It shall be as you ask; and I tell you truly: if any man in great distress is mindful of you, and he then invokes your worthy name on behalf of his concern, then I shall help the man in his distress.' Then Christopher completed his martyrdom. Then a bishop, who was Peter by name, bought his body with money, and brought it to his city and set it on a certain lake from which formerly a flood had flowed and overturned the city; and afterwards, to the glory of God, the city was kept from the flood.

MAY

When the month which we call Easter-month is ended, then the night is ten hours long and the day fourteen hours. In the fifth month in the year there are thirty-one days; the month is called in Latin *Maius* and in our language 'Three-milk', because formerly there was in Britain, and also in the land of Germany from whence the nation of the Angles came into this Britain, such plenty that in that month they milked their beasts three times a day.

3 May: The Invention of the Cross[1]

On the same day [the third day of the month] is the festival of when Christ's cross was first found, so holy writings tell us, on the day we call *quinta nonas Maias*. There came up from the earth the smell of a delightful perfume where the cross was found; and the same day the cross was found, the wood was placed over a dead man's body, and he immediately rose up; and through that miracle it was manifested that that was truly Christ's cross.

6 May: St Eadberht

On the sixth day of the month is the passing of the venerable father St Eadberht, who was bishop in Britain after St Cuthbert in the holy monastery which is called Lindisfarne. Forty days before Easter and forty days before Christ's nativity, that is before Yule, this Eadberht was always accustomed to dwell in a secret place, at his prayers and in spiritual labours; and the place was surrounded with the flood of the sea. Then, when in the Lenten fast in which the brothers of the monastery took St Cuthbert's body from the earth and they found that it was as sound as if he still lived eleven years after he was buried, they carried part of the shroud to the bishop Eadberht, and he kissed it with pure love and wept so that he could say scarcely a word, and said: 'What man can explain the grace of the Lord! He grants to those that love him that their souls live for ever in the heavenly height, and he keeps the dead bodies undecayed under the earth, until they shall rise again alive, when this middle earth will tremble and angels' trumpets sing from above.' He said: 'I certainly know that the place in which St Cuthbert's body rests will not be vacant long and it will be a very blessed man to whom the Lord gives rest in the place.' Then not long after this, Bishop Eadberht, God's dear one, became infirm; and after forty-seven days he sent his spirit to God, and his body was put in the same place where St Cuthbert's body rested before.

8 May: St Michael on Garganus & St Victor

On the eighth day of the month is the day that St Michael's church was first discovered on Mount Garganus, where the man was shot with his own arrow, with which he intended to shoot the bull that

---

[1] See generally below, pp. 114–21.

stood in the cave's entrance.[1] On the same day is the passion of the martyr St Victor, whose body rests in the city of Milan. This Victor, he was of the race of the Moors, and he was a soldier of the heathen emperor Maximianus, but he was a Christian. Then the emperor instructed him to relinquish belief in Christ. Then, when he did not consent to that, they threatened him with torments. He ordered him to be drenched with boiling lead, but that did not injure him any more than cold water. Then he ordered his buffoons to lead him to the wood that is called *ad ulmos* and behead him there. Then he said to those who led him: 'You tell the Emperor Maximianus that he will be dead this year, and his shanks will be broken before he is buried.' Then the emperor commanded that nobody was to bury the body after he was beheaded, but that wild beasts and serpents should devour it. Then two wild beasts came thither and guarded the body, one at the head the other at the foot,[2] until the bishop St Maternus came there and honourably buried it.

9 May: the Beginning of Summer

On the ninth day of the month is the beginning of summer. The summer has ninety days; then the seven stars rise at dawn and set in the evening.

JUNE

In the sixth month in the year are thirty days. The month is called in Latin *Junius*, and in our language the Earlier Mildness, because the air and the winds are gentle, and then men are accustomed to sail on the waters of the sea.

23 June: St Æthelthrytha[3]

On the twenty-third day of the month is the passing of the holy queen St Æthelthrytha. She was wed by two men, but nevertheless she was a pure virgin. First she was wed by Tondberht, Ealdorman of the South Gyrwe, and after that she was given as queen to Ecgfrith, King of the Northumbrians, because she was daughter of Anna, King of the East Anglians. And she was twelve

---

[1] Cf. the Blickling Michaelmas sermon, below, p. 129.
[2] Cf. 'The Passion of St Edmund', below, p. 161.
[3] Cf. the Cambridge thegns' veneration, above, p. 33.

years with Ecgferth the king, and he could not change her mind for anything. Then she took the veil in the monastery which is called Coldingham. A year after this she built a monastery for virgins in the place we call Ely. And she was abbess there, and thereafter wore woollen clothes, and she seldom bathed in a hot bath, except before Easter and before Quinquagesima and before the day of Christ's baptism; and she seldom went to meals more often than once a day, and from the time of matins until day-time she always remained in church at her prayers; and through God's spirit she prophesied to herself when she should depart from the middle-earth. And then she departed; and she was buried in the earth sixteen years; and then, when they took the body up again, it was found as undecayed as if she had passed away the same day. And there was a great open wound in the neck when they put her in the grave, and then, when they took her out again, it was healed so that there was nothing but the mark.

24 June: the Solstice

On the same day [the twenty-fourth day of the month] is *Solstitia*, that is in our language the station of the sun, because the sun stands in the middle of the sky. As St Arculf says,[1] he saw in Jerusalem a certain pillar in the middle of the city, which was set up on the place where the dead man came to life when they placed the Lord's cross over him.[2] Then it happens wonderfully in the summer station of the sun at midday: when the sun is in the middle of the heavens, the pillar doesn't have any shadow. When the station of the sun has run on three days, and the day is somewhat shorter, then the pillar first has a little shadow; and as the days go on shortening, so the pillar's shadow is longer. This pillar proves that the city of Jerusalem is set in the centre of the earth; and it is called *umbilicus terrae*, that is, the navel of the earth, because in the middle of the summer at midday the sun shines from the middle of the heavens alike on either side of the pillar which stands in the centre of the earth.

[1] Related by Adamnan of Iona, *De Locis Sanctis*, PL., LXXXVIII 787–8.
[2] Cf. above, p. 81; below, pp. 119–20.

AUGUST

In the eighth month in the year are thirty-one days. This month they call in Latin the month of Augustus. The nobles of the Romans first called it by that name because on the first day of that month he established the kingdom of the Romans, and overcame those who earlier destroyed it. And in our language we call the month Weed-month, because in that month they grow most.

13 August: St Cassianus

On the same day [the thirteenth day of the month] is the festival of the martyr St Cassianus, who was a teacher of young men in God's law. But then there came a certain heathen emperor who let the boys slay him with their writing-tablets and stab him with their pens; and his suffering was the longer and the harder because their hands were too weak to kill him.

31 August: St Aidan

On the thirty-first day of the month is the passing of the bishop St Aidan, whose soul St Cuthbert saw when in the middle of the night angels brought it to heaven in a great light. The bishop was Scottish, and the holy king St Oswald gained him for this nation. And both living and departed, he did many miracles; and his bones are half in Scotland, half in Glastonbury in St Mary's monastery.

SEPTEMBER

When the month which we call Weed-month is ended, the night is ten hours long and the day fourteen hours. In the ninth month in the year are thirty days. The month is called in Latin *Septembris*, and in our language Holy-month, because our ancestors, for as long as they were heathen, worshipped their idols in that month.

8 October: SS Dionysius, Rusticus & Eleutherius

On the eighth day of the month is the festival of the holy martyrs the bishop St Dionysius and his two deacons whose names were Rusticus and Eleutherius. They were in the city which is called Paris. There they were urged to worship idols; then, when they would not consent, they were martyred for Christ. Then the executioners wanted to throw their bodies into deep water in the river which is called the Seine. But a certain Christian woman invited them to a banquet, and then they showed her the bodies of the saints, and she then ordered her men to steal the bodies at night and bury them in her field; and thereafter the field grew a hundred times better than it did before. Afterwards Christian men built a church there, and there blind men receive their sight, the lame their mobility and the deaf hearing.

NOVEMBER

In the eleventh month in the year are thirty days. The month is called in Latin *Novembris*, and in our language Blood-month, because our ancestors when they were heathen, always sacrificed in that month, that is, they dedicated and committed to their idols the cattle they wanted to give.

28 November: St Chrysanthus

On the same day [the twenty-eighth day of the month] is the festival of the fine man St Chrysanthus, whom his parents committed in his boyhood to a certain learned man in the city of Alexandria, that from him he should learn the seven arts in which all worldly knowledge is found: that is, first arithmetic, that is the art of numbers; and astrology, that is the art of stars; and astronomy, that is the way of the stars; and geometry, that is the measurement of earth; and music, that is the art of harmony; and mechanics, that is the art of worldly works; and medicine, that is the art of remedies. Then, when he had looked through all these arts, he came to a certain mass-priest, then he instructed him in divine writings. Then he abandoned the secular writings and loved the divine writings, and received baptism and served God in purity. Then, when he became a youth, his parents began to urge him to marry.[1]

Then he rejected that. Then the father ordered a certain house to be decorated with great beauty, and ordered many kinds of entertainment to be brought into that house, and ordered the boy to be led into that house, and ordered five richly adorned girls to

---

[1] Literally, 'began to invite him to a marriage-ceremony'.

go into that house. Then the holy boy bent his face downwards and did not want to see them – the more so because five adders crept into that house; and then immediately sleep came over the girls, and they slept day and night for as long as they were in the house. Then the father ordered him to be led to a very clever woman who was decked with gold and with jewels, that she should change his mind, whose name was Daria. Then he instructed her in Christ's faith, and they lived together in purity, and together ended their lives in martyrdom, and together rest in one grave, and the spirits together rejoice in one glory. And through them God did many miracles, both through their living and through their passing away.

DECEMBER

When the month is ended which we call Blood-month, then the night is sixteen hours long, and the day eight hours. In the twelfth month in the year are thirty-one days. The month is called in Latin *Decembris* and in our language Early Yule. The two months[1] are called by one name, the one the Early Yule, the other the Later, because the one of them goes in front of the sun, before it turns to lengthen the day, the other after.

21 December: St Thomas

On the twenty-first day of the month is the festival of the apostle St Thomas, who was called *didymus* in Greek and in Latin *geminus*, that is in our language 'twin'. He was so called because he was like our Saviour in human appearance; and after Christ's ascension he instructed many nations in Christ's faith: Parthians and Medes and Persians and Hyrcanians, and Bactrians, and two peoples of India. And he journeyed through the country of heathen people and the eastern part of the middle-earth. And with the Indians he built in heaven a hall for their king, who was Gundaforus by name; and the king's brother, whose soul was led to heaven by God's angels, saw that the hall was built inside and out with green and with azure and with white – and afterwards he was alive on earth – who said that it was built thus in heaven. But among the other people of India, the king Mygdæg[2] – and his

---

1 I.e. January and December, cf. above, p. 72.
2 Properly Mazdai.

Ealdorman who was Caritius by name – he insisted that this Thomas worship a sun idol. There was the likeness of the sun made of gold, and it was a golden chariot, and there were golden horses to it, and the reins on them were tied back as if they were galloping up to heaven. Then, when Thomas went in there, a terrible devil went out of the gold-work and stood in front of him, and the gold-work fell away, just as wax melts at fire. Then one of the heathen bishops slew the thegn of Christ; and writings sometimes say that he was stabbed through with a sword, sometimes they say that he was pierced with spears. He suffered in the Indian city of Calamina, and his body was brought out of India to the city which is called Edessa; there he is set in a silver chest – and it hangs on silver chains. Nor may any heretic live in that city, nor any of those who worship idols, nor ever afterwards could any foreign nation harry the city.

THE LIFE OF ST GUTHLAC

The Mercian hermit Guthlac died at Crowland in the fens of south Lincolnshire in 714. Shortly after, and probably between about 730 and 740, a Latin account of his life was written by one Felix at the request of Ælfwald, King of the East Anglians c. 713–49. We know little or nothing about the author, and no other known work of his survives. But he betrays a clear knowledge of earlier saints' lives, and was influenced especially by Aldhelm and by Bede – in particular by Bede's prose *Life of St Cuthbert*.

Guthlac became an especially popular cult figure in the old Middle-Anglian region, where several ancient church-dedications to the saint are found. His festival was celebrated by the Anglo-Saxon Church on 11 April. He was the subject of two Old English poems in the Exeter Book: *Guthlac A* and *Guthlac B*, and a Middle English verse life was included in the *Early South-English Legendary*. There are several later Latin accounts of the saint in both prose and verse. And particularly notable is the so-called Guthlac Roll (British Library Harleian Roll, Y6), a twelfth-century collection of narrative scenes depicting incidents from the saint's life.

The Old English version of the *Life* is by no means a pedestrian translation of the Latin original, although it follows the narrative outline quite closely. It occurs at the end of an eleventh-century collection of biblical translations and other writings by Ælfric, now British Library MS. Cotton Vespasian D xxi, ff. 18–40ᵛ. A fragment corresponding to the greater part of sections 4 and 5, and adapted for use as a homily, is found at the end of the Vercelli Book. As might be expected, its linguistic forms show some indication of Mercian origin. There is a critical edition, printed together with a comparative Latin text and facsimile illustrations from the Guthlac Roll, by Paul Gonser, *Das angelsächsische Prosa-Leben des heiligen Guthlac* (Anglistische Forschungen, 27), Heidelberg, 1909.

Prologue. To him who truly believes in our Master, world without end, to my dearest lord above all other men, earthly kings, Ælfwald, King of the East Angles, ruling the kingdom with justice and with propriety. I, Felix, confirm the true faith and the eternal blessing of salvation for all of God's faithful people, and send greetings. I have obeyed your words and commands; I have written the book which you asked for concerning the life of Guthlac of venerable memory, with clear words and evidence.

Wherefore I entreat and beseech the learned and the faithful that if he find any ridiculous phrase here he blame us not for it. But let each of those who detract and deride, remember and think that the kingdom of God does not dwell in words but in steadfastness of holy faith. And remember and reflect that the salvation of the world was not devised by idle thoughts, but preached and told by fishermen. But if any man reproach our design and work – for I know many among the English who might have written this book themselves, gilded with beautiful letters, beautifully and clearly set down – let him not blame us, inasmuch as we obeyed compulsion and command, and carried out an instruction. Therefore, O reader, if you deride me after the fashion of those who detract, beware yourself, lest while you look for laughter you are not suddenly blinded with the obscurity of darkness. It is the fashion of the blind that, when they are in the light, they do not know but that they wander in the dark. In the holy scriptures folly is often termed blindness, since from there the beginning of all evil first comes. For this reason then, reader, I exhort you not to rebuke strangers, lest afterwards you as a stranger be rebuked by others. But lest I longer burden the mind of readers with talking of the detraction of strangers, let me sail, as it were, over a great and powerful sea, and come now to that most peaceful harbour, the life of Guthlac.

Because you commanded me to write and tell about Guthlac's actions and the example of his life, I therefore obeyed you and accordingly wrote as those informants who best knew his life told me – first what its beginning was, and then to what end he brought it. I composed this book for this reason, that those who knew the life of the blessed man might be adequately reminded of his life; and for those others who did not know about it before, I might, as it were, show them a broad and open path. I learned the things which I write here from conversations with the venerable abbot Wilfrid. Also many others who were with the blessed man and observed his life with their own eyes, told about it. I do not doubt anything that my informants were able to remember and tell – all the miracles of this blessed man; they were very widely known and famous throughout the land of the English.

I have therefore obeyed your instructions and satisfied your word and will, and have set down the text in this present document as best I could with the knowledge of my predecessors and their elders. I have put the beginning at the beginning and the end at the end.

1. In the days of Æthelred, the famous King of the Mercians,[1] there was a certain nobleman in the great kingdom of Mercia who was called Pendwald. He came from the oldest and noblest family, who were called Iclings. He was prosperous in the world and had

---

[1] Æthelred reigned from 675 to 704, then abdicated to become a monk, and died in 716.

great riches; and then when he was most prosperous and had most riches, he longed to take himself a wife. From out of a multitude of girls he chose the one who was the prettiest and from the noblest family. She was called Tette.

And they were together until the time that God ordained that the woman was pregnant with a child. Then when the time came that she should give birth to the child, suddenly a sign came from heaven and marked out the child clearly with a seal. In fact, coming out of heaven men saw a hand of the most beautiful red hue; and it held a golden cross, and was manifested to many men, and tilted down in front of the door of the house in which the child was born. Then all those men who saw it hurried there because they wanted to see and to perceive the sign more clearly. Then the hand returned with the cross up into heaven. Then all the men who saw the sign prostrated themselves on the earth and prayed to God that he would make known to them what the sign and portent was which was so suddenly manifested to them there. Then when they had finished that prayer, a certain woman came running in great haste out of the house in which the child was born, and called and spoke to the men thus: 'Be steadfast and heartened, for a man of future glory is born here on this earth.' Then when the men heard this word, they said among themselves that it was a divine sign that was manifested there, because the child was born there. Some of them then said that by divine dispensation eternal bliss was a pre-ordained gift for him, by the holy sign that was manifested to them at his birth. Men were quite amazed at the matter and at the sign which was manifested there, and indeed, before the sun had gone to its rest, it was known and famous all over the land of the Middle Angles.

2. Then about eight nights afterwards, when they brought the child to the holy bath of the baptismal font, he was given a name after the name of the family and of the people – Guthlac, as though it were done by divine dispensation that he were named thus, for wise scholars among the English say that the name consists of two terms: the name Guthlac is in Latin *Belli munus*, because he not only endured many hardships with worldly toil, but also by conversion received the gift of eternal bliss with the victory of eternal life, saying thus with the apostle:[1] *Beatus vir, qui suffert temptationem, quia cum probatus fuerit, accipiet coronam*

---

[1] James, I 12.

vite, quam repromisit dominus diligentibus se. That is in English: 'Blessed is the man', he says, 'who endures manifold labours and hardships here in the world, for when he is tempted and afflicted, then he receives the eternal crown; and that God has promised to all those who love him.'

Then after he was bathed with the bath of holy baptism, he was taken back to his father's hall and there nursed. When the age came that he could speak in a child's fashion, he was not at all difficult, nor disobedient to the commands of his elders, nor to those who nursed him, whether old or young. Neither did he engage in boyish wantonness, nor in the idle chatter of vulgar men, nor in unseemly flattery or dissimulation. Nor did he care about the various bird songs, as is often the custom of boyish years. But he grew in acuteness and became cheerful of face, and pure and clean in his spirit, and innocent in his ways. And the light of spiritual brightness shone so much in him that all men who looked at him could see what would happen to him.

Then when, after the passage of time, his power grew and was strengthened in him in his youth, he thought about the valiant deeds of the heroes of old and of the great men of the world. Whereupon, as if he had awoken from sleep, his mood changed, and he gathered a great troop and band of his friends and equals, and took up weapons himself. Then he wreaked his displeasure on his enemies, and burned their fortress and ravaged their villages; and he made a great slaughter widely throughout the land, and killed and took men's property from them. Then, of a sudden, he was divinely admonished within, and instructed that he should command thus: he ordered that of all that he had taken, the third part should be given back to those men from whom he had previously taken it.

It was about nine years that the blessed Guthlac was engaged in hostile raids, and himself strayed amidst the tumults of this present world. Then it happened one night when he had come in from an expedition and he rested his weary limbs, and thought over many things in his mind, that he was suddenly inspired with the fear of God, and his heart within was filled with spiritual love. And when he awoke he thought about the ancient kings of old, who forsook this world with a wretched death and with a miserable departure left this wicked life. And he saw the great wealth which they formerly owned all quickly pass away. And he saw his own life daily hurry and hasten towards the end. Then suddenly he was so very inspired with godly fear that he vowed to God that, if he would spare him until morning, he would be his servant. When the darkness of night had passed away and daylight came, he rose up and signed himself with the seal of Christ's cross. Then he asked his companions to find themselves another commander and leader of their company; and he confessed and told them that he wanted to be a servant of Christ. When his companions heard these words they were very surprised and greatly afraid of the words which they heard. Then they all bowed to him and begged him that he would never carry out the things he had said. He did not heed their words, however, but wanted to follow through the very thing that he had previously intended. The love of God burned so strong within him that he scorned not only the world, but his parents' riches and his home, and even his very companions, so that he forsook it all. He was twenty-four years old when he forsook all worldly pomp and put all his hope in Christ.

And after that he went to the monastery which is called Repton[1] and there, under Abbess Ælfthryth, received the mystic tonsure of the Apostle St Peter. And indeed, after he received the tonsure and the monastic life, he would not taste any intoxicating liquor. And for this reason the brethren hated him, because he was so abstinent. But soon afterwards, when they perceived the purity of his mind and the cleanness of his life, they all loved him. He was large in appearance, clean in body, cheerful in mood and handsome of face; he was gentle and modest in his speech and he was patient and humble; and divine love was always hot and burning in his heart. When he was drawn to letters and learning, he longed to learn his psalms. Then the fertile breast of the blessed man was filled with the grace of God and with the teaching of the best of God's masters, so that he was instructed and learned in divine discipline. When he had spent two years in that study, he had learned his psalms and canticles and hymns and prayers according to ecclesiastical routine. Then he began to observe the good habits of those who were virtuous in that way of life: humility and obedience, patience and long-suffering and bodily continence. And he cultivated the virtues of all those good men.

After he had thus lived for about two years of his life in the monastic order, he began to long for the wilderness and a hermit's

---

[1] In Derbyshire, burial-place of the Mercian kings.

cell. When he heard tell and learned about the anchorites of old who, for the name of God, longed for the wilderness and hermits' cells, and lived their lives there, his heart was inwardly inspired by the grace of God, so that he longed for the wilderness. Then, a few days later, he begged leave from the servants of God who were the elders there that he might depart.

3. There is in Britain a fen of immense size, which begins from the River Granta not far from the city of the same name, called Grantchester. There are immense swamps, sometimes dark stagnant water, sometimes foul rivulets running; and also many islands and reeds and tummocks and thickets. And it extends to the North Sea with numerous wide and lengthy meanderings.

When the aforesaid man, Guthlac of blessed memory, heard of this uncultivated place of broad wilderness, he was supported by divine aid and at once made his way there by the most direct route. And when he came there he asked the inhabitants of the country where he might find himself a place to live in the wilderness. Whereupon they told him many things about the vast extent of the wilderness. Then a certain man called Tatwine said that he knew of a certain particularly obscure island, which many men had often tried to occupy but no man could endure because of various horrors and fears and because of the loneliness of the broad wilderness; and because of that everyone ran away from it. When the holy man heard these words, he bade him immediately show him the place; and he did so straightaway. Then he went on a boat and they both travelled through the wild fenlands until they came to the place which they call Crowland. The land was such, situated in the middle of the wilderness of the aforesaid fen, very obscure. And as no man could ever live there before the blessed Guthlac came there, because of the dwelling-place there of the accursed spirits, very few men knew of it except the one who showed it to him. And the blessed Guthlac at once scorned the temptation of the accursed spirits and was strengthened with heavenly support so that he began to live alone amidst the swampy thickets of the wilderness.

It happened by divine providence that he came to the island on the festival of the Apostle St Bartholomew, since he sought his assistance in everything. And he loved the obscurity of the place, and then he vowed that he would serve God on that island all the days of his life. After he had been there a few days, he surveyed the circumstances of the place. Then he thought that he would go back to the monastery and greet his brethren, because he had gone away from them earlier without taking leave. Then in the morning when daylight came, he went back to the monastery. He stayed there with the brethren for ninety days; and after he had taken leave of them, he turned again to the place in the beloved wilderness with two boys. It was the 25th of August, which they observe as the festival of St Bartholomew the Apostle, when the blessed Guthlac came to the aforesaid place, Crowland, because he sought his assistance first in everything to do with the hermitage. He was twenty-six years old when, endowed with heavenly grace, God's champion first settled in the wilderness.

Then straightaway, in order that he might shield himself against the darts of the wicked spirits with spiritual arms, he took the shield of faith in the Holy Spirit, and dressed himself in the mail of heavenly hope; and he put on his head the helmet of pure thoughts; and he continually shot and fought against the accursed spirits with the arrows of holy psalms. And now, how greatly must we wonder at the secret might of our Lord, and his merciful judgements; who can tell them all? As the noble teacher of all nations, St Paul the Apostle, whom our Lord Almighty God fore-ordained to preach the Gospel to his people – he was previously a persecutor of his holy church, and while he journeyed to the town of Damascus he was delivered from the dark errors of the Jew's unbelief by the sound of a heavenly voice – so Guthlac, of venerable memory, was led from the tribulation of this world to the battle for the life eternal.

4. *Concerning the holy man; how he lived in the place.* I will now begin concerning the life of the blessed Guthlac, just as I heard those who knew of his life, Wilfrid and Cissa, tell; and I will tell it in that order.

There was on the island a certain great burial-mound built over the earth, which men of old had dug into and broken up looking for treasure. On one side of the burial-mound there was dug, as it were, a great reservoir. Over this reservoir the blessed Guthlac built himself a house. From the beginning, as soon as he settled in the hermitage, he resolved that he would use neither woollen nor linen clothing, but that he would live all the days of his life in garments of skins; and thenceforward he did so. Each day from the time that he began to live in the wilderness, the frugality of his diet was such that he tasted nothing but barley-bread and water; and he partook of the food by which he lived, after the sun had set.

One day soon after he began to live in the wilderness, it happened that, when he had sung his psalm in his accustomed manner and fell to his prayers, that the ancient foe of mankind (who even as a roaring lion went about the grassy plain, widely scattering the poison of his temptations), while he scattered the might of his wickedness and the poison of his fierceness so that he might injure the hearts of men thereby, then suddenly, as if from a bended bow, fixed the arrow of his temptation in the heart of Christ's champion. Then when the blessed man was wounded with the accursed spirit's poisoned arrow, the blessed man's heart was greatly troubled within him about the undertaking which he had begun, to live alone in the wilderness thus. Then he turned it over continually in his mind, and remembered the former sins and wickednesses which he had performed and committed, and how he himself had done greater and more enormous things than he imagined he could ever atone for. So the devilish arrow had wounded him with despair. For three days the blessed man Guthlac was wounded with despair, so that he himself did not know where to turn his heart. It was on the night following the third day that he firmly withstood these doubting thoughts; and thereupon he sang with prophetic mouth and cried to God and said: *In tribulatione mea invocavi dominum,* et cetera,[1] that is in English: 'My Lord, I cry to you in my distress and you hear me and aid me in my tribulation.' Then it was soon after that that his faithful support, St Bartholomew, came to him; and he did not appear to him while asleep, but he saw and looked upon the apostle in angelic splendour while awake. And forthwith the blessed Guthlac was very joyful because of the heavenly visitor. And immediately his heart and mind was completely enlightened; and he rapidly abandoned the evil and irresolute thoughts. And the heavenly visitor, St Bartholomew, comforted him and confirmed and strengthened him with words, and commanded him not to doubt but to be resolute, and said that he would be a help to him in all his troubles. When the holy Guthlac heard these words of his faithful friend, he was filled with spiritual bliss, and confirmed and fixed his faith fast on God himself.

5. It also happened on one occasion, while he was considering the conduct of his life, how he might live most acceptably to God, suddenly there came to him two devils, slipping down from the

---

[1] Psalm XVII 7.

sky, and spoke to him familiarly and said: 'We are acquainted with your life, and we are aware of the firmness of your faith, and we also know your patience to be unconquered; and in that we tested and tried you when we sent our weapons against you with manifold cunning. Now henceforth we will no longer trouble nor irritate you. Not only will we now not hinder you from what you previously intended, but we will tell you also about all those who inhabited the wilderness of old, how they lived their lives. First Moses and Elijah, they fasted; and also the Saviour of all the world, he fasted in the wilderness; and also the famous monks who were in Egypt, and lived in the wilderness there; they, through their abstinence, struck down and killed all vice in themselves. Therefore if you wish to wash from you the sins that you formerly committed, then you should afflict your body with abstinence; because to the extent that you severely afflict yourself here in the world, so afterwards you will be the more firmly strengthened in eternity; and to the extent that you endure more distress in this present life, you will afterwards receive so much in the future; and when you get down to fasting here in the world, then you will be raised up in God's eyes. Therefore your fasting must not be for a space of two days, or three, or every day, that you should congratulate yourself on such a very great abstinence; but it takes a fast of seven days' space to cleanse a man. As God first fashioned and adorned the beauty of all the earth in six days and on the seventh rested himself, so then it behoves you similarly to adorn the spirit with a six-day fast, and then on the seventh day to take food and rest the body. When the blessed Guthlac heard these words, he at once arose and cried to God and said: 'Let my foes be forever repulsed, my Lord God, for I know and understand you, for you are my Creator.' Then immediately after these words the accursed spirit vanished from before his face, just like smoke. Then he scorned the devilish doctrine, for he perceived that it was entirely vain; and he took modest nourishment, that is, the barley-bread, and ate it and sustained his life. Then when the accursed spirits realized that he completely scorned them and their doctrines, they lamented with a wailing voice that they were conquered. And the blessed man was so triumphant that he scorned the blasphemy of their doctrines and their temptations.

It also happened some time not many days later, that he spent the night keeping watch with holy prayers, when in the quiet of the night it suddenly happened that there came great multitudes of the accursed spirits; and they filled all the house with their presence and they poured in on every side, from above and below and everywhere. They were terrible in appearance; and they had huge heads and a long neck and a scraggy face; they were filthy and squalid in their beards; and they had shaggy ears, and crooked nose and cruel eyes and foul mouths; and their teeth were like horses' fangs, and their throats were filled with flame, and they were harsh of voice; they had crooked shanks and huge knees, big in the rear, and shrivelled-up toes; and they shrieked hoarsely with their voices, and came with such excessive noises and such immense horror, that it seemed to him that everything between heaven and earth resounded with their dreadful cries. Without delay after they had come into the building they immediately bound the holy man in all his limbs and dragged and brought him out of the cell, and then led him into the black fen and flung and immersed him in the filthy water. After that they brought him to the wild places of the wilderness among dense thickets of brambles, so that he was all wounded in the body. After they had tormented him thus in the dark for a long time, then they let him stay and stand a while. Then they commanded him to leave the wilderness; or if he would not do so, then they would afflict and try him with more filthiness. He, the blessed Guthlac, did not heed their words. But with prophetic mouth, he spoke thus: 'The Lord is at my right hand, therefore I shall not be moved from you.'[1]

Thereupon the accursed spirits seized him and beat him with iron whips; and then after that they brought him on horrible wings amidst the cold regions of the sky. Then when he was at that height in the air he saw all the northern part of heaven as if it were surrounded by the blackest clouds of intense darkness. Then suddenly he saw an immense host of accursed spirits come towards him; and at once they gathered together, and immediately all then led the holy man to the black places of torment and brought him to hell's door. Then when he saw the foulness of the smoke and the burning flames and the terror of the black depths, he soon forgot all the torments and punishments which he had previously suffered and endured from the accursed spirits. Then the accursed spirits promptly rushed in and fell among the

[1] Psalm XVI 8.

terrible flames, and there they tormented the souls of wicked men with manifold punishments. Then, when the blessed Guthlac saw the greatness of those punishments, he was very afraid for dread of them. Then the accursed spirits at once cried out with a great crying, and spoke thus: 'Power is granted to us to thrust you into the torments of this abyss, and here is that fire which you yourself set alight within you; and because of your sins and crimes the door of hell opens before you.' When the accursed spirits had threatened him with these words, he answered them thus, and said: 'Woe to you, children of darkness and fruits of perdition! You are dust and ashes and cinders; who granted you wretches that you should have power to send me into these punishments? Well, I am here present and ready, and await the will of my Lord; so why should you frighten me with your false threats?' Then those accursed spirits at once motioned against the blessed man, as if they would thrust him in there. Then suddenly the inhabitant of heaven, the holy Apostle St Bartholomew, came shining with heavenly brightness and glory amidst the dark gloom of black hell. Those accursed spirits were not able to remain there because of the splendour of the holy visitor, but they hid themselves in the darkness. Then when the blessed man Guthlac saw his faithful friend, he was very glad, with spiritual bliss and heavenly joy. Whereupon the holy Apostle St Bartholomew commanded and ordered them to be subject to him and to bring him again with gentleness to the same place from which they had previously abducted him. And then they did so, and brought him thus with all gentleness, and carried and conveyed him on their wings, so that he could not have been conveyed more pleasantly in a ship. When they came to the midst of the height of the sky, there came towards him a company of holy spirits, and they all sang and spoke thus: *Ibunt de virtute in virtutem*, et cetera,[1] that is, in English: 'Holy men shall go from strength to strength.' Then in the morning when it was about to become day, they set him down again in the place from where they had previously taken him.

Then when he was about to complete his morning period of prayer to God, he saw two of the accursed spirits standing there, greatly weeping and lamenting. When he asked them for what reason they wept, they answered him and spoke thus: 'We are weeping because our power is all broken through you, and we

---

[1] Psalm LXXXIII 8.

cannot now come to you, nor have any conversation with you; but you have mocked at us in every way, and overcome all our strength.' Then after those words the accursed spirits passed from his sight, just like smoke.

6. *How the Devils spoke in Celtic.* It happened in the days of Cœnred, King of the Mercians,[1] that the British nation, enemy of the English people, annoyed the English with many skirmishes and various battles. Then it happened one night when it was cock-crow and the blessed Guthlac fell to his morning prayers, he was of a sudden lulled into a light sleep. Then Guthlac started up from that sleep, and immediately went out and looked and listened. Then he heard a great host of the accursed spirits speaking in Celtic; and he knew and understood their speech because some time previously he had been in exile among them. Then immediately after that he saw all his house filled with fire, and thereafter they all struck him down with the points of spears, and hung him up in the air on the spears. Then the strong champion of Christ immediately perceived that these were the terrors and torments of the accursed spirits. Without fear he then at once thrust the darts of the accursed spirits away from him, and sang the psalm: *Exurgat deus et dissipentur*, et cetera.[2] As soon as he had sung the first verse of the psalm they vanished from his sight just like smoke. Then when the blessed Guthlac fought and contended with the accursed spirits so frequently, they realized that their power and activity was vanquished.

7. *Concerning the priest Beccel.* There was a certain priest whose name was Beccel. He came to the holy man and begged that he would take him in, and promised that he would live humbly in God's service by his instructions. Then the accursed spirit sprinkled and mingled the heart and mind of that same priest with the poison of his treacheries; the accursed spirit urged him to strike down and slay Guthlac, and suggested to his heart thus: 'If I slay and kill him, then later I can possess the same place after him, and then men of the world will honour me as they now do him.' It happened that the same priest came to the holy man one day in order to shave him – as his custom was to wash himself every twenty days – when he was overcome by a very strong desire to shed the holy man's blood. Guthlac immediately recognized the cunning of the accursed spirit (since through the grace of God, all

[1] Cœnred reigned from 704 to 709, when he abdicated and went to be a monk at Rome.
[2] Psalm LXVII 2.

future things were known to him, and similarly those present, and he could see and survey the man within as well as without). And he spoke to him thus: 'Oh my Beccel, why have you hidden the accursed fiend beneath your foolish breast? Why will you not spew out from you the deadly draught of that bitter poison? I see that you are deceived by the accursed spirit and the wicked thought of your heart. The tempter of mankind and the enemy of the world has given birth to those incessant recurrences of that evil thought in you; but turn yourself away from the evil teaching of the accursed spirit.' Then he realized at once that he had been deceived by the accursed spirit, promptly fell at the feet of the holy man, and in tears immediately confessed his sin to him. Then the holy Guthlac not only forgave him that sin, but also promised him that he would be of assistance to him in all his troubles.

8. *How the devils departed.* One night when the holy Guthlac fell to his prayers it happened that he heard the bellowing of cattle and various wild beasts. Shortly afterwards he saw the shape of all sorts of creatures and wild beasts and serpents coming towards him. First he saw the face of a lion, and it threatened him with its bloody fangs; also the likeness of a bull and the face of a bear, as when they are enraged; also the shape of vipers, and a pig's grunting, and the howling of wolves, and croaking of ravens, and the various whistlings of birds; that by their appearance they might turn the mind of the holy man. Then the holy Guthlac armed himself with the weapon of Christ's cross and with the shield of holy faith, and scorned the temptations of the accursed spirits, and spoke thus: 'Oh you wretched, perverse spirit, your power is seen and your might is made known. Now, wretch, you take on the form of wild beasts and birds and serpents, you who formerly exalted yourself when you wanted to be on a par with God. Now I command you in the name of the eternal God, who made you and flung you from the height of heaven, to cease from this disturbance.' Thereupon all the manifestations of the accursed spirits immediately passed away.

9. *How the writing was recovered.* It happened one night that there came a certain man to speak to the holy man. When he had been there some days, it happened that he wrote some writing on a piece of paper. Then, when he had written the writing, he went out. Thereupon there came in a raven; as soon as it saw the paper it immediately took it and went into the fen with it. The aforesaid visitor came back again directly and saw the raven carrying off the

paper; whereupon he was at once very distressed. When at the same time the holy Guthlac came out of his church, he saw the brother sorrowful. Then he comforted him and said to him: 'Do not be sorrowful, brother; but as the raven flies up through the fens, so you row after him; then you will find the writing.' Shortly afterwards the same man who had written the writing went into a boat. Then, when he rowed through the fens, he came to a certain mere which was very near the island; and there was in the middle of the mere a certain reed-bed; and the paper hung on a reed, just as if a man's hand had hung there. And straightaway, joyfully he seized the paper and marvelling brought it to the man of God; and then he, the holy Guthlac, said that it was not due to his merit but to the mercy of God. There were, living in that same island, two ravens so greedy that they would carry away whatever they could seize; nevertheless, he put up with and endured all their greediness, so that he might later give men the example of his patience. And not only were the birds subject to him, but all the fishes and wild animals of the wilderness also obeyed him; and daily from his own hand, he gave them food appropriate to their kind.

10. *How the swallows sat on him and sang.* Then one time it happened that there came to him a venerable brother whose name was Wilfrid, who had for long been united with him in spiritual communion. While they pondered their spiritual life with much discussion, there suddenly came flying in two swallows; and lo, they lifted up their song, rejoicing, and after that settled fearlessly on the shoulders of the holy Guthlac, and lifted up their song; and afterwards they settled on his breast and on his arms and on his knees. Then when Wilfrid, marvelling, had long beheld the birds, he asked him why the wild birds of the broad wilderness settled on him so submissively. He then, the holy Guthlac, answered him, and said to him: 'Have you not learned in holy scriptures, brother Wilfrid, that the wild beasts and wild birds come closer to him who has led his life in God's will? And the angels come nearer to him who would live his life apart from men of the world; whereas he who frequently wishes for the conversation of worldly men cannot fall in with angelic discourse.'

11. *Concerning the gloves which the ravens carried off.* Also at one time there occurred a prophetic miracle concerning this holy man. There was a certain prominent man of the royal house in Mercia whose name was Æthelbald. When he wanted to come and speak with the holy man, he prevailed upon Wilfrid to bring him

to the man of God; and at once they went into a boat and journeyed to the island where the holy Guthlac was. Then when they came to the holy man, Wilfrid had left his gloves in the boat. And when they spoke with the holy man, the blessed Guthlac asked them whether they had left anything behind them in the boat (for God had made all hidden things known to him). Then Wilfrid answered him and said that he had left his two gloves in the boat. Shortly afterwards, as soon as they came out from inside, they saw the raven up on the thatch of the house tearing the glove with its black beak. Then the holy Guthlac immediately rebuked the raven with his voice, for its mischief; and it obeyed his voice, and so the bird flew westward over the wilderness. Whereupon Wilfrid reached the glove from the roof of the house with a stick. Also, not long after, there came three men to the landing-stage and sounded the signal there. Then the holy man Guthlac went out to the men directly, with cheerful face and good humour. He then spoke with the men. Then, when they wished to leave, they brought out a glove and said that it had fallen from the mouth of a raven. Smiling, the holy man immediately took it, and gave them his blessing, and they went away. And he returned the glove to him who had previously owned it.

12. *How Hwætred recovered his health.* There was in the land of the East Angles a certain man of noble family whose name was Hwætred. While he was daily dutifully subject to his parents, it happened on one occasion when he was at his father's home that the accursed spirit entered into him so that he went out of his mind. And the accursed fiend afflicted him with madness so severely that he bloodied and wounded his own body, both with iron and with his teeth; and he not only wounded himself with his savage teeth, but he likewise also tore at whomever he could. It happened that on one occasion there was a great company of men of his kin gathered, and also other of his close friends, that they might bind him and bring him under control. He then took a winged axe and struck three men to death with it, and wounded many others with them. He was afflicted with madness thus for four years. Then at last he was taken by his family and brought to the holy monastery so that priests and bishops might wash and cleanse him from the madness. But, despite many attempts they could not drive out the evil power of the accursed spirit. Then finally they journeyed home again with the kinsman, sorrowful; and they wished him dead rather than that he should trouble men

THE LIFE OF ST GUTHLAC

any longer. Then eventually the rumour was noised in the province that in the middle of the fen on an island which was called Crowland was a certain hermit who abounded with various powers before God. Then immediately they found out about the holy man, they thought they would bring the man there, if it should be God's dispensation that they might find help there. And they did so: journeyed there so that they came to a certain island which was very near that on which the man of God was; and they spent the night there with the sick man. Then when it dawned in the morning they came to the aforesaid island, and then in the customary manner made the signal. He then, the holy Guthlac, went to them directly with the great power of God's love. When, weeping, they had told him of their case, he was at once filled with pity. He promptly took the sick man and led him into his church, and there remained for three days, incessantly at his prayers. Then when the sun rose on the third day, he bathed him in holy water and blew on his face, and with that, all the power of the accursed spirit in him broke. And it was as if the same man, stretching, awoke from a deep sleep. And he recovered his health, and went home; and the sickness never troubled him afterwards for as long as he lived.

13. *Concerning Æthelbald's companion.* It also happened on one occasion that a companion of the aforesaid exile Æthelbald,[1] whose name was Ecga, was troubled because of the accursed spirit; and it afflicted him so severely that he did not know what he was doing. Whereupon his family brought him to the man of God. Then as soon as he came to him he put his girdle around him. No sooner was he girded with the girdle, than all the uncleanness passed away from him, and the sickness never troubled him again. Moreover, the blessed man Guthlac flourished and prospered in the prophetic spirit, and he made known the future to men as clearly as the present.

14. *Concerning the abbot.* It happened that on one occasion there came to him a certain abbot, who had for long been united with him in spiritual communion. While he journeyed there, his two servants who were with him asked him for permission to travel by another route, and added that it was inevitable and necessary for them. Whereupon the abbot granted them what they requested of him. Then, when the abbot came there to talk

[1] See p. 101. In the Old English version the fact of his exile is not mentioned until section 19, p. 107.

with the blessed man, they drank together from the well of holy scriptures; then amidst their talk of the holy scriptures, Guthlac said to him: 'But where did those two go who turned aside from you earlier?' Then he answered him and said: 'They asked leave of me; they had other business, so that they could not come here.'

Then Guthlac answered him – inasmuch as God revealed all future things to him, so that they were as clear to him as the present – and began to tell him the doings of those brothers, and said to him: 'They went to the home of a certain widow, and were intoxicated there by too much drinking.' And not only did he tell him of their course, but also about their refreshment and even the very words which they spoke there; he told it all to him in order. After the abbot had received his blessing, he left. When the aforesaid brothers returned to the abbot, he asked them where they had been. Whereupon they answered him and said that they had much wearied themselves in their necessary business. Then, when he questioned them whether it was so, they swore stoutly that it was so. Then he said to them: 'But why do you both swear false? for you were at the home of this widow, and lived your life there thus, and spoke these words there, thus!' Then when they realized their misdeeds, they fell at his feet and begged forgiveness of him, and confessed to him that it was just as he had previously said.

15. *Concerning the brethren who came to him.* Also at one time there came to him two brethren from a certain monastery. While they journeyed there they had with them two flagons filled with beer. Then it was agreed between them that they should hide them under a turf so that they should have them again when they journeyed home. Then, when they came to him, he strengthened them with his instruction and edified their hearts with his exhortation. When they had spoken about many things between them, then with cheerful face and laughing voice the blessed Guthlac said to them: 'Why did you hide the flagons under a turf, and why did you not bring them with you?' Then they greatly marvelled at the words of the holy man, and bowed to him and begged his blessing. And he blessed them and then they journeyed home again.

At the same time men of various ranks sought out the aforesaid man, both ealdormen and bishops and abbots, and men of every rank, lowly and powerful. And men sought him out not only from the great kingdom of Mercia, but also all those in Britain who heard of this blessed man, so that they hurried and hastened to him from everywhere – and those who were either sick in body, or afflicted and taken with the accursed spirit, or with other evils, with various griefs and pains by which mankind is surrounded. And hope failed in none of those whom they brought to him, because there was no sick person that left him undoctored, no devil-possessed that was not of sound mind again, nor anyone sick who did not depart from him healed.

16. *Concerning Æthelbald's companion.* It happened that while many men came to him about various matters, there came among others a companion of the aforesaid exile Æthelbald, whose name was Offa, that he might visit and speak with the saint. It happened that on the second day he was on the journey there, he trod on a thorn in the night; whereupon the thorn stuck in the foot and the prick of the thorn was so great that it went through the foot. And after that he travelled on his way with difficulty and, with much effort, came to the aforesaid island on which the blessed man Guthlac lived. And then when he was there at night, over half the body from the loins to the feet swelled up, and he was so grievously afflicted with the pain that he could neither sit nor stand. Then, when they told that to the man of God, Guthlac, he ordered that they should bring him to him. Then when he was brought to him, he told him the manner in which he was first so hurt, and how the trouble first came upon him. Whereupon Guthlac immediately undressed himself and the garment which he wore next his skin he slipped onto the aforesaid man. No sooner was he dressed with the clothing of so great a man, than the wound could not remain. Straightway that same thorn leapt from the man, just like an arrow leaves the bow, and went some distance away. And at the same time all the swelling and all the pain immediately left him. And at the same time, he forthwith spoke to the holy man with a cheerful spirit. And he left without the pain of any injury. So it happened that all men who heard of these things marvelled and gloried in them and praised the God of heaven.

17. *Concerning the holy Bishop St Headda.* Moreover we should not omit, through neglect, that miracle how by prophetic power he knew and made things known to men; because it was granted to him through the grace of God, that he should know the words of those who were absent as readily as of those present which were said in front of him.

It happened on one occasion that a certain bishop came to him, whose name was Headda,[1] just as though he were urged by a heavenly thought, that he should go to speak with the man of God. The bishop had with him then in his company a certain learned man whose name was Wigfrith. While he journeyed there amongst other of the bishop's thegns, they began to say many things about the holy man, and told many things about his miracles. Some spoke of the hardship of his life, the miracles which he worked; some then spoke dubiously about his life, and said that they did not know whether he did those things in the strength of God or through the power of the Devil. Then as they discussed these things between themselves, the scholar said to them: 'I can test and find out whether he practises divine piety', he said, 'because I lived for a long time among the Irish people and saw there many good men who led their life well in the service of God; and through God's power they shone before the eyes of men with many miracles and signs. From the life of the men which I saw there, I can recognize what kind this man's life is, whether he works the miracles through the strength of God or does it through the power of the Devil.'

When the aforesaid bishop came to speak with Guthlac, the man of God, together they drenched themselves with the wines of evangelical sweetness. The brightness of God's grace shone so greatly in the blessed Guthlac that whatever he preached and taught was as though he preached and taught those words with the voice of an angel. There was also great wisdom, heavenly prudence, in him, so that whatever he taught he confirmed with the divine lessons of holy scriptures. And then suddenly in the middle of the discussion which they held between them, the bishop humbly bowed to the man of God and earnestly begged and entreated him that he should receive the sacerdotal office at his hands, so that he might ordain him a priest, and to the ministry of the Lord's altar. Thereupon Guthlac at once consented to his requests, and prostrated himself on the ground, and said that he would do what was God's will and the bishop's.

Then, when they had finished the service and he was consecrated, as I have said, then the bishop asked the holy man to take a meal with him. And he did so, although it was contrary to the custom of his life. Then when they sat down to the meal as I have

[1] Bishop of Lichfield from 691 and of Leicester from 709; later confused, in the Guthlac Roll and elsewhere, with his contemporary, Hæddi, Bishop of Winchester.

described, Guthlac looked at the bishop's thegns. When he saw the aforesaid brother Wigfrith, he spoke to him thus: 'And now, brother Wigfrith, what do you now think of the priest of whom yesterday you said that you would ascertain whether he were good or wicked?' Then straightaway Wigfrith got up and bowed down to the earth and confessed his sin to him. Whereupon the holy man at once embraced him and granted and gave him his pardon.

The consecration of the island of Crowland, and also of the blessed Guthlac, was at harvest-time, five days before the feast of St Bartholomew.

18. *Concerning Abbess Ecgburh*. It also happened on one occasion that the venerable virgin, Abbess Ecgburh, the daughter of King Aldwulf,[1] sent a lead coffin, and a shroud for it, to the venerable Guthlac, and entreated him through the holy name of the Heavenly King, that after his death they should put his body in it. She sent a message by a certain brother of venerable life, and instructed him to ask who was to be the keeper of that place after him. When he had courteously received the greeting of the venerable virgin, then he answered concerning that about which he was asked – who should be the keeper of the place after him – and said that the man was among a heathen people and not yet baptized, but that he should soon come, however, and should then receive the sacrament of the baptismal font. And thus it came about, for the same Cissa who subsequently held the place came to Britain shortly afterwards, and they baptized him there as the man of God foretold.

19. *Concerning Æthelbald the King*. Also we should not omit, through neglect, the marvel which this holy man Guthlac foretold and made known to men. It happened one time that the aforesaid exile Æthelbald came to him; and Ceolred the King[2] hunted him far and wide, hither and thither, and he fled and escaped his persecution and hatred. Then he came to speak with this holy Guthlac; for when human aid failed him, divine aid comforted him nevertheless. When he came to the man of God and told him his troubles, Guthlac then spoke to him thus: 'Oh my son, I am not forgetful of your struggles and troubles; for that reason I took pity on you, and because of your troubles I prayed God that he would have mercy on you and help you. And he has heard my

[1] King of the East Anglians 663–713.
[2] King of Mercia 709–16.

request, and he will grant you dominion and power over your nation; and those that hate you shall all flee before you, and your sword shall destroy all your adversaries, because the Lord is your helper. But be patient, for you will not gain the kingdom by seizure in a worldly way, but you will gain your kingdom with the help of the Lord; for the Lord shall bring down those who now hate you, and the Lord will remove that kingdom from them, and has remembered and appointed you.'[1] Then when he heard these words, Æthelbald immediately confirmed his hope and faith in God himself, and he trusted and believed all those things which the holy man foretold – how kingdoms are overturned and taken away, and how it is forever hastening towards the end; and how strong death seizes and takes all alike: the powerful and the lowly, the learned and the unlearned, and young and old.

20. *Concerning the length of the holy man's life, and his death.* When some time after this, it happened that Guthlac, the beloved servant of God, had led his life according to God's will for fifteen years, then God wished to lead his beloved servant away from the conflict of this world's troubles to the everlasting rest of the heavenly kingdom. Then it happened at a certain time when he was at his prayers in his church that he was suddenly attacked by sickness. And he realized at once that God's hand was laid upon him; and rejoicing, he began to prepare himself for entry into the heavenly kingdom. He was afflicted with that sickness for seven days, and on the eighth day he was brought to the crisis. The sickness attacked him on the Wednesday before Easter, and on the same day in the Easter week following he sent his life from the body.

A certain brother was with him whose name was Beccel, through whom I learned about the death of the blessed man. When he came to him on the day when the sickness attacked him, he asked him about certain things. Whereupon he answered him slowly and drew breath from the breast with long gasps. Then when he saw the holy man so distressed in spirit, he said to him: 'What a transformation has come over you now! Has some illness befallen you in the night?' Then he answered him and said to him: 'Sickness befell me in the night.' Then again he asked him: 'Do you know the cause of your sickness, my father, or to what end do you think the illness will come?' Then the holy man answered him

---

[1] Æthelbald came to the throne on Ceolred's death and reigned for forty-one years until 757.

again and said to him: 'The cause of my illness is this, that the spirit must be taken away from this body; for there will be an end to my illness on the eighth day. Therefore it is proper that the spirit be prepared, so that I may follow God.' Then, when the aforesaid brother Beccel heard these words he wept greatly and began to mourn, and in great grief repeatedly made his cheeks shine with tears. Then the man of God, Guthlac, comforted him and said to him: 'My son, do not be grieved, since it is no hardship for me to be going to my Lord God.' There was such a depth of holy faith in him and he had so great a love of God also, that with regard to good deeds the known and unknown seemed all alike to him.

Then four nights later when the first day of Easter came, the blessed Guthlac gave praise to God in his illness and sang mass. And after he offered the precious sacrifice of Christ's blood, he then began to preach the gospel to the aforesaid brother; and he moved him so deeply with his teaching, that he never before nor after heard the like. When the seventh day of his illness came, the aforesaid brother came to visit him about the sixth hour of the day. Then he found him leaning in the corner of his chapel against the altar. However, he could not speak with him for he saw that his illness troubled him very much; nevertheless, afterwards he begged that he would leave his words with him before he died. Then the blessed Guthlac raised his tired limbs a little from the wall, and spoke to him thus: 'It is now very near the time, my son, so take heed of my last instructions. After my soul leaves the body, go then to my sister and say to her that I avoided her presence here on earth and would not see her, in order that afterwards we two might see each other again in heaven before the face of God. And bid her set my body in the coffin, and wrap me in the shroud that Ecgburh sent me. I would not be dressed in linen clothing while I lived, but now for the love of Christ's virgin I will put the gift she sent me to the use for which I kept it. When body and soul part, let them wrap the body in that garment, and lay it in the coffin.'

When the aforesaid brother heard these things, then he spoke thus: 'Now that I see and understand your illness, and I realize that you must leave this world, I entreat you my dear father to tell me about something which I never dared ask you about before. Since the time that I first lived with you in this wilderness, I have heard you speak in the evening and in the early morning – with whom I know not. Wherefore I beg and entreat you never to leave

me troubled and anxious about this matter after your death.'
Then the man of God drew the breath from his breast with a long
gasp, answered him and said: 'My son, do not be troubled; the
things which I would not tell to any man of the world before for as
long as I lived, I will disclose and make known to you. From the
second year I lived in this wilderness, in the evening and in the
early morning God himself has sent to me an angel for my
consolation, who revealed to me the heavenly mysteries which it is
permitted no man to tell, and quite relieved the hardness of my
struggle with heavenly angelic conversation; who made known
and revealed to me things absent as well as present. And now my
son, beloved one, preserve my words and tell them to no other
men save Pega my sister and Ecgberht the hermit, if it happen that
you should speak with him. Then when he had spoken these
words he leaned his head against the wall, and drew the breath
from his breast with a long gasp. When he recovered and got his
breath back again, there came a fragrance from the mouth like the
scent of the sweetest flowers. And on the following night, when
the aforesaid brother fell to his nightly prayers, he beheld all the
house surrounded outside with a great brightness; and the
brightness remained there till daylight.

Then when it was morning, the man of God again stirred a
little, and lifted up the tired limbs. Then he spoke to him thus: 'My
son, prepare yourself to go on the journey which I commanded
you; because it is now time that the spirit must leave the tired
limbs and go to unending bliss, to the kingdom of heaven.' Then
when he had said these things, he stretched his hand towards the
altar and strengthened himself with the heavenly food, Christ's
body and his blood. And after that he lifted his eyes to heaven, and
stretched out his arms, and then with joy and bliss sent his spirit to
the eternal bliss of the heavenly kingdom. In the middle of those
things, the aforesaid brother saw all the house suffused throughout with heavenly light; and he saw there a fiery tower from the
earth to the height of heaven, the brightness of which was unlike
anything else; and because of its beauty, all the brightness of the
sun itself at midday was turned to paleness. And he heard angelic
songs throughout the regions of the air; and all the island was
completely filled with a great fragrance of a wonderful scent.

Then the aforesaid brother was immediately struck with great
fear, and went into a boat and travelled to the place which the
man of God had previously instructed, and then came to Pega and

told her all those things, in order, as the brother had ordered him. Then, when she heard that the brother had passed away, she immediately fell on the earth, and was filled with great grief so that she could not say a word. Then, when she recovered herself, she drew a long sigh from within her breast, and gave thanks to the Almighty for his will. Then on the following day, according to the instruction of the blessed man, they came to the island and there they found all that place and the building filled with the fragrance of the herb ambrosia. Then for a period of three days she commended the holy man to God with holy hymns, and on the third day, as the man of God had instructed, they buried the body with honour in the chapel.

The Divine Goodness wished openly to display to men in how great a glory the blessed man was after he was buried; for formerly he shone and was resplendent with so many miracles before the eyes of men. So after his death, when he had been buried twelve months, God put it into the mind of the Lord's servant that she should remove the brother's body to another tomb. Then she gathered together there God's servants and priests and those in ecclesiastical orders, on the same day twelve months after the blessed man had died; and they opened the tomb. Whereupon they found the body as entirely sound as it formerly was, and as though he were still alive; and in the flexibility of the joints and in all things it was much more like a sleeping man than a dead one. Moreover the garments were as pristine as when they were first put round the body. When they who were assembled there saw these things they were very afraid because of what they saw there; and they were so struck with fear that they could say nothing. Then when Christ's servant Pega saw that, she was immediately filled with spiritual bliss, and then with hymns in honour of Christ wrapped the holy body in another shroud which Ecgberht the hermit had previously sent him, when alive, for the same service. Moreover, they did not put the coffin back into the earth but they set it in a more memorable and a more honourable place. Now the place where the triumphant body of the holy man rests in spirit has since been honourably dignified with various buildings by Æthelbald the King. And the man who seeks out that place with all his might shall, through the mediation of that holy man, carry out and accomplish what he desires.

The blessed Guthlac was a man elect in godly deeds and a treasure of all wisdom. And he was steadfast in his duties; also he was so earnestly occupied in Christ's service that there was never anything else in his mouth except Christ's praise, nor in his heart except piety, nor in his mind except peace and love and gentleness. Nor did anyone see him angry or negligent in Christ's service, but in his face one might always perceive love and peace. And there was always sweetness in his mood and wisdom in his breast, and there was so much joy in him that he always seemed the same to friends and strangers.

21. *Concerning King Æthelbald.* After these things Æthelbald, the aforesaid exile, heard in distant lands of the death of the holy man, St Guthlac; for he alone was formerly his refuge and comfort. Thereupon he was suddenly moved with sadness, and travelled there to the place where the body of the man of God was, because he hoped that through the holy man God would grant him comfort in his struggle. Then when he came to the tomb of the holy man, weeping tears he said thus: 'My father, lo, you know my miseries, you were always a help to me in my difficulties. Where shall I turn now; who shall comfort me if you forsake me?'

After he had said these and many other things weeping at the tomb, when night-time came, he was there in a certain house where he had sometimes lived as a guest while Guthlac was alive. Then while he was in the house, he was turning his thoughts hither and thither in his unhappy mind, when at last his eyes were closed in sleep. Then suddenly afraid, he started up, when he saw all inside the cottage filled with heavenly light. While he was in fear of the uncommon sight, then he saw the blessed Guthlac stand before him in the form of an angel and say to him: 'You shall not be afraid, but be resolute, for God is your help; and I have come to you because God heard your prayer through my mediation. But do not be sad, for the days of your miseries have passed, because before the sun has gone a twelve-month circuit round about you will rule this kingdom, for which you have long fought.' And not only did he tell him of the future kingship, but he also described to him the entire course of his life. God wrought these signs through the merit of the holy man after he was dead and buried.

22. There was a certain head of a household of the aforesaid exile Æthelbald in the district of the Wisse, whose eyes had been covered over with the white spot and with cloudiness for twelve months. Then when his doctors had for a long time treated him with salves, and this had brought about no cure, he was divinely admonished within that if they brought him to Guthlac's place, he should then recover his health and sight. His friends brought him

to the Crowland place shortly after, and they spoke to Christ's servant, Pega; and she heard of the man's firm and fixed faith. Whereupon she led him into the church where Guthlac's venerable body was, took some of the consecrated salt which Guthlac himself had previously consecrated, and moistened it and dropped it in the eye. And then, before she put another drop in the other eye, he could see with the other; and he easily saw what there was there; and he went home whole and sound.

To our Lord be praise and glory and honour, and to the blessed St Guthlac, world without end, for ever in eternity. Amen.

THE FINDING OF THE HOLY CROSS

The story of how the true cross was eventually discovered, was one of the most popular legends of the early Church. The 'invention' (i.e. discovery) of what was believed to be the cross on which Jesus of Nazareth was killed, took place, it was said, in about 326 A.D. as the result of an expedition to Palestine by St Helena, mother of Constantine the Great, first Christian Emperor of Rome. This legend was of particular interest to the Anglo-Saxons, inasmuch as Helena was thought (wrongly) to have been a British princess – and certainly Constantine was in Britain when he was proclaimed emperor. The success of Helena's divinely inspired excavations resulted in a proliferation of cross-relics and an exotic cross-cult marked by its own feast day (cf. Calendar, above, p. 81). The cult spread rapidly to Merovingian France and Anglo-Saxon England, where its best literary remains are the poems *Elene* and *The Dream of the Rood*.

Here cast in homiletic form, this text represents a re-working of the Latin *Inventio Sanctae Crucis*, versions of which were circulating in the East from the end of the fourth century (cf. *Acta Sanctorum*, May, pp. 361–6). It is found on an individual parchment quire written in the second half of the eleventh century and inserted in a Glastonbury collection of ninth-century Latin tracts: Oxford, Bodleian Library MS. Auct, F.4.32, ff. 10–18ᵛ. A later copy is found in a volume of homilies produced, probably at Rochester, in the twelfth century: Corpus Christi College, Cambridge, MS. 303, pp. 76–82.

The text is edited by R. Morris, *Legends of the Holy Rood*, EETS., OS. XLVI, London, 1871, pp. 3–17, and by M. C. Bodden, *The Old English Finding of the True Cross*, Cambridge, 1987. There is a facsimile introduced by R. W. Hunt, *Saint Dunstan's Classbook from Glastonbury*, Amsterdam, 1961.

Now hear what I want to say to you about the holy cross on which Christ suffered – how it was found on this day.[1]

When there had passed a hundred-and-thirty-three years after Christ's suffering and ascension into heaven, there reigned in the city of Rome the noble Emperor Constantine. He was pious in customs and virtuous in deeds, a supporter of Christian men, but was not yet baptized however. Then in the sixth year in which Constantine reigned, a great foreign nation was assembled at the river which is called Danube and were ready to fight against the emperor and against the Roman race. Then it was immediately made known to the noble Emperor Constantine, and he immediately gathered a great army, and, anxious in spirit, advanced against his enemy, and frequently looked heavenward, earnestly

[1] This homily was presumably intended to be read on 3 May, the Feast of the Invention, cf. Calendar, above, p. 81.

praying for divine support. Then, when they came to the river, he saw there the mighty and innumerable armies of his enemies. Then he was very sorrowful and saddened unto death, because he thought that they must all perish.

Then on that same night that Constantine slept and rested himself, there came to him a certain very beautiful angel in white shining raiment, and roused him and said: 'Constantine, don't you be sad, but look up now into this heaven.' And he immediately then looked up into the heavens; and there saw the sacred sign of Christ's cross set opposite him and outlined in the brightness of a great light; and above the cross were written these words: 'Constantine, in this sign you shall overcome and overwhelm all your enemy.' He then awoke, joyful because of the beautiful vision and because of the noble promised victory; and in honour of God he marked the holy cross sign on his head and on his banner. Then immediately in the morning, the Emperor Constantine commanded a golden cross to be made in the same form which he had seen shining so nobly in the heavens, and he commanded it to be carried before him against the heathen. Immediately they looked on that holy cross sign they immediately became frightened and turned to flight. And the noble Emperor Constantine then had the victory, and his army slew the heathen, and also some were drowned in the river.

On this day Almighty God granted a great victory to the noble King Constantine through the great might of the noble cross of Christ. After that the noble emperor returned home to his own city, into Rome. Then he commanded to be summoned to him all the elders and the scribes of the Jewish people, and asked them what sign that might be which he had seen so nobly shining in the heavens. They said then: 'It is that great and that noble heavenly sign on which the Son of the living God suffered.' Then, when those who were Christians there learned this, they came swiftly to the noble Emperor Constantine and with very joyful spirit preached to him about the Holy Trinity and about the holy advent of the begotten Son of God – in what manner he was born through the human body of the holy woman St Mary; and told him of the sufferings which our Saviour suffered on the cross for the salvation and redemption of mankind, and how our Lord was buried in the tomb, and on the third day, immortal, rose from death, and harrowed hell and bound the old devil,[1] and

[1] See generally The Gospel of Nicodemus, below, pp. 217–25.

afterwards ascended into heaven and prepared a way thither for those who wish to earn it. Then, when this was told to the noble Emperor Constantine he became very joyful in spirit; and then sent his mother Helena with a great company to the city of Rome to the bishop, to earnestly ask that he come swiftly to him and baptize him. Then the bishop immediately thanked God and baptized him in the name of Father and Son and of the Holy Ghost and strongly confirmed him in the true faith. And he then broke in pieces and overthrew all of their idols, and there he consecrated churches and appointed all ecclesiastical orders by rank. Then afterwards the noble Emperor Constantine was confirmed in the true faith. He then began to learn the divine teachings and to read the holy books of Christ. Then, when he had learned in the holy books in which place our Lord was hanged on the cross, he sent his mother, the holy woman Helena, with a great company, to the glorious city of Jerusalem in order that she should there enquire about the holy cross. And he instructed her that she should build churches in the same place where she, through God's assistance, might find the holy cross.

The blessed Queen Helena then firmly placed her trust in Almighty God and set off. Then, when she entered into the glorious city of Jerusalem, she commanded that they assemble before her all the Jewish people. When they came in front of her, then she spoke to them and said thus: 'I know, and have learned from your prophetical books, that you were from the beginning chosen by Christ himself. And you know how our Lord worked divine miracles: he enlightened many blind, and to the deaf gave hearing, and he drove out devils from men, and he cleansed the leprous, and the dead he raised to life, and many diverse sicknesses he healed. And your ancestors, through the devil's teaching, condemned to death the Almighty Lord, the world's redeemer, and hanged him on a cross; and on the third day he arose from death. And still your hearts are hardened so that you cannot acknowledge nor know the most true creator of the world, Saviour and Redeemer. But the curse remains over you which your ancestors themselves asked for in the sufferings of our Lord, when they said, "Let his blood and the vengeance of his blood be upon us and upon our children."[1] But you, choose now the wisest men of your tribe, so that they may correctly answer that which I

[1] Cf. Matthew, XXVII 25.

wish to ask them.' And then with great fear they went out and earnestly considered what the question would be. And then they chose a thousand of the best of the most learned Jewish men, and led them in front of the holy queen. Then spoke the holy Queen Helena: 'Take heed now of my words! Well! How haven't you learned from your prophetical books about the advent of the only-begotten Son of God; that our Saviour was hanged on the cross, as was his own will! You yourselves know and understand all these things thus; and yet you still don't want to acknowledge what I want to ask you.' They answered her and said: 'Tell us, lady, why you speak to us thus so sternly.' She answered and said: 'Go out and choose you from among these men those best learned, so that they may make known to me, on this day, all those things about which I want to ask them.' Then with great fear they went out from the queen, and had a debate amongst themselves and earnestly considered what the question might be. Then spoke there one who was called Judas: 'I know for certain that this question will be about the holy cross on which our elders hanged the Nazarene Saviour. If this queen wants to ask about this, then watch out whether you want to make it known to her, because we know for certain that afterwards all of our elders' decrees will be overthrown.' He then spoke again: 'My grandfather Zaccheus told my father and my father told me and said to me: "My dearest child, when the question occurs about the holy cross on which our elders hanged the Saviour Christ, then you take care that you make it known to them before you are tortured to death, because the Jewish people shall never rule any longer; but then the kingdom of men will be for those who believe in Almighty God, because he is truly the Son of the living God." Then I answered my father and said: "My father, if our elders knew that he was Christ, Son of the living God, why did they hang him on the cross?" Then my father said to me: "Judas, my dearest child, I was never in their plan nor supported them in their discussion. But I constantly spoke strongly against them because I always recognized the holy and glorious name of him, the Son of the living God, whom our elders in envy hanged and in rage condemned to death. And they hanged him on the cross, and he was laid in the tomb, and on the third day truly rose from death. And after his glorious resurrection he revealed himself to his chosen disciples, and your brother Stephen firmly believed in him, and therefore the Pharisees and scribes condemned him to death and killed him by hurling stones. Then he said: 'My Lord, do not blame them for these sins which they do against me' ".[1] Then my father said to me again: "I urge you, my dear child, that you resolutely and firmly believe in Christ, Son of the living God; then you will have life with him for ever in eternity." These things my father, Simon, said to me, as I have now said to you. Now, if she wants to ask you about this, consider whether you want to make it known to her.' They answered and said: 'We never before heard these words nor these things which you now say. If this queen wants to ask about this, then take care that you never make it known to her. We neither know nor understand.' Then, when they were speaking thus among themselves, the queen's soldiers called them thither and commanded them that they swiftly come in front of the noble queen. When they stood before her, then she said to them: 'Truly, I say that unless you make known to me truly the holy cross of Christ, I shall command that you all burn in fire.' Then they immediately became very frightened, and gave her the one who was called Judas, and said to her: 'Lady, this is honest; he is the wisest of our learned, and he can make known to you all the things about which you asked us.' The queen then released them all, and took Judas alone, and said to him: 'Now, both your life and your death are in your own power; choose now whichever you want.' He, Judas, then answered her and said: 'If any man be grievously starving and they lay before him stones and loaves, whoever is so stupid that he will want to eat the stones and leave the loaves!' Then the noble Queen Helena said to him: 'If you want to live in heaven or on earth, then make known to me where the holy cross of Christ is preserved.' Judas answered her and said: 'I neither know it nor understand, because it was done more than a hundred years ago and I'm young and don't remember that.' The noble queen answered him: 'I have read in the holy books of Christ that the place is called Calvary in which our Saviour's cross is preserved. But make known to me where the place is, or I will command you to be killed by starvation.' Then Judas answered her again and said: 'I don't know the place; I wasn't yet born then.' Then the Queen Helena ordered that they take him and put him in a deep pit without food and without water; and he remained there seven days and seven nights. And then on the seventh day, then Judas called up from the pit and said thus: 'I beg

[1] Cf. Acts, VII 60.

and implore you that you pull me up from this pit, and I will show you the holy cross of Christ.' Then, when he was out of the pit, he went to the place where our Saviour was hanged. Then, when he came thither he stretched out his hands and prayed to Christ and said thus: 'My Lord Saviour Christ, you who created heaven and earth and sea and all creatures which are in them, now I pray you, Lord, for your great compassion, that you reveal to us your holy cross on which you suffered and redeemed mankind, and cause that there ascend up from that place the sweetest scent of all precious perfumes, so that I then may firmly believe that you are king of all kings, you who live and reign for ever in eternity.' Then, when Judas had finished this divine prayer, immediately all the place quaked, and there ascended up from that place the sweetest scent of all most precious perfumes. Immediately then Judas marvelled greatly, and spoke thus: 'Truly I say that the only-begotten Son of God is Saviour and preserver of all mankind who wish to believe in him. I now beg and implore you, my Lord Saviour Christ, that you blot out my sins so that I might be in the number with my brother Stephen of whom many good deeds are written among the marvellous acts of the apostles.' When Judas had said these words, then he took a spade and dug into the earth. Then, when he had dug twenty feet into the earth, he found three crosses. Immediately then he was very joyful. Then he took the three crosses and carried them to the glorious city of Jerusalem in front of the noble Queen Helena. She then said to Judas: 'Tell me on which of these crosses our Saviour was hanged. I know that two are those of the two criminals who were hanging on either side of him.' Then Judas did not know what to say to her, but took then the three crosses and set them in the middle of the glorious city of Jerusalem, and there awaited the glory of the Lord. Then it was at the noon of that day when they carried in a young boy who had passed away. Then Judas was very joyful at this, and said to the noble Queen Helena: 'Lady, now you may discern the might of our Lord Saviour Christ.' Well, Judas then commanded them to set down the body, and then took one cross and laid it upon the dead man; then prayed very earnestly that God almighty for his name and for his noble compassion – and commanded all the people to pray likewise – that God almighty should disclose through his noble might, which might be the cross on which he himself was hanged for the salvation of mankind. The body lay just as dead as it was before. When he took the second, it was all the same. Then, when he took the third, the boy immediately rose living and sound, and blessed the name of the Lord. And all those who were there blessed and praised and magnified the name of the Lord.

Then the malicious devil in hell was stirred to wrath and fury. And he then roared very loudly and said thus: 'Well, who is it that has now betrayed me? Alas, you Nazarene Saviour, through your suffering you have drawn to yourself all the souls that I through myself had earlier betrayed! Alas, you Judas, what is this that you have now done to me! Earlier, through one Judas, the betrayer of Christ, I was honoured, and I drew many people to hell. Now through this Judas I am overthrown.' Then Judas became filled with the Holy Ghost, and said thus: 'May the Saviour who lives and reigns sink you into the deep abyss of hell.' Then immediately the devil was nowhere seen nor heard there. Then, when the blessed Queen Helena heard this, she marvelled much at the great faith which Judas had in God. And she commanded that the holy cross of Christ be adorned with gold and with silver and with precious jewels; and commanded churches to be built in that same place in which the cross was found, as her son Constantine had earlier instructed.

And Judas then received baptism by the city bishop; and the bishop changed the name Judas and called him Cyriacus after he was baptized. And then afterwards he flourished so nobly that, after the bishop passed away, he was chosen and consecrated bishop.

Then St Helena began very earnestly to ask about the nails which were driven through our Saviour's hands and feet. She commanded them to fetch her the holy bishop Cyriacus, who was earlier called Judas, and said to him: 'I beg and implore you that you find out about the nails with which our Saviour was fastened to the cross.' And immediately he, the holy bishop with his mass-priests and with his deacons and with the faithful people, went thither to the place Calvary, and commanded that the holy cross be carried with him. Then, when they came to the place, he raised his eyes up to heaven and secretly beat on his breast and said thus: 'My Lord Saviour Christ, I beg and implore you for your great noble compassion, that you make known to me the nails with which your holy body was fastened to the cross.' Then, when he had said these words, all the people said: 'Amen!' And there came a great light up from the place in which the holy cross was found.

And there were revealed the nails, and in the earth they shone and glinted as the purest gold. All those who were there spoke and said thus: 'Now we may know and perceive truly that the only-begotten Son of God is Saviour and Redeemer of all mankind who believe in him.' And then he, the bishop St Cyriacus, with very great joy and with gladness, took the nails and brought them to the worshipful Queen Helena. And she immediately bent her knees and bowed her head to the earth; and inwardly she prayed to the nails, and earnestly began to consider what she might best do about the nails. Then came a voice from heaven and said: 'Take the nails, Helena, and command them to be forged into the bridle of your son the Emperor Constantine; then he will secure victory and peace in every battle.' And she then did just as she was instructed through the Holy Ghost. And she then gave many things to the bishop Cyriacus. And the holy bishop had such great grace from God that through his divine prayers he healed a host of various sicknesses. And she, the blessed Queen Helena, returned again to the city of Rome and made known all these things to the noble Emperor Constantine. And they ordered all the people that they should always keep this day in which Christ's holy cross was found, in great honour.

The Jews, through the devil's teaching, took the holy cross of Christ and hid it under the earth one hundred-and-thirty-three years. Then the compassionate Lord would not permit that that on which he voluntarily suffered – and by the sign of the cross redeemed all mankind – that it should be hid any longer, but should gloriously disclose it, just as we earlier read out to you, on this holy day, for his praise and honour, and for our salvation and protection against all the devil's temptations.

It behoves us that we always honour this day with church-going and with charitable deeds and with holy prayers, that we may bless ourselves through the holy cross of Christ, so that we can and may avoid all the devils in this life – and their future humiliation and company. May the Lord, who suffered on the holy cross, help us so that we may so keep what our Lord's will is – and is necessary for ourselves. To him be always thanks because he suffered for us, and to him be always praise and glory for all his goodness which he has made known to mankind, through all worlds for ever in eternity. Amen.

THE BLICKLING HOMILIST

AN EASTER DAY SERMON

Blickling Homily 7

The Blickling Homiliary is a late tenth- or eleventh-century collection of eighteen sermons for Sundays and saints' days, arranged roughly in order of the Church year. An internal reference in the eleventh sermon, for Ascension Day, indicates that this sermon at least was composed in or shortly before the year 971, and perhaps the whole collection belongs to roughly the same date.

The manuscript apparently belonged to the Corporation of Lincoln from the late thirteenth to the early seventeenth centuries, and seems to have been used as a mayoral oath-book. There is some evidence for its having had a Mercian origin, and perhaps it had been written for one of the monastic foundations in or around Lincoln. Subsequently it came into the possession of the Marquis of Lothian of Blickling Hall, Norfolk, but was sold in 1932 and now forms part of the John H. Scheide Library at Princeton, New Jersey.

There is an edition of *The Blickling Homilies* by R. Morris, EETS., OS., LVIII, LXIII, LXXIII, London, 1874–80, and a facsimile of the manuscript was edited by R. Willard, EEMF., X, Copenhagen, 1960. This sermon occupies ff. 50–8ᵛ of the MS.

For the general theme of the Harrowing of Hell, which occupies the first half of the sermon, see the apocryphal *Gospel of Nicodemus*, pp. 217–25. More immediately, however, the author seems to have drawn on a sermon attributed to Augustine (*PL*, XXXIX 2059–61). The dialogue between Christ and Adam and Eve has much in common with the fragment of a Latin Harrowing preserved in the probably ninth-century Mercian *Book of Cerne*, edited by A. B. Kuypers, Cambridge, 1902, pp. 196–8. And part of a similar dialogue is recorded in the Old English Church Calendar (see above, p. 78.). The apocalyptic signs which were believed to herald the end of the world, an account of which forms the second half of this sermon, derive ultimately from such biblical references as: II Esdras, V, Matthew, XXIV 29–31 and Revelation, XVI 15–16, XX 12–13. The subject is dealt with by various Church fathers, but the author probably based his account on the so-called *Apocalypse of Thomas*, an Old English version of which was printed by M. Förster, *Anglia*, 73 (1955), 17–33. Of many representations of the Last Days in Old English poetry, perhaps *Judgement Day II* (the translation of a poem attributed to Bede) and *Christ III*, are best known.

Dearly beloved, this Easter mystery presents to us a clear example of the life eternal, as we can now listen to it related and explained, so that none need doubt but that the event must come about in this present time, that the same Creator will sit on his judgement seat. There will be present before him all of the race of angels and of the race of men, and of the wicked spirits also. And there every man's actions will be investigated. And he who is now humble and with his whole heart mindful of the Lord's suffering and his resurrection, shall receive a heavenly reward; and he who now scorns to keep God's commandments, or to bear in mind the Lord's humility, shall there receive a stern judgement and afterwards dwell in eternal torments, which will never come to an end. Therefore this time is of all times the highest and holiest, and at this time we should have a divine joy – and a worldly also – because, as an example to mankind, the Lord rose up from death after his suffering, and after the bonds of his death and after the fetters of hell's darkness, and laid torment and eternal misery on the prince of devils, and delivered mankind; as the prophet David prophesied concerning this time, saying thus: 'Our Lord delivered us'.[1] And he brought to pass what he had long threatened the accursed spirits. And he made known to men at this present time all those things which were ever before prophesied by the prophets about his suffering and about his resurrection and about his harrying in hell and about his many miracles which were foretold – all that he fulfilled. Let us now listen and consider what he did, and by what means he made us free.

He was not compelled by any necessity, but came down to earth by his own will, and here suffered many plots and snares by the Jews and by the miserable scribes; and then finally he allowed his body to be fastened to the cross with nails; and he endured death for us because he wanted to grant us eternal life. And then he sent his glorious spirit into the depths of hell, and there bound and humbled the prince of all darkness and of eternal death and greatly troubled all his gang. And he completely smashed the gates of hell and their bronze bolts; and all his chosen he led out from there; and he overcame the darkness of the devils with his shining light. Then, very fearful and terrified, they spoke thus: 'Where does this come from, so strong and so bright and so terrible? The world was subjected to us for long, and death paid us great tribute before; it has never happened to us before that death has been put to an end thus, nor ever before has such terror been ordained for us in hell. Indeed, who is this who now enters our confines so unafraid? and not only does not fear our punishments, but wishes to deliver others from our bonds? We think this is he, through whose death we imagined all the world should be subjected to us. Do you hear, our prince? This is the same one for whose death you

[1] Psalm CVII 13 ff.

have long made a play; and in the event you promised us much plunder. But what will you do about him now? and what can you do to overthrow him? He has now put all your darkness to flight with his brightness, and he has broken up all your prison, and all of those whom you previously held captive he has released, and he has turned their life to joy; and those who formerly sighed in our bonds now mock at us. Why do you bring this man here, who in his coming has restored all his chosen to their former happiness? Though they formerly despaired of eternal life, they are now very glad. No weeping and no wailing is now heard here, as was formerly customary in this place of torment. Now alas, the wealth that in the beginning you our prince got from the boldness and disobedience of the first man, and from the loss of Paradise – all that he has now taken away from you. And through Christ's cross all your joy has turned to grief. When you longed to know that Christ hung on a cross, you did not know how many troubles should come upon us all by his death. You always wanted to corrupt him, in whom you knew no wrong at all. Why do you bring this noble and innocent one here? Now, in his coming here, he has condemned and humiliated all the guilty.'

Then, immediately after the infamous speech of those who dwelt in hell, and their lamentation was heard, then it was that, because of the coming of the Kingdom of the Lord, all the iron bolts of hell's locks were broken without any delay. And at once, the countless host of holy souls who were previously held captive bowed down before the Saviour and prayed to him with weeping entreaties and spoke thus: 'You came to us, Redeemer of the world; you came to us, the hope of those who dwell in heaven and earth, and our hope also, because of old the prophets told us of your coming, and we looked forward to and hoped for your coming here. On earth you granted forgiveness of men's sins. Now redeem us from the power of the devil and from the imprisonment of hell. Now that you have descended into the pit of hell for us, do not now leave us to live in torment, when you return to your kingdom on high. You set up the sign of your glory in the world; now set up the symbol of your glory in hell.' This prayer was heard without delay, and immediately at the Lord's command the countless host of holy souls were lifted up from the burning sulphur, and he cast down the old Devil and threw him, bound, into the pit of hell. Then the holy souls cried to the Lord with indescribable joy, and spoke thus: 'Now, Lord Saviour

Christ, ascend, now that you have plundered hell and bound the prince of death in these torments. Now make known joy in the world, that all your chosen may rejoice and trust in your Ascension.'

As yet Adam and Eve had not been set free, but were held in bonds. Then Adam with a weeping and wretched voice cried out to the Lord, and said: 'Be merciful to me, Lord, be merciful to me in your great mercy and blot out my unrighteousness; for I have sinned against you alone and have done great wrong in your sight. I have erred, just like the sheep that perished. Seek out your servant now, Lord, for your hands created and shaped me; do not leave my soul with those who live in hell; but show me your mercy and lead me out of these bonds and out of this prison-house, and out of the shadow of death.' Then the Lord Saviour was merciful to Adam, and quickly his bonds were released, and having clasped the Lord's knees, he said: 'My soul shall bless the Lord, and all that is within me shall bless his holy name. You yourself have had mercy on all my unrighteousness; you yourself have healed my infirmities, and you released my life from eternal destruction, my longing you satisfied with good things.' As yet, Eve remained in bonds and in woe. She said: 'You are just, Lord, and your judgements are righteous; therefore I suffer this deservedly. I lived in honour in Paradise, and I did not realize it; I was perverse and became like the foolish animals. But you, Lord, shield of my youth, and mine, be not mindful of my lack of wisdom, nor turn away your face nor your mercy from me, nor depart in anger from your servant. Gracious God, listen to my voice with which I, wretched, cry to you; for my life and my years have been wasted in sorrow and in lamentation. If you consider my unrighteousness Lord, you will know my substance, that I am dust and ashes. I entreat you now, Lord, for the sake of your servant St Mary, whom you have honoured with heavenly glory. For nine months you filled her womb with the price of all the world; you know that you were born of my daughter, Lord, and that her flesh comes from my flesh and her bones from my bones. Forgive me now, my Lord, for the honour of her glory; forgive me, unhappiest of all women, and be merciful to me, my Maker, and save me from the bonds of this death.' Then the Lord Saviour had mercy upon Eve, and immediately her bonds were loosed. Then she cried out, and spoke thus: 'May your name be blessed in the world, Lord, because your mercy towards me is great; now you have saved my soul from lower hell.' Then the patriarch Abraham, with all the holy souls that had been held captive from the beginning of the world, cried out with a joyful voice and said: 'We give thanks to you, Lord, and praise you, for you redeemed us from the author of death and have enriched us in your coming.'

With that, the Lord, with the plunder that he had taken in hell, quickly went out living from his grave, raised up by his own strength; and afterwards arrayed himself in his immaculate body and showed himself to his followers because he wanted to remove every doubt from their hearts. And he also showed the wounds and the scars of the nails to unbelieving men, because he did not want there to be any lack of faith concerning his resurrection. And then afterwards in the sight of many men he ascended into the heavens, and he sat on the right hand of God the Father, from whence, in his divinity, he was never absent, but was established there always. Now therefore let all faithful people rejoice and be glad, because God's blood was shed for us. Let us all be joyful in the Lord, we who celebrate his resurrection; for when he took on human body and redeemed us from the power of the devil, he diminished his divinity no whit. Now we hear, dearly beloved, how many things the Lord suffered for us when he bought us with his blood from the captivity of hell. Let us therefore consider what recompense we are able to offer him, when he recounts and tells all this, at this same time when he sits on his judgement seat; when with our souls alone we must repay and make amends for all those things which previously we have done against his commandment – or have neglected to do, which we ought.

Let us now consider how great a terror will come upon us created things, in this present time, when the Judgement draws near; and the revelation of that day will be very terrible to all created things. In that day heaven and earth and the sea, and all the things that are in them, will pass away; so also, because of the same happening, sun and moon will pass away, and so will all the light of the stars. And the cross of our Lord, which now puts wicked spirits to flight on earth, will be raised up into the concourse of the stars. And in that day heaven will be folded up like a book; and in that day the earth will be burned to ashes; and in that day the sea will dry up; and in that day all the power of the skies will be turned and stirred. And six days before this day, marvellous signs will occur every day. At noon on the first day, there will occur a great lamentation of all created things, and men will hear a great noise in the skies, as if an army were being assembled and set in order there; then a great bloody cloud will arise from out of the north and obscure the sky; and after the cloud will come lightning and thunder all day; and in the evening bloody rain will rain down. On the following day a great sound of the preparation of armies will be heard in the skies; and the earth will be moved out of her place, and the sky will be open at one end, in the east; and in the evening a great power will come forth through the open part, and obscure and cover up the sky; and a bloody and fiery rain will strive to devour and burn up this earth; and the sky will fall to the four ends of the earth, and all the earth will be covered up with darkness at the eleventh hour of the day. And then all people will say: 'Now may the Lord have mercy and spare us, who when he was born in Bethlehem, was praised by ranks of angels when they cried out and spoke thus: "Glory be to God on high, and in earth [peace] to men of goodwill." '[1] The third day the northern part and the eastern part of the earth will speak together; and the deeps will rage and want to devour the earth. Then all the power of the earth will be changed, and a great earthquake will occur on that day. After nine o'clock on the fourth day there shall be great thunderings in the skies; and then all idols will fall down; and then it will be sunset, and yet no light will show; and the moon will be quenched, and darkness will come to pass over all the earth, and the stars will run widdershins the whole day, and men will be able to see them as clearly as on a night when it freezes hard. And then in that day they will hate this world's wealth and the things that now they love. At nine o'clock on the fifth day the sky will be rent asunder from the eastern part to the western part; and then all the race of angels will gaze through the opening onto mankind. Then all men will see how it will be at this world's end. Then they will flee to the mountains and hide because of the sight of the angels; and then they will call to the earth and beg it to swallow and hide them, and will wish that they were never born of father or mother. So it was prophesied of old about this in Christ's books, saying thus: 'Blessed are those who were barren, and blessed are the wombs that have never conceived, and the breasts which have never given suck.' And then they shall say to the hills and to the mountains: 'Fall on us, and cover and hide us so that we need no longer endure

[1] Luke, II 14.

this terror from these angels. Now everything is visible which we formerly kept hidden.'[1] Before nine o'clock on the sixth day all the world will be filled with accursed spirits from the four ends of the earth, who will strive to seize a great plunder of men's souls, as Antichrist did before; and when he comes, then he will threaten to send those souls who will not obey him into eternal punishments. And then at last he himself will be driven into everlasting woe. So then on that day St Michael will come with a heavenly host of holy spirits, and will then slay all those accursed ones and drive them into the pit of hell for their disobedience to God's commands, and for their wickednesses. Then all created things shall see the power of our Lord, although now human beings do not want to acknowledge or recognize it. Then after these things the seventh day will be near; and then the archangel St Michael will order the four trumpets to be blown at these four ends of the earth, and will rouse up all the bodies from death, though they had previously been covered with earth, or drowned in water, or eaten by wild animals, or carried off by birds, or torn by fishes, or departed from this world in any fashion. Then they will all have to arise and go forth to the Judgement in such fashion as they previously adorned themselves. Not with gold or with purple clothing, but with good and holy deeds must we be adorned if we want to be at the right hand of the Lord Saviour Christ then, with those righteous and chosen souls whom he will send into eternal light.

Therefore we should now consider the need of our souls while we may and are able, lest we put off this permitted time, and then wish to repent when we cannot. Let us be humble and merciful and charitable, and remove and banish malice, lies and envy from our hearts, and have a righteous spirit towards other men; for God himself will not then heed any man's repentance; nor will there be any intercessions. But he will then be fiercer and more severe than any wild animal, or any anger might ever be. And to the extent that a man's power is the greater and he is the richer in this world, so much more will the Supreme Judge require from him, since he will earn for himself and receive a fierce and stern judgement; as it is written concerning such: the man who now judges the poor without mercy, shall afterwards be ordained a harsh judgement.[2]

Now, dearly beloved, let us think about these things very

---

[1] Luke, XXIII 29–30 and cf. Revelation, VI 16–17.
[2] Cf. Matthew, XVIII 35.

prudently and wisely, so that through just works and acts of mercy we may find our Judge merciful, and through humility and through the true love of God and men we may merit eternal bliss with our Lord, where he lives and reigns in eternity for ever without end. Amen.

A MICHAELMAS SERMON
Blickling Homily 17

This sermon occupies ff. 120–7 of the Blickling Homiliary (see p. 122). The opening lines suggest that it was probably composed for the dedication of a church to the archangel Michael; Ælfric tells the same story on a similar occasion (Catholic Homily, I 34; see p. 136); and it is referred to in the Old English Church Calendar (see above, p. 81). But it is found in its fullest form in an eighth- or ninth-century Lombardic account (*MGH. Rerum Lang. et Italicarum*, 541–3).

St Paul's vision of hell, described in the last part of the sermon, is familiar because of its similarity to the *Beowulf*-poet's account of Grendel's mere. Both may have used a common source. But none of the known versions of the *Visio Pauli* include all the details these share in common, and probably the Blickling homilist knew the poem and drew on its imagery. An unprinted independent Old English translation of the *Visio* is found in the eleventh-century homiliary, Bodleian MS. Junius 85–6, ff. 3–11ᵛ. And an early Middle English version is included in the *Early South-English Legendary*.

Dearly beloved, the dignity and blessedness of the high and holy archangel's festival reminds us and suggests that we should say something about the blessed memory of him who is to be honoured and glorified throughout the globe in his churches, consecrated both by his own work and in his name. And it first became apparent and was made known to men thus.

It does not shine in the beauty of gold and silver then, but stands glorified through divine power with distinct honour. Moreover it is unpleasant in appearance outside; but inside it is adorned with eternal virtue. Thus it might well be that the holy archangel should have come from heaven and remembered the infirmity of men, so that he humbled himself in order to found and create it with his own hands, because he wished that mortal men might there yearn for the citizenship on high and the eternal fellowship. The holy church of Michael, then, is set upon the high summit of a certain mountain, and was revealed in the form of a cave. And the church lies there on the borders of the land of Campania. Again, there is in the neighbourhood, towards the sea called the Adriatic, a certain very famous town set on Mount Garganus, which is called Sepontus. And measured from the walls of the town up to the high summit of which I spoke before, it is twelve miles to the archangel's church. And it stands flourishing in joy and in bliss. This church was revealed and made known in the beginning by the very book which was discovered and found in the church. In it, it says that there was in the town a certain man, powerful and wealthy in the sight of the world, whose name was Garganus. The rich man gave the mountain the same name as himself. The man possessed great riches; whereupon the rich man's endless herds and countless numbers of oxen and all kinds of cattle increased and flourished, until he spread over and covered all the mountain pasture with his property. Then it happened that a certain bull-ox scorned the company of the other cattle and dwelt as a solitary in the wilderness, and did not ultimately return again to the oxen and to the cattle and to their dwelling. The bull scorned the keeper's herd, and dwelt in the wilderness at the mouth of a certain cave. When the lord found out that the bull had wilfully gone into the wilderness thus, then he was enraged because he thought the bull had gone frenzied throughout the wide-spread mountain. Then he gathered together a great band of his men, and turned in all directions through the woods, and looked for the wilful bull. Then he found it at last on the summit of the mountain, and saw that it stood at the mouth of a certain cave. Then he was greatly moved with anger, because it had gone about so madly and wandered so arrogantly. Then he took his bow and bent it, and with a poisoned arrow made to shoot towards where he saw the bull standing. Then immediately the arrow was in flight a great gust of wind came against it, so that the arrow was instantly turned back and pierced that same rich man by whom it had been sent, so that he promptly died. When the townspeople saw that, they became very afraid because of the disaster, for they had never seen such a marvel. And then they dare not approach the place where they saw the bull standing. There was at that same time in that city of theirs called Sepontus, a holy bishop. Then they sought him out and told him the marvel, and they asked him for instruction as to what to do about it. Then he instructed them and advised them to fast for three days and to entreat Michael that God should make known what was hidden and kept secret from men. When they had done so, both with fasting and with singing psalms and with alms-giving, then there appeared at night to that same bishop, the high and holy archangel Michael. And humbly and lovingly he then addressed him, and spoke thus: 'You acted with worldly wisdom when you sought from God in heaven what was hidden from men on earth. Know also of the man who was shot with his own arrow – that that was done by my will. And my name is Michael. I am the árchangel of the Heavenly King, and I stand ever in his sight. I tell you now that I love this place here on earth especially, and I have chosen it in preference to all others, and will also make known by all the signs that happen there that I am the creator and guardian of that place especially.' When that was told and made known to the townspeople, they sought out the place with their holy bishop, very happy and rejoicing; and in their manner they earnestly prayed to the living God and to the holy archangel Michael; and they humbly offered gifts to God. And there they saw two doors in the church, of which the south door was somewhat larger in form. And so steep was it where they had to go, they could not as yet get over to the cave, before they had cleared and constructed the ascent. But every day they earnestly engaged in their prayers outside. At the same time, their neighbours the Neapolitans were still erring in heathen practices and served devils. Then they began to challenge the townspeople of Benevento and Sepontus, as they were called, to a combat, and to ravage their land shamefully, and gave them no reparation but arrogant hostility and threats. Then their holy bishop instructed them and advised them to perform a three-day fast, and various alms and holy songs of praise, and to entreat the archangel Michael, as the most faithful guardian, for protection and assistance so that they might escape and overcome the contrivances of the enemy. Then at the same time the heathen shamefully and wickedly called upon their false gods with various idols to aid them. Then at the same time the blessed angel Michael was revealed to their bishop in a vision, and promised them imminent victory and said that their prayers were heard by God; and instructed them to set forth against their foes at nine o'clock in the morning. And he promised them also that he would himself watch their action, and would be of assistance to them there. Then in the morning they were very glad and went out rejoicing against the heathen. And because of the angel's statements, they were assured both of their victory and also of the flight and destruction of the heathen men. And then immediately at the opening of the battle, Mount Garganus, over which they had to fight, was completely overcome with a great trembling and with terror; and a fierce storm rose up from the mountain, and the summit of the mountain was entirely covered over with a dark cloud. Then the lightnings flew like fiery arrows against the heathen people so thickly that they could not look at it at all because of the blaze of the light. Then what the prophet foretold was fulfilled; and he praised the Lord and spoke thus: *Qui facit angelos suos spiritus et ministros suos ignem urentem,*[1] 'Sometimes the same God sends his angel-spirits as messengers; sometimes he sends through the flame of fire.' Then the heathen people fled; and they were killed alike by the lightning, and laid low and borne down by the Christians with their weapons, until they had severely vanquished the Neapolitans and the heathen people who left their city half alive, and fell upon those who had survived the danger and distress. Then it was made known to us Christian people that God's angel had come there for aid and protection; and immediately all humbly bowed down to the King of kings, to Christ himself. And all the heathen people submitted to them, and lived according to Christian teaching, and received baptism; and they readily perceived that the angel of God had come as a help and protection to those Christian peoples. When the Christians fully examined it, they looked and reckoned that there were six hundred men killed by the lightning and by the fiery arrows alone, beside those whom they had destroyed and slain with their weapons. Then victorious thus, and crowned with great bliss, they journeyed home. And at the holy church they at once humbly and gladly gave thanks to Almighty God and to the archangel Michael for the victory they had attained. Then moreover, on the marble in front of the north door of the church, they found, as it were, a man's tracks, just as if a man had stood there. And those footprints were clear and visible in the stone as if they had been impressed on wax. Then they plainly perceived that the blessed Michael had been present there as a help to them while they were at the battle, and himself had set down that token of the victory and made it known in the deep sleep. Then forthwith over that stone they built a church and in it built and beautifully adorned an altar. And afterwards those who had great love and faith in the church honoured and venerated the place with great joy. And a great fear also came upon the people; and they were greatly troubled in spirit and in much doubt as to what they dare do about

[1] Psalm CIII 4.

it: whether they should consecrate the church, or what might be the will of God and the holy craftsman who created it by his hand. Then they found it advisable at first to erect a church to the east of the place, and to consecrate it in the name of St Peter, the holy servant of Christ; and in it they put two altars, and consecrated one in the name of St Mary, Christ's mother, and the other to St John the Baptist, Christ's father in baptism. Then their venerable bishop proposed to them a happy and salutary plan, and advised that they send at once to Rome to the pope, and that they ask and enquire from the pope and the papal see what they considered advisable, whether they dare consecrate the church in another fashion. Then the blessed pope sent back this message, and spoke these words: 'If it be one's place that one has to consecrate a church, then it is altogether most fitting that it should be on that day in which the victory was granted; if the holy guardian should favour and prefer anything else concerning the place, however, then it is altogether best to find out what his will might be about the day. And when the time approaches then let both of us two perform a four-day fast with our townspeople, and earnestly pray the holy Trinity to lead forth and produce that gift which they first revealed to men through the holy archangel, a wonderful sign which they manifested for men to follow.' Then, as their noble bishop advised, they all humbly performed a four-day fast. Then on the night in which they had completed the fast, St Michael appeared to the bishop in a vision and said to him: 'You need not be anxious about consecrating the church, because I made it and I have consecrated it. Now you go inside there and wait on me, and trust readily in the patron of the place, and visit it frequently with prayers. Your part, then, is that tomorrow you sing masses in it, and this people attend Eucharist after their custom; my part is that with a solemn sign I reveal and make it known that I myself have consecrated and blessed it.' Then forthwith in the morning, greatly rejoicing because of that answer, they came there with a great concord of prayers and with offerings of holy hymns; and then they all went into the church. It was evident that the tracks, which I previously said were first found in the marble, had first begun to go in an outwards direction across the threshold coming out of the porch door. This church with this porch might receive and hold about five hundred men. Then, against the south wall in about the middle of the wall, the noble altar was revealed. Moreover it was covered and spread over with a fine purple cloth.

And that same house had sloping walls, not at all in the manner of human works in which the walls would be straight, but it seemed much more like a cave; and frequently the stones jutted out steeply as if from a cliff. Moreover the roof was of various heights; in one place it was such as a man might scarcely reach it with his hands, in another easily touch it with his head. I believe, therefore, that the archangel of our Lord looked for and loved purity of heart much more than the ornamentation of stones. The summit was then as it is now known. The mountain is large outside, and it is overgrown here and there with patches of broom; other parts are covered with green fields. And then, after the holy hymns and masses were finished, they turned again to their houses, with great joy and gladness and with the angel's blessing. Then the bishop appointed good singers and mass-priests there and all sorts of church servants who thereafter should worship daily in a fitting manner. However, there was no man who dared ever come into the church at night time. But at daybreak, after first light, they assembled inside for hymns. Also there was flowing out from the very stone of the church roof to the north side of the altar a very sweet and pure stream, used by those who still lived in the place. And by this body of water there was a glass vessel hung on a silver chain, which received the pleasant liquid. It was the custom of the people when they had gone to the Eucharist, to climb up to the glass vessel by means of ladders and there take and taste the heavenly liquid. It was sweet to taste and wholesome to the stomach. It is a sign also that many men with fever and with various other illnesses were immediately healed through a taste of this liquid. In other ways also, countless illnesses of men were often and frequently healed there. And various miracles similar to these, the power of which was proper and sacred, were and still are displayed and made known, but most frequently on that day which is his festival and commemoration. Then the people come from there from the surrounding regions, and it is to be believed and surely known that there manifold and various illnesses of men are healed, and there the angel's power and his miracles reverenced, and most often manifested on that day. As St Paul said: *Qui ad ministrum summis*[1] . . . 'Angels are as ministering spirts sent hither into the world by God to those who in spirit and in virtue deserve from God the eternal home, so that they should

---

[1] Cf. Hebrews, I 14.

be a help to those who must forever fight against the accursed spirits.' But let us now beseech the archangel St Michael and the nine orders of holy angels to be of help to us against the hell-fiends. They were the holy ones in defence of men's souls.

As St Paul was gazing towards the northern part of this world, where all waters pass below, he also saw there above the water a certain grey stone. And to the north of the stone there had grown very frosty groves; and there were dark mists; and beneath the stone was the dwelling place of water-monsters and evil spirits. And he saw that on that cliff many black souls bound by their hands were hanging in the icy groves; and the devils in the shape of water-monsters were clutching at them, just like ravenous wolves. And the water under the cliff below was black; and between the cliff and the water was about twelve miles. And when the twigs broke, the souls which hung on the twigs dropped below and the water-monsters seized them. These were the souls of those who had sinned wickedly here in the world, and would not turn from it before their life's end. But let us now earnestly beseech St Michael to lead our souls into bliss, where they may rejoice in eternity without end. Amen.

ÆLFRIC

SERMON ON THE EPIPHANY OF THE LORD

Catholic Homily, I 7

Ælfric's Catholic Homilies consist of two series of forty and forty-five sermons respectively, intended for use on the principal festivals of the Church year. Each series is preceded by prefaces in both Latin and Old English. Both series are dedicated to Sigeric, Archbishop of Canterbury 990–4, and must therefore have been written while Ælfric was a monk at Cerne Abbas, Dorset.

Ælfric acknowledges a wide variety of sources: Augustine, Jerome, Gregory, Bede, Smaragdus 'and sometimes Haymo'; and others also are discernible. Several were conveniently available in the collective homiliary of Paul the Deacon.

A relatively large number of MSS. of the Catholic Homilies exist, the best of which, Cambridge University Library MS. Gg.3.28, was used as the basis of the edition by Benjamin Thorpe, *The Homilies of the Anglo-Saxon Church*, The Ælfric Society, London, 1844–6. It is a contemporary or nearly contemporary MS., probably no more than one stage removed from Ælfric's holograph. Since the twelfth century, at least, it seems to have belonged to the cathedral library at Durham. The Feast of the Epiphany occurs on 6 January (cf. Calendar, above, p. 72); and this sermon occupies ff. 22ᵛ–6ᵛ of the MS.

Ælfric's initial exposition follows that of the liturgical celebration of Epiphany, which mentions the Wise Men, Christ's baptism and the miracle at the wedding feast in Cana. Otherwise his main source seems to have been either an Epiphany sermon by Augustine (*PL.*, XXXVIII 1033–5), or more probably one by Fulgentius, *c.* 467–533 (*PL.*, LXV 732–7). The moral interpretation of the Wise Men's gifts found towards the end of the sermon (p. 142) was taken from an Epiphany sermon by Gregory (*PL.*, LXXVI 1110–14).

Dearly beloved, a few days ago now we read through before you the gospel which belongs to this day's service, for the interpretation of the gospel narrative; but we did not treat the text more than was appropriate to the dignity of that day. Now, we will run over the same gospel narrative, and explain it in respect of this present festival.

Matthew the evangelist said: *Cum natus esset Iesus in Bethleem Iudae, in diebus Herodis regis, ecce Magi ab oriente venerunt Hierosolimam, dicentes: 'Ubi est qui natus est Rex Iudeorum?'* et cetera.[1] 'When the Saviour was born in Bethlehem of Judea, in the days of Herod the King, behold, there came from the eastern part

[1] Matthew, II 1–2.

of the world three astrologers to the city of Jerusalem, asking
thus: "Where is he who is born King of the Jewish nation?" ' et
cetera.

Today is called *Epiphania Domini*, that is the day of God's
manifestation. On this day Christ was manifested to the three
kings who sought him out from the eastern part of the world with
three-fold gifts. Again, in the course of years, he was on this day
manifested to the world at his baptism, when the Holy Spirit
rested upon him in the shape of a dove, and the voice of the Father
sounded loud from heaven, saying thus: 'This is my beloved Son,
with whom I am well pleased; listen to him.'[1] On this day also he
changed water into fine wine, and by that manifested that he is the
true Creator, who might change his creatures. For these three
reasons this festival is called 'the Manifestation of God'. On
the first day of his birth he was revealed to three shepherds in
the Jewish country, through the proclamation of the angel. On the
same day he was made known to the three astrologers in the east,
through the bright star; for on this day they came with their gifts.
It was appropriate that the prudent angel should make him
known to the prudent Jews who knew God's law, and that he
should be manifested to the heathens who did not know the divine
purpose, not through a voice but through a sign.

The Jewish shepherds signified the spiritual shepherds, that
is the apostles, whom Christ chose from the Jewish people as
shepherds and teachers for us. The astrologers, who were dwelling in heathenism, had the significance of all heathen peoples
who should be turned to God through the teaching of the apostles,
who were of the Jewish nation. The psalmist wrote truly, concerning Christ, that he is the corner-stone which joins the two walls
together,[2] for he united his chosen from the Jewish people and
the faithful from the heathen like two walls to one church;
concerning which the Apostle Paul said: 'In his advent the Saviour
preached peace to us who were afar off, and peace to those who
were at hand. He is our peace, who has made both one, abolishing
the former enmities in himself.'[3] The Jews who believed in Christ
were nearer to him geographically, and also through knowledge
of the old law. We were very distant, both geographically and

---

[1] A confusion of Matthew, III 17 with an altogether different event recorded in Mark, IX 7.
[2] Psalm CXVIII 22.
[3] A paraphrase of Ephesians, II 14 ff.

through ignorance; but he joined us with one faith to the great corner-stone, that is, the unity of his Church.

The eastern astrologers saw a bright new star, not in heaven amongst other heavenly bodies, but a solitary between heaven and earth. Then they realized that the unfamiliar star signified the birth of the true King in the land over which it glided; and therefore they came to the kingdom of Judea, and greatly terrified the infamous King Herod with their announcement. For when the greatness of heaven was revealed, earthly wickedness was without doubt confounded.

It is clear that the astrologers understood Christ to be a true man, since they asked: 'Where is he who is born?' They knew him to be a true king, since they said: 'King of Judea.' They worshipped him as a true God, since they said: 'We have come that we might adore him.' God could easily have directed them to the city in which the child was, by the star, just as he had manifested his birth by the star's rising; but he wanted the Jewish scribes to read the prophecy concerning it and thus manifest his birth-place, so that, if with the astrologers they wanted to worship Christ, they might be saved; and if they would not, that they might be condemned by that manifestation. The astrologers went and worshipped; and the Jewish scribes, who had identified the place by means of book-learning, remained behind.

All creatures acknowledged their Creator's advent, save only the impious Jews. The heavens acknowledged their Creator when at his birth they displayed a new star. The sea acknowledged him when Christ in his might walked over its waves, with the soles of his feet dry. The sun acknowledged him when at his passion it hid its beams from midday till three o'clock. The rocks acknowledged him when at his death they burst into pieces. The earth acknowledged him when it all trembled at his resurrection. Hell acknowledged him when it unwillingly released its prisoners. And yet for all those signs, the hard-hearted Jews would not recognize the true Creator, whom dumb creation knew and manifested by signs. They were not all equally unbelieving, however, but from their race there were both prophets and apostles and many thousands of believing men.

When the astrologers turned to the king, the star became invisible to them; and afterwards, when they turned to the child, they saw the star again, and then it led them to the house in which he dwelt. It did not glide in front of them all the way, but after they came to the Jewish land it was their guide there, until it stood above Christ's inn.

Herod had the signification of the Devil; and he who turns from God to the Devil loses God's grace, that is the enlightenment of his spirit, just as the astrologers lost the star when they turned to the cruel king. If he then afterwards resolutely forsakes the Devil, he will have found again the grace of the Holy Spirit, which enlightens his heart and leads to Christ.

We should also realize that there were some heretics who said that every man is born according to the position of the stars and that his destiny befalls him as a result of their course; and they advanced in support of their error the fact that a new star sprang up when the Lord was corporeally born, and said that the star was his destiny. May this error depart from believing hearts, that there is any destiny except for the Almighty Creator, who provides life for every man according to his merits. Man is not created for the stars, but the stars are created for men as a light in the night-time. When the star glided and led the astrologers and pointed out the child's inn to them, then it manifested that it was Christ's creature and served its Creator aright; but it was not his destiny. Again, we entreat that no believing man defile his faith with this error. Indeed, Isaac's wife, Rebecca, gave birth to two twins, Jacob and Esau, at one time, so that at his birth Jacob held the elder brother Esau by the foot; and yet they were similar neither in conduct, nor in life's merits. Indeed, holy scripture says that God loved Jacob and hated Esau; not because of destiny, but because of various merits. It will very often happen that the queen and the maid-servant give birth at the same time, and yet the prince receives a lofty throne because of his birth, and the maid-servant's son lives all his life in servitude.

Now foolish men often say that they must live according to destiny, as if God compels them to evil deeds! But we will quench the empty lies of these foolish men with the profundity of the divine scriptures. The Almighty Creator created angels by his divine power, and in his great righteousness gave them their own free will, that through obedience they might remain in everlasting bliss, and also might lose that bliss, not because of destiny, but because of disobedience. His profound righteousness would not compel them to either, but granted them their own free will; for that is righteousness, that everyone be permitted his own free will. Because his righteousness would be put aside if he subjected them to his service by compulsion, or if he pushed them into evil. Then some angels perverted their own free will, and through pride wrought themselves into accursed devils.

Again, when the Creator, ruling in glory, made mankind, he gave Adam and Eve their own free will, whether through obedience they with all their offspring would remain without death in bliss for ever in eternity, or whether through disobedience they would become mortal. But when they transgressed God's command and obeyed the accursed Devil's instruction, then they became mortal and guilty through their own free will, they and all their offspring. And although mercy should never be shown to mankind afterwards, any more than to the devils, nevertheless God's righteousness would be altogether irreproachable. But afterwards, the great mercy of our Lord redeemed us through his incarnation, if we will obey his commandments with our whole heart. Certainly, those who now forsake God of their own free will and the Devil's allurement, God also will forsake to everlasting destruction.

The Almighty Creator well knew what was to happen before he created his creatures. He knew exactly the number of both chosen angels and chosen men; also of those proud spirits and wicked men who perish because of their wickedness. But he predestined no one to evil, for he himself is all goodness; nor did he destine anyone for destruction, for he is true life. He predestined the chosen to the eternal life, because he knew they would come to such through his grace and their own obedience. He would not predestine the wicked to his kingdom, because he knew they would come to such through their own transgression and perversity.

Keep this fast in your hearts, that the almighty and the righteous God compels no man to sin, but nevertheless he knows beforehand which will sin of their own will. Why then will he not justly avenge the evil that he abhors? He loves every good and righteousness, because he is by nature good and righteous; and he hates all those who work unrighteousness, and destroys those who speak falsehood. Assuredly, those who believe in God are guided by the Holy Spirit. The conversion to God is not of ourselves, but by the grace of God; just as the apostle says: 'Through God's grace you are saved by faith.'[1]

---

[1] Ephesians, II 8.

Those who do not believe refuse by their own choice, not through destiny, because destiny is nothing but a false imagination; in fact nothing happens by destiny, but all things are arranged by the judgement of God, who said through his prophet: 'I try the hearts of men, and their loins, and give to each according to his ways and according to his own invention.'[1] Let no man ascribe his evil deeds to God, but ascribe them first to the Devil who deceived mankind, and to Adam's transgression, but most of all to himself, since evil pleases him and good does not please him.

However, it frequently happens that the offspring are condemned through their forefathers' wicked deeds, if they imitate them in evil. But if the offspring is righteous, then he will live in his righteousness and will not bear the sins of his parents at all. Let no man be so impious that he curse Adam or Eve, who now reign with God in heaven. But rather let him earn God's mercy, so that he turn of his own free will to the obedience and commandments of his Creator. For no man will be saved except by the grace of Christ the Saviour; that grace he prepared and preordained in eternal wisdom before the foundation of the world.

My brothers, you have heard now about the false imagination which vain men call destiny. Let us now take up the explanation of the gospel where we left it previously.

The astrologers went into the child's inn, and found him with his mother. Then with prostrate bodies they worshipped Christ, and opened their treasure-chests and offered him three-fold gifts: gold, and incense and myrrh. Gold befits a king; frankincense belongs to the service of God; with myrrh they treat the bodies of dead men so that they decay less rapidly. These three astrologers worshipped Christ and offered him significant gifts. The gold signified that he is a true king, the frankincense that he is the true God, the myrrh that he was then mortal; but now he remains immortal in eternity.

There were some heretics who believed that he was God, but did not believe that he reigned at all anywhere; they offered incense to Christ spiritually, and would not offer him gold. Again, there were other heretics who believed that he was a true king, but they denied that he was God; these without doubt offered him gold, and would not offer him incense. Some heretics confessed that he was true God and true king, and denied that he took on

---

[1] Jeremiah, XVII 10.

mortal flesh; these assuredly brought him gold and frankincense, and would not bring myrrh for the mortality taken on.

My brothers, let us offer our Lord gold because we confess that he is true King and rules everywhere. Let us offer him frankincense, because we believe that he was always God, who at that time appeared to man. Let us bring him myrrh, because we believe that he who is incapable of suffering in his divinity was mortal in our flesh. In his incarnation he was mortal before his passion, but he is henceforth immortal, as we shall all be after the general resurrection.

We have said about these three-fold gifts, how they apply to Christ; we want also to say how they apply to us, in a mortal sense. Assuredly, by gold wisdom is signified; just as Solomon said: 'A desirable treasure lies in the wise man's mouth.'[1] With frankincense holy prayer is explained, concerning which the psalmist sang: 'Lord, let my prayer be sent forth like burning frankincense in your sight.'[2] By myrrh is figured the destruction of our flesh, about which the holy congregation says: 'My hands dripped myrrh.'[3] We bring gold to the born King if we are shining in his sight with the brightness of wisdom from on high. We bring him frankincense if, through diligence of holy prayers, we kindle our thoughts on the altar of our heart, so that through heavenly desire we may smell somewhat sweet. We offer him myrrh if, through continence, we quell the fleshly desires. Myrrh, as we said earlier, acts so that dead flesh does not easily rot. Certainly the dead flesh rots rankly when the mortal body is enslaved to overflowing lust; just as the prophet said of some: 'The cattle have rotted in their dung.'[4] As the cattle rot in their dung, so fleshly men end their days in the stench of their lust. But if we spiritually offer myrrh to God, then our mortal body will be preserved through continence from the stenches of lust.

The astrologers pointed out something important when they returned to their country by another way. For our country is Paradise to which we cannot return by the way we came. The first-created man and all his offspring were driven from the delight of Paradise through disobedience and for eating the forbidden food, and through pride when he wanted to be greater

---

1 Proverbs, XXI 20, Septuagint text.
2 Psalm CXL 2.
3 Song of Solomon, V 5.
4 Joel, I 17.

than the Almighty Creator had created him. But it is very necessary for us that we should, by another way, avoid the treacherous Devil, so that we may come happily to our homeland, for which we were created.

We should, by obedience and continence and humility, proceed with one accord to our home-land, and with holy virtues attain that country which we lost through faults. The treacherous Herod was justly deceived by the astrologers, and he did not get to Christ because he sought him with deceitful heart. He signified those false hypocrites who seek God with dissimulation, and never find him. He is to be sought with a truthful heart and resolute mind, he who lives and reigns with the Father and the Holy Spirit, world without end. Amen.

SERMON ON THE GREATER LITANY

Catholic Homily, I 18

The first of three sermons for Rogation week, occupying ff. 53ᵛ–6ᵛ of the Cambridge MS. edited by Thorpe (see p. 136).

A Gallic festival in origin (see fn. 1), the Rogation days were three days of ceremonial penitence and prayer, immediately preceding Ascension Day. A similar service was held on St Mark's Day, 25 April. The second series contains a further three sermons for Rogation week.

Ælfric acknowledges Augustine as the source of his exposition of the gospel for the day – apparently the homily PL., XXXVIII 618–25.

These days are called *Letaniae*, that is 'Prayer-days'. On these days we should pray for abundance of earthly crops, and for health for ourselves, and peace, and what is more, forgiveness for our sins.

We read in books[1] that this observance was established at the time when a great earthquake occurred in a city which is called Vienne; and churches and houses fell down, and wild bears and wolves came and devoured a large number of the people, and the king's palace was burnt with heavenly fire. Then the bishop, Mamertus, ordered a three-day fast, and then the tribulation

[1] The events at Vienne in Burgundy were referred to by Sidonius Apollinaris, Bishop of Clermont, writing to Mamertus c. 473, and telling of his institution of a similar period of penance with the hope of alleviating the distress of a siege by the Visigoths (MGH. Auct. Antiq. VIII 103–4). An unprinted sermon 'de letania maiore' found in the Wulfgeat homiliary (see p. 185) and perhaps attributable to Wulfstan, tells the same story with additional narrative details.

ceased; and the custom of the fast survives in the faithful Church everywhere.

They took the example of the fast from the people of Nineveh. The people were very sinful; then God intended to destroy them, but they placated him with their repentance. God spoke to a prophet who was called Jonah: 'Go to the city of Nineveh, and there preach the message that I tell you.'[1] Then the prophet was afraid and wanted to flee from the sight of God, but he could not. Then he went to the sea and went on board ship. Then when the sailors came out onto the sea, God sent them a great wind and tempest, so that they despaired of their lives. Then they threw their merchandise overboard, and the prophet lay down and slept. Then they cast lots between them and prayed that God would make clear from whence that misfortune came upon them. Then the prophet's lot came up. They demanded of him who he was and where he wanted to go. He said that he was a servant of God who created sea and land, and that he wanted to flee from God's sight. They asked: 'What shall we do about you?' He answered: 'Throw me overboard; then this tribulation will cease.' Then they did so, and the tempest was stilled. And they offered their sacrifice to God, and went on their way.

Then God prepared a whale, and it swallowed up the prophet and carried him to the land where he had to go, and spewed him out there. Then again God's word came to the prophet and said: 'Arise now and go to the great city of Nineveh, and preach just as I told you before.' He went, and preached that the wrath of God was about to descend on them if they would not submit to God. Then the king rose up from his throne, and threw off his costly clothing and put sackcloth on his body and ashes upon his head, and commanded that each man should so do; and that both men and nursing children, and also the cattle, should not eat anything for three days. Then, through that conversion they ceased from evil; and because of that strict fast, God took pity on them and would not destroy them in the way he had previously burnt up the inhabitants of the two cities Sodom and Gomorrah with heavenly fire, because of their sins.

On these days we should also go about our prayers, and process in and out with our relics,[2] and praise the Almighty God with

---

[1] Purportedly Jonah, I 2, although the actual wording anticipates that of God's subsequent command, Jonah, III 2, cited below.

[2] Processions with relics were prescribed as a specific part of the Rogation week ritual by the Council of Cloveshoh in 746 (Haddan and Stubbs, *Councils*, II 368).

fervour. We will now explain to you this gospel, which was read here just now: *Quis vestrum habebit amicum, et reliqua.*[1] The Saviour said to his disciples: 'Which of you has a friend, and goes to him at midnight, and says,' et cetera.

The holy Augustine[2] explained this gospel and said that the night signified the ignorance of this world. This world is filled with ignorance. Now therefore, everyone should rise up from that ignorance and go to his friend; that is, he should submit to Christ with all fervour, and pray for the three loaves, that is faith in the Holy Trinity. The Almighty Father is God, and his Son is Almighty God, and the Holy Spirit is Almighty God; not three Gods, but they are all one, Almighty God, indivisible. When you attain to these three loaves, that is to an understanding of the Holy Trinity, then you have in that faith life and food for your soul, and with it might also feed another stranger; that is, you might teach the faith to another friend who shall ask it of you. He said 'a stranger' because we are all strangers in this life, and our native land is not here; but here we are like wayfaring men; one comes, another goes; one is born, the other departs and gives up his seat to him. Now therefore everyone should desire faith in the Holy Trinity, for the faith will bring him to the eternal life.

We want to speak more about the faith, for much good may be drawn from the explanation of this gospel. The head of the household who had gone to rest with his children is Christ, who sits in heaven with his apostles and with the martyrs and with all the saints whom he fetched in this life. We should call to Christ and pray for the three loaves. If he should not grant us them straight away, we should not cease from prayer as a result. He delays, but wants to give nevertheless. He delays so that we should be possessed of a strong desire, and hold God's gift in high esteem. Whatever a man gets easily is not so precious as that which is got with difficulty. The Saviour said: 'If he continue knocking, then the head of the household will arise because of the other's importunity and will grant him what he asks, not because of friendship but because of his clamour.'[3] He said 'not because of friendship' because no man would be worthy of either the faith or the eternal life, if God's mercy towards mankind were not so great. Now we should knock and call out to Christ, for he will give

[1] Luke, XI 5 ff.
[2] *PL.*, XXXVIII, 620–1.
[3] Paraphrase of Luke, XI 8.

to us. As he himself said: 'Ask, and it will be given to you; seek and you will find; knock and it will be opened to you.' To each of those who prays fervently, and does not cease from prayer, God will grant the life everlasting.

Then he spoke a second parable. 'What father will give his child a stone if he asks him for bread? or a serpent if he asks for a fish? or a scorpion beetle if he asks for an egg?' God in his mercy is our Father, and the fish signifies faith, and the egg the holy hope, and the bread the true love. God gives these three things to his chosen, for no man may have the kingdom of God unless he has these three things. He must have proper faith, and have hope in God and true charity towards God and towards men if he wants to come to the kingdom of God. The fish signifies faith because its nature is that the more it is tossed by the waves, the stronger it is and the more it improves. So also the believing man; the more he is oppressed because of his faith, the stronger the faith will be, wherever it is sound. If it falls away under persecution, then it is not faith, but is hypocrisy. The egg signifies hope, for the birds do not bring forth young like other animals, but it is an egg first, and then with hope the mother hatches the egg into a chick. So also our hope does not yet attain that for which it looks, but is, as it were, an egg. When it has that which is promised it, it will be a bird. Bread signifies the true love, which is greatest of all virtues, just as bread is the foremost of all foods. Faith is a great virtue and the true hope is great; nevertheless love excels them because it will be forever in eternity and the other two will come to an end. We now believe in God, and we hope in him; but afterwards, when we come to his kingdom as he has promised us, then faith will be ended because we shall be in possession of that for which we previously hoped; but love will never cease: now therefore it is the best of them.

In the gospel the serpent is set against the fish. The devil deceived Adam in the form of a serpent; and he is forever striving against our faith now; but defence comes from our Father. The scorpion beetle, which is set against the egg, is poisonous and stings to death with the tail. The things which we see in this life are perishable; those which we do not see and are promised to us, they are eternal. The man who despairs of God's mercy looks behind; then his hope is poisoned with the scorpion's tail. But both in difficulties and in fortune and misfortune, we should say, as the prophet said: 'I will praise my Lord at all times.'[1] Should it befall

1 Psalm XXXIII 2.

us well in body, should it befall us ill, our hope will be saved from the beetle's sting.

A stone is set against the bread, because hardness of the spirit is contrary to true love. The man who will not, for love, do good to others where he can, is hardhearted. The gospel says: 'If you, who are evil, know how to give good things to your children, how much more will your heavenly Father give a good spirit to those asking him.' What are the good things that men give to their children? Transitory goods, such as the gospel touched on: bread, and fish and an egg. These things are good of their kind, because the earthly body needs food. Now you prudent men will not give your children a serpent instead of a fish; neither will our heavenly Father give us the devil's unbelief if we pray to him to give us true faith. And you will not give your child a scorpion instead of an egg; neither will God give us despair instead of hope. And you will not give your child a stone instead of bread; neither will God give us hardness of heart instead of true love. But the good heavenly Father gives us faith, and hope and the true love, and causes us to have a good spirit, that is, good will.

We ought to ponder the words which he said: 'You who are evil.' Evil we are, but we have a good Father. We have heard our name: 'You who are evil.' But who is our Father? The Almighty God. And of what men is he the Father? It is said clearly: of evil men. And of what kind is the Father? Of whom it is said: 'No one is good, but God alone.'[1] He who is forever good will bring us who are evil to be good men, if we turn away from evil and do good. The man Adam was created good, but by his own free will, and the Devil's allurement, he and all his offspring became evil. He who is sinful is evil, and there is no man alive without some sin. But our good Father cleanses us and heals us; just as the prophet said: 'Heal me Lord, and I shall be healed, save me and I shall be saved.'[2]

Let him who wishes to be good call on him who is forever good, to make him good. A man has gold – that is good in its way; he has land and wealth – they are good. But the man will not be good in consequence of these things, unless he do good with them; as the prophet said: 'He distributed his wealth and divided it among the poor, and his righteousness endures forever in the world.'[3] He

[1] Mark, X 18; Luke, XVIII 19.
[2] Jeremiah, XVII 14.
[3] Psalm CXII 9.

diminished his wealth and increased his righteousness. He diminished that which he must relinquish, and that which he shall have to eternity will be increased. You praise the merchant who gets gold for lead, and will not praise him who gets righteousness and the kingdom of heaven for perishable wealth! The rich and the poor are wayfarers in this world. The rich man now carries the heavy burden of his treasures, and the poor man goes empty. The rich man carries more provisions than he needs, the other carries an empty bag. The rich man should therefore share his burden with the poor; then he will diminish the burden of his sins, and help the poor. We are all God's poor; let us therefore acknowledge those poor who ask of us, so that God might acknowledge us when we ask him for what we need. Who are those who ask of us? Men wretched, and weak and mortal. From whom do they ask? From men wretched, and weak and mortal! Except for possessions, those who ask and those from whom they ask are alike. How could you, for shame, ask anything from God, if you deny your fellow what you might so easily grant him? But the rich man looks at his costly clothing and says: 'The beggar in his rags is not my fellow.' But the Apostle Paul takes him by the nose with these words: 'We brought nothing into this world, nor can we take anything away with us.'[1]

If a rich woman and a poor one give birth together, let them go away; you will not know which is the rich woman's child, which the poor one's. Again, if one opens the graves of dead men, you will not know which are the rich man's bones and which the needy one's. But greed is the root of all evil things; and those who devote themselves to greed wander from God's faith, and they fall into various temptations and harmful lusts which sink them into perdition. It is one thing for a man to be rich if his forebears have bequeathed him possessions; another if anyone become rich through greed. This man's greed is accused before God, not the other's possessions, if his heart is not kindled with greed. For such men the Apostle Paul enjoined:[2] 'Enjoin the rich that they be not proud, nor trust in their uncertain wealth; but let them be rich in good works, and give to God's poor with a generous spirit, and God will repay them with a hundredfold whatever they do for the poor, for love of him.'

The rich and the poor are necessary to each other. The wealthy

---

[1] 1 Timothy, VI 7.
[2] 1 Timothy, VI 17 f.

man is made for the poor, and the poor for the wealthy. It behoves the prosperous to lay out and distribute; it behoves the destitute to pray for the distributor. The poor's is the way that will lead us to the kingdom of God. The poor man gives to the rich more than he receives from him. The rich man gives him bread which will turn into dung, and the poor gives to the rich man the life eternal; yet not he, but Christ, who spoke thus: 'What you do for one of the poor in my name, that you do for myself,'[1] he who lives and reigns with the Father and the Holy Spirit, ever without end. Amen.

SERMON ON THE SACRIFICE ON EASTER DAY

Catholic Homily, II 15

Because of its particular theological content, this homily aroused the interest of Protestant reformers in the reign of Elizabeth. First published under the direction of Archbishop Parker in 1567, it may fairly be considered the origin of Old English studies. It occupies ff. 185ᵛ–9ᵛ of the Cambridge MS. edited by Thorpe (see p. 136).

Ælfric apparently drew his parallel between Passover and Eucharist from an Easter homily by Gregory (PL., LXXVI 1174–81). But his major source was a tract 'De Corpore et Sanguine Domini' by Ratramnus, monk of Corbie, fl. c. 860 (PL., CXXI 125–70). Condemned and ordered to be destroyed after the Synod of Vercelli in 1050, this tract was itself of some importance at the Reformation.

Dearly beloved, you have frequently been told about our Saviour's resurrection, how on this present day he rose up in strength from death after his passion. Now, by the grace of God, we will explain to you about the holy Eucharist to which you must now go, both according to the Old Testament and according to the New; lest any doubt concerning the living food might harm you.

The Almighty God commanded Moses, the leader in the land of Egypt, that he should command the people of Israel on the night in which they left that country for the promised land to take a year-old lamb on each hearth and offer that lamb to God: and afterwards cut it up and make the sign of a cross on their doorposts and lintels with the blood of the lamb, and afterwards eat the lamb's flesh roasted, and unleavened loaves with wild lettuce.

God said to Moses: 'Eat nothing of the lamb raw, nor boiled in

---

[1] Matthew, XXV 40, end of Mark, IX 41.

water, but roasted in the fire. Eat the head and the feet and the entrails and let nothing of it be left until morning; if there is anything left, burn it. Eat it in this manner. Gird your loins, and be shod, have your staff in hand, and eat in haste; this time is God's passover.'[1] And on that night, in every house throughout Pharaoh's entire kingdom the first-born child was slain; and God's people Israel were delivered from that sudden death through the offering of the lamb and the marking with its blood. Then said God to Moses: 'Keep this day in your remembrance, and celebrate it solemnly in your generations with eternal observance, and at this festival eat unleavened bread continually for seven days.' After this deed, God led the people of Israel over the Red Sea with dry feet, and drowned in it Pharaoh, who had persecuted them, and all his host together; and afterwards fed the people of Israel for forty years with heavenly food, and gave them water out of the hard rock, until they came to the promised homeland. We have expounded part of this narrative elsewhere; we will now explain that part which appertains to the holy Eucharist.

Christian men may not now keep the old law bodily, but it behoves them to know what it signifies spiritually. The innocent lamb which the old Israel then slaughtered had the significance, in the spiritual sense, of Christ's passion, who innocent, shed his holy blood for our redemption; about which the servants of God sing at every mass: *Agnus dei, qui tollis peccata mundi, miserere nobis*. That is in our language, 'Lamb of God, who takes away the sins of the world, have mercy upon us.' The people of Israel were delivered from sudden death and from Pharaoh's slavery through the sacrifice of the lamb, which had the significance of Christ's passion, through which we are redeemed from eternal death and the power of the cruel Devil, if we believe properly in the true redeemer of all the world, Christ the Saviour. The lamb was sacrificed in the evening, and our Saviour suffered in the sixth age of this world; that age is considered the evening of this transitory world. With the blood of the lamb they marked a Tau, that is a sign of the cross, on their doors and lintels, and were thus protected from the angel who slew the first-born children of the Egyptians. And we should mark our foreheads and our bodies with the sign of Christ's cross, so that we may be saved from

---

[1] Exodus, XII 9–11.

destruction, when we are marked both on the forehead and in the heart with the blood of the Lord's passion.

The people of Israel ate the flesh of the lamb at their Easter-tide, when they were delivered; and we now partake spiritually of Christ's body and drink his blood when with true faith we partake of the holy Eucharist. They kept the time in which they were delivered from Pharaoh and departed out of the land, as their Easter-tide, with great honour for seven days; so also we Christian men keep Christ's resurrection as our Easter-tide for seven days, because we are redeemed through his passion and resurrection, and we shall be cleansed by attendance at holy Eucharist: just as Christ himself said in his gospel: 'Truly, truly, I say to you, unless you eat my flesh and drink my blood, you have no life in you. He who eats my flesh and drinks my blood, dwells in me, and I in him; and he has the life eternal, and I will raise him up at the last day. I am the living bread which came down from heaven. Not the heavenly food such as your forefathers ate in the wilderness, and afterwards died; he who eats this bread will live to eternity.'[1] He consecrated bread before his passion, and distributed it among his disciples, saying thus: 'Eat this bread; it is my body, and do this in remembrance of me.' Afterwards he blessed wine in a cup and said: 'Drink you all of this; this is my blood, which shall be shed for many in forgiveness of sins.'[2] The apostles did as Christ commanded, in that they afterwards consecrated bread and wine for a Eucharist in remembrance of him. So also their successors and all priests, according to Christ's command, consecrate bread and wine for a Eucharist in his name, with the apostolic blessing.

Now certain men have often questioned, and still frequently question, how the bread which is prepared from grain and baked by the heat of the fire, can be changed into Christ's body; or the wine, which is pressed out from many grapes, becomes changed, by any blessing, into the Lord's blood? Now we say to such men that some things are spoken of Christ figuratively, some literally. It is a true and certain thing that Christ was born of a virgin, and of his own will suffered death, and was buried, and on this day arose from death. He is called 'bread' figuratively and 'lamb' and 'lion' and so forth. He is called 'bread' because he is our life, and the angels'; he is called 'lamb' on account of his innocence; a 'lion'

---

[1] Paraphrase of John, VI 53–8.
[2] A conflation of Matthew, XXVI 26–8 with I Corinthians, XI 24–5.

on account of the strength with which he overcomes the powerful devil. But nevertheless according to true nature, Christ is neither bread, nor lamb, nor lion. Why then is the holy Eucharist called Christ's body, or his blood, if it is not truly that which it is called? In fact the bread and the wine which are consecrated through the priests' mass, appear one thing to human understanding from without, and cry another thing to believing hearts from within. From without they seem bread and wine, both in form and in taste; but after the consecration they are, through a spiritual mystery, truly Christ's body and his blood. A heathen child is baptized, but it does not alter its outward form, although it is changed within. It is brought to the font sinful because of Adam's transgression, but it is washed from all sins within, although it does not change its outward form. So also the holy font-water, which is called the well-spring of life, is like other waters in appearance, and is subject to corruption; but the power of the Holy Spirit approaches the corruptible water through the priests' blessing, and afterwards by spiritual power it can wash body and soul from all sins. Indeed, we see two things in this one substance. By true nature the water is a corruptible liquid and by a spiritual mystery it has healing power; so also, if we consider the holy Eucharist in a bodily sense, then we see that it is a corruptible and changeable substance. But if we perceive the spiritual power in it, then we understand that there is life in it, and that it confers immortality on those who partake of it with faith. The difference between the invisible power of the holy Eucharist and the visible form of its own nature is great. By nature it is corruptible bread and corruptible wine, and by the power of the divine word it is truly Christ's body and his blood; not, however, bodily but spiritually. The difference between the body in which Christ suffered, and the body which is consecrated for Eucharist is great. In fact, the body in which Christ suffered was born of the flesh of Mary with blood and with bones, with skin and with sinews, with human limbs, quickened by a rational soul; and his spiritual body, which we call Eucharist, is assembled from many grains, without blood and bone, limbless and soulless; and nothing in it is to be understood bodily, therefore, but everything is to be understood spiritually. Whatever there is in the Eucharist which gives us the essence of life, comes from its spiritual power and invisible efficacy; therefore the holy Eucharist is called a mystery, because one thing is seen in it, and another thing understood. That which is seen there has a bodily form, and that which we understand by it has spiritual power. Assuredly, Christ's body which suffered death and rose up from death, will henceforth never die, but is eternal and incapable of suffering. The Eucharist is temporary not eternal, corruptible, and is distributed piece-meal, chewed between teeth and sent into the stomach; but it is nevertheless through spiritual power entire in every part. Many receive the holy body, and it is nevertheless, through a spiritual mystery, entire in every part. Although a smaller part should be allotted to one man, nevertheless there is no more power in the larger part than in the smaller; because through its invisible power it is whole in each man.

This mystery is a pledge and a symbol; Christ's body is truth. This pledge we keep mystically until we come to the truth, and then this pledge will come to an end. Truly, as we said before, it is Christ's body and his blood, not bodily but spiritually. You ought not to question how this is done, but to hold to your faith that it is thus done.

We read in the book that is called *Vitae Patrum*[1] that two monks prayed to God for some manifestation concerning the holy Eucharist, and after the prayer they attended mass. Then they saw a child lying on the altar at which the priest said mass, and the angel of God stood with a knife waiting until the priest broke the Eucharist. Then the angel dismembered the child in the dish, and poured its blood into the chalice. Afterwards, when they went to the Eucharist, it was changed into bread and wine, and they received it, thanking God for that manifestation. The holy Gregory also prayed to Christ that he would show a doubting woman a great proof of his mystery. She went to the Eucharist with doubtful mind, and straightway Gregory obtained of God that the piece of the Eucharist which she should eat appear to both of them as if there lay in the dish the joint of a finger, all bloodied; and the woman's uncertainty was then rectified.[2] Now let us hear the words of the apostle about this mystery.

Paul the Apostle said of the old people of Israel, writing thus in his epistle to faithful men: 'All our forefathers were baptized in cloud and in sea, and they all ate the same spiritual food, and they

---

[1] Attributed to Jerome, *PL.*, LXXIII 979.
[2] This and a similar story is referred to by Paschasius Radbertus, Ratramnus' superior at Corbie, in a tract of his own, also entitled 'De Corpore et Sanguine Domini' (*PL.*, CXX 1317–20).

all drank the same spiritual drink. Truly, they drank from the stone that followed them, and the stone was Christ.'[1] The stone out of which the water then flowed was not Christ in person, but it symbolized Christ, who declared to all faithful men thus: 'Whoever thirsts, let him come to me and drink, and out of his belly shall flow living water.'[2] He said this about the Holy Spirit, whom those received who believed in him. The Apostle Paul said that the people of Israel ate the same spiritual food and drank the same spiritual drink, because the heavenly food which fed them for forty years, and the water which flowed out of the stone, had the signification of Christ's body and his blood, which are now offered daily in God's Church. They were the same which we now offer, not bodily but spiritually.

We told you a little while ago, that before his passion Christ consecrated bread and wine for Eucharist, and said: 'This is my body and my blood.' He had not yet suffered, but nevertheless by invisible power he changed the bread into his own body and the wine into his blood, just as he had done before in the wilderness before he was born as man, when he changed the heavenly food into his flesh, and the water which flowed out of the stone into his own blood. Many men ate of the heavenly food in the wilderness and drank the spiritual drink, and nevertheless died, just as Christ said. Christ did not mean the death which no one can avoid, but he meant the eternal death, which some of the people deserved because of their unbelief. Moses and Aaron and many others of the people who pleased God, ate the heavenly bread but did not suffer eternal death, although they died the common death. They saw that the heavenly food was visible and corruptible, and partook of it spiritually. The Saviour said: 'He who eats my flesh and drinks my blood, shall have eternal life.' He did not command the body in which he was enclosed to be eaten, nor the blood which he shed for us to be drunk; but by those words he meant the holy Eucharist, which is his body and his blood spiritually; and he who tastes that with a faithful heart has that life eternal.

Under the old law faithful men offered to God various gifts which had the future significance of Christ's body, which for our sins he himself afterwards offered as a sacrifice to his heavenly Father. Assuredly this Eucharist which is now consecrated at God's altar, is a remembrance of Christ's body, which he

[1] I Corinthians, X 1–4.
[2] John, VII 37–8.

sacrificed for us, and of his blood, which he shed for us; as he himself commanded: 'Do this in remembrance of me.'

Christ suffered once in himself, but nevertheless his passion is renewed daily through the mystery of the holy Eucharist at the holy mass; wherefore, as has been made clear so often, the holy mass greatly benefits both the living and the departed. We should also consider that, by a spiritual mystery, the holy Eucharist is both the body of Christ and of all faithful people; just as the wise Augustine[1] said of it: 'If you want to understand about the body of Christ, listen to the Apostle Paul, saying thus: "You are truly the body and limbs of Christ." '[2] Now your mystery is laid on God's table, and you receive your mystery, which you yourselves are. Be what you see on the altar, and receive what you yourself are. Again, the Apostle Paul said of this: 'We many are one bread and one body.'[3]

Now understand and rejoice; many are one bread and one body in Christ. He is our head and we are his limbs. The bread does not come from one grain, but from many; nor the wine from one grape but from many.[4] So we also should have unity in our Lord, just as it is written of the company of those who believed, that they were in as great a unity as if they had all one soul and one heart.[5]

Christ consecrated on his table the mystery of our peace and our unity. He who receives the mystery of unity and does not keep the bond of true peace, does not receive the mystery for himself, but as a witness against himself. It is very good for Christian men to attend Eucharist frequently, if they carry to the altar innocence in their hearts, if they are not weighed down with sins. For the evil man it comes to no good but to perdition, if he tastes the holy Eucharist unworthily. Holy books[6] enjoin that one should mix water with the wine used for the Eucharist because water symbolizes the people, just as the wine does Christ's blood; and therefore neither ought to be offered at the holy mass without the other, so that Christ may be with us, and we with Christ, the head with the limbs, and the limbs with the head.

We wished earlier to explain about the lamb which the

---

[1] In the course of an Easter sermon, now lost but partially preserved in a letter of Fulgentius (PL., LXV 391–2).
[2] I Corinthians, XII 27.
[3] I Corinthians, X 17.
[4] Cf. Augustine, PL., XXXVIII 1099–1100.
[5] Acts, IV 32.
[6] Cf. Cyprian, PL., IV 383–4.

old Israel sacrificed at their Easter-tide, but we wished first to explain to you about this mystery, and then how one ought to partake of it. The symbolic lamb was sacrificed at their Easter-tide, and the Apostle Paul said in the epistle for today,[1] that Christ is our Easter-tide, who was sacrificed for us, and on this day rose up from death. Israel partook of the flesh of the lamb, just as God commanded, with unleavened bread and wild lettuces; and we ought to partake of the holy Eucharist, Christ's body and his blood, without the leaven of evil and wickedness. Just as leaven changes substances from their nature, so also sins change the nature of man from innocence to corruption. The apostle taught that we should not feast on the leaven of evil, but on the unleavened loaves of sincerity and truth. The plant which they were to eat with the unleavened loaves is called lettuce; it is bitter to eat; and we should cleanse our hearts with the bitterness of true repentance if we wish to partake of Christ's body. The people of Israel were not accustomed to raw flesh; however, God commanded them not to eat it raw, nor boiled in water, but roasted in the fire. He will partake of God's body raw who, without reason, imagines that he was an ordinary man like us and not God. And he who will question the mystery of Christ's incarnation with human wisdom, he acts as if he seethed the flesh of the lamb in water, for in this instance water signifies human knowledge. But we must understand that all the mysteries of Christ's incarnation were ordained through the power of the Holy Spirit; so we partake of his body roasted in fire, because the Holy Spirit came in the form of fire to the apostles in various tongues. Israel was to eat the lamb's head, and the feet, and the entrails, and nothing could be left overnight; if anything was left, it was to be burnt in the fire; and they were not to break the bones. In a spiritual sense we eat the lamb's head when we accept the divinity of Christ in our faith. Again, when with love we accept his humanity, then we eat the lamb's feet, for Christ is the beginning and the end, God before all worlds, and man at the ending of this world. What are the lamb's entrails, but Christ's secret commands? Those we eat when we accept the word of life with avidity. Nothing of the lamb might be left until morning, because the sayings of God are to be considered with very great carefulness, so that in the night of this present life all his commandments might be contemplated with understand-

[1] I Corinthians, V 7 ff.

ing and exertion before the last day of the universal resurrection should appear. But if we cannot investigate all the mysteries of Christ's incarnation, then with true humility we should entrust the remainder to the power of the Holy Spirit, and not too daringly question those deep secrets beyond the range of our understanding.

They ate the lamb with girded loins. In the loins is the lust of the body, and he who wishes to partake of the Eucharist should bind up lust and receive the holy meal with purity. They were also shod. What are shoes but the hides of dead cattle? We shall be truly shod, if by our course and work we imitate the lives of men departed, of those who prospered in God by keeping his commandments.

They had staff in hand at the meal. The staff symbolizes care and guardianship. Those who know better, and can, should take care of other men and support them with their aid. Those who ate together were commanded that they should eat hastily, for God abhors slackness in his servants, and he loves those who seek the joy of eternal life with God's speed. It is written: 'Do not delay to turn to God, lest the time be lost through slothful delay.'[1] Those who ate together might not break the bones of the lamb, nor might those soldiers who crucified Christ break his holy legs, as they did those of the two thieves who hung on either side of him. But the Lord rose up from death whole without any corruption; and at the great Judgement they shall see him whom they cruelly wounded on the cross.

In the Hebrew language this season is called *Pascha*, that is in Latin *Transitus*, and in English 'Passover', because on this day God's people passed from the land of Egypt over the Red Sea, from slavery into the promised land. Our Lord also passed at this time, as the evangelist John said,[2] from this world to his Heavenly Father. We should follow our fountain-head, and pass from the Devil to Christ, from this fickle world to his steadfast kingdom; but first, we should pass in our present life from sins to holy virtues, from bad habits to good conduct, if we want after this transitory life to pass to the eternal, and after our resurrection to Christ the Saviour. May he lead us to his living Father, who gave him up to death for our sins. For which munificence be to him glory and praise, world without end. Amen.

[1] Ecclesiasticus, V 7.
[2] Cf. John, XVI 16–17; XX 17 etc.

THE PASSION OF ST EDMUND, KING AND MARTYR

Edmund came to the throne of East Anglia in 855 while still in his 'teens, and ruled until 870, when he was killed in a confrontation with a Danish army wintering in Norfolk. Within forty years Edmund was honoured as a saint in East Anglia, and subsequently acquired a veneration on a par only with that of Cuthbert and Thomas à Becket. From the tenth century at least, his martyrdom was commemorated on 20 November.

Ælfric's acknowledged source is the *Passio Sancti Eadmundi* by Abbo of Fleury, one of the most learned men of his time in Europe, who had visited England some time between 985 and 987 to teach at the newly founded monastery at Ramsey, Huntingdonshire. It was at the special request of the monks of Ramsey that Abbo wrote the *Passio*. There were several later Latin re-workings of the story, beginning in the eleventh and twelfth centuries with those by Hermann the Archdeacon, Osbert de Clare and William of Ramsey. Of Middle English versions, that in the *Early South-English Legendary* and those by Lydgate and Caxton are most important.

Ælfric's *Lives of the Saints* were compiled, probably some time during the last decade of the tenth century, at the request of his two noble patrons, Æthelweard, Ealdorman of Wessex beyond Selwood, who died in about 1002, and his son Æthelmær, founder of the monasteries at Cerne Abbas and Eynsham. Like his 'Catholic Homilies', Ælfric's *Lives* consists of a series of homilies intended for use on the major saints' days and other festivals of the Church year.

Several MSS. of the *Lives* exist, the best of which, British Library MS. Cotton Julius E vii, was used by W. W. Skeat as the basis of his edition of Ælfric's *Lives of Saints*, EETS., OS., LXXVI, LXXXII, XCIV, CXIV, London, 1881–1900. This is a nearly contemporary MS., written some time at the beginning of the eleventh century. Since the thirteenth century at least, it had been at Bury St Edmunds, where, probably because of the special interest in the saint there, it was known as *Liber sancti Ædmundi regis et martyris*. The Passion of St Edmund itself occupies ff. 203–7. There is a useful separate edition by G. I. Needham in *Ælfric: Lives of Three English Saints*, 2nd ed., Exeter, 1976.

In the time of King Æthelred a certain very learned monk came from the south over the sea from St Benoit sur Loire[1] to Archbishop Dunstan, three years before he died; and the monk was called Abbo. Then they talked together until Dunstan told the story of St Edmund, just as Edmund's sword-bearer had told it to King Athelstan when Dunstan was a young man and the sword-bearer was a very old man. Then the monk set down all the information in a book; and afterwards, when the book came to us a few years later, then we translated it into English, just as it stands hereafter. Then within two years the monk Abbo returned home to his monastery and was straightway appointed abbot in that very monastery.

The blessed Edmund, King of East Anglia, was wise and honourable, and by his noble conduct ever glorified Almighty God. He was humble and virtuous, and continued resolutely thus so that he would not submit to shameful sins; nor did he alter his

[1] The monastery of Fleury, which had received the remains of St Benedict during the later seventh century, and was now the centre of the Benedictine Revival.

conduct in any way, but was always mindful of that true teaching:
'You are appointed ruler? do not exalt yourself, but be amongst
men as one of them.'[1] He was as generous as a father to the poor
and to widows, and with benevolence always guided his people
towards righteousness, and restrained the violent, and lived
happily in the true faith.

Then eventually it happened that the Danish people came with
a pirate force, harrying and slaying widely throughout the land, as
their custom is. In that fleet, united by the devil, were the very
important leaders Ivar and Ubbi;[2] and they landed with warships
in Northumbria, and wasted the land and slew the people. Then
Ivar turned eastwards with his ships and Ubbi remained behind in
Northumbria, having won victory with savagery. Then Ivar came
sailing to East Anglia in the year in which Prince Alfred (he who
afterwards became the famous King of Wessex) was twenty-one
years old; and the aforesaid Ivar abruptly stalked over the land
like a wolf, and slew the people: men and women and the innocent
children, and humiliated the honest Christians.

Then immediately afterwards he sent an arrogant message to
the king that if he cared for his life, he should submit to do him
homage. The messenger came to King Edmund and quickly
announced Ivar's message to him: 'Ivar our king, brave and
victorious by sea and by land, has subdued many nations and now
suddenly landed here with an army, so that he might take winter
quarters here with his host. Now he orders you to divide your
secret treasures and the wealth of your forebears with him quickly,
and if you want to live, you will be his under-king, because you
haven't the power to be able to resist him.'

Well, then King Edmund summoned a certain bishop who was
very near at hand,[3] and discussed with him how he should answer
the savage Ivar. Then the bishop was afraid because of the
unexpected disaster, and for the king's life, and said that he
thought it advisable that he should submit to what Ivar commanded. Then the king was silent and looked at the ground, and
then eventually said to him, regally: 'Oh bishop! this wretched
nation is humiliated, and I would rather fall in battle against him
who might possess my people's land.' And the bishop said: 'Alas,
dear king, your people lie slain, and you have not the forces to be

---

[1] Ecclesiasticus, XXXII 1.
[2] Two of the three sons of the great Viking king, Ragnar Lothbrok.
[3] Probably Humberht, Bishop of Norfolk, whose cathedral was at Elmham.

able to fight; and these pirates will come and bind you alive, unless
you save your life by flight, or save yourself by submitting to him
thus.' Then said King Edmund, very brave as he was: 'Thus I
desire and wish with my heart, that I alone should not be left, after
my beloved thegns, who with wives and children were suddenly
slain in their beds by these pirates. It was never my custom to take
flight, but I would rather die for my own country if I must; and
Almighty God knows that I would never turn away from his
worship, nor from his true love, whether I die or live.'

After these words he turned to the messenger that Ivar had sent
to him and said to him, unafraid: 'You would certainly deserve
death now, but I would not dirty my clean hands in your filthy
blood, for I follow Christ, who set us an example thus; and I will
cheerfully be slain by you if God so ordains it. Go very quickly
now and say to your savage lord: "Edmund will never while living
submit to the heathen war-leader, Ivar, unless he first submit in
this land to Christ the Saviour in faith." '

Then the messenger went away quickly and met the savage Ivar
on the way hastening to Edmund with his entire army, and told
the wicked man how he was answered. Then Ivar resolutely
commanded the men of the warships that they should all seize
only the king, who had scorned his behest, and immediately bind
him. Well, then when Ivar came, King Edmund stood within his
hall, mindful of the Saviour, and threw aside his weapons; he
would imitate the example of Christ, who forbade Peter to fight
against the savage Jews with weapons. So, then those wicked men
bound Edmund and insulted him shamefully, and beat him with
cudgels, and afterwards led the faithful king thus to a tree rooted
in the ground, and tied him to it with tight bonds, and afterwards
flogged him with whips for a long time; and amidst the floggings
he unceasingly called on Christ the Saviour with true faith; and
then, because of his faith, the heathen became insanely angry
because he called on Christ to help him. Then, as if for sport, they
shot at him with darts, until he was entirely covered with their
missiles, like the bristles of a hedgehog, just as Sebastian was.[1]
When the wicked pirate Ivar saw that the noble king would not
renounce Christ, but ever called on him with steadfast faith, he
ordered him to be beheaded; and the heathens did so. While he
still called on Christ the heathens dragged the saint away to

[1] A Roman martyr, whose death is described elsewhere in Ælfric's *Lives of the Saints*.

slaughter and with one blow struck off his head, and his blessed soul went to Christ. There was at hand a certain man, hidden from the heathen by God, who heard all this and afterwards told it just as we tell it here.

Well, then the pirate force returned to ship, and hid the head of the holy Edmund in the dense brambles, so that it would not be buried. Then after a time, when they had gone away, the inhabitants who were left there came to where their lord's headless body lay, and were very sorrowful at heart because of his slaughter, and in particular because they did not have the head to the body. Then the observer who previously saw it, said that the pirates had taken the head with them, and he thought, as was perfectly true, that they had hidden the head somewhere in the wood. Then they all went in a body to the wood, searching everywhere through bushes and brambles, to see if they could find the head anywhere.

There was moreover a great miracle, in that a wolf was sent by God's guidance to protect the head against the other beasts by day and night. Then they went searching, and continually calling out, as is usual among those who frequent the woods, 'Where are you now, comrade?' And the head answered them: 'Here, here, here!', and called out frequently thus, answering them all, as often as any of them called out, until they all came to it by means of the calling. There lay the grey wolf who watched over the head, and had embraced the head with his two feet, ravenous and hungry, and because of God dare not eat the head, but kept it safe from the beasts. Then they were amazed at the wolf's care, and thanking the Almighty for all his miracles, carried the holy head home with them; but as if he were tame, the wolf followed the head along until they came to the town, and afterwards turned back to the wood again. Then afterwards the inhabitants laid the head with the holy body, and buried it as best they could in such haste,[1] and erected a chapel over it forthwith.

Then in time, when after many years the raids stopped and peace was restored to the afflicted people, they joined together and built a church worthy of the saint, because miracles were frequently performed at his grave in the oratory where he was buried. They wished then to carry the holy body with universal veneration and lay it within the church. Then there was a great

[1] Perhaps at Hellesdun, near Norwich; but translated some time during the first half of the tenth century to the abbey subsequently known as Bury St Edmunds.

miracle, in that he was just as whole as if he were alive, with unblemished body; and his neck, which was previously cut through, was healed, and there was, as it were, a silken thread red about his neck as an indication to men of how he was slain. Likewise the wounds which the savage heathens had made in his body with repeated missiles, were healed by the heavenly God. And he lies uncorrupt thus to this present day, awaiting resurrection and the eternal glory. His body, which lies here undecayed, proclaims to us that he lived here in the world without fornication, and journeyed to Christ with a pure life. A certain widow called Oswyn lived in prayer and fasting at the saint's tomb for many years afterwards; each year she would cut the hair of the saint and cut his nails, circumspectly, with love, and keep them as relics in a shrine on the altar.

Then the inhabitants venerated the saint with faith, and Bishop Theodred[1] richly endowed the monastery with gifts of gold and silver in honour of the saint. Then at one time there came wretched thieves, eight in a single night, to the venerable saint; they wanted to steal the treasures which men had brought there, and tried how they could get in by force. One struck at the bolt violently with a hammer; one of them filed around it with a file; one also dug under the door with a spade; one of them with a ladder wanted to unlock the window. But they laboured in vain and fared miserably, inasmuch as the holy man miraculously bound them, each as he stood, striving with his tool, so that none of them could commit that sinful deed nor move away from there, but they stood thus till morning. Then men marvelled at how the villains hung there, one up a ladder, one bent in digging, and each was bound fast in his labour. Then they were all brought to the bishop, and he ordered them all to be hung on a high gallows. But he was not mindful of how the merciful God spoke through his prophet the following words: *Eos qui ducuntur ad mortem eruere ne cesses*,[2] 'Always redeem those whom they lead to death'; and also the holy canons forbid those in orders, both bishops and priests, to be concerned with thieves, for it is not proper that those who are chosen to serve God should be a party to any man's death, if they are the Lord's servants. Then after Bishop Theodred

---

1 There were two bishops of Elmham with this name in the second half of the tenth century, at least one of whom was a generous benefactor of Bury St Edmunds. Or it may refer to Theodred, Bishop of London (*c.* 915–60), who was also a benefactor of the monastery.
2 Proverbs, XXIV 11.

had examined his books, he repented, with lamentation, that he had appointed so cruel a judgement to those wretched thieves, and regretted it to the end of his life, and earnestly prayed the people to fast with him a whole three days, praying to the Almighty that he would have mercy on him.[1]

There was in that land a certain man called Leofstan, powerful before the world and foolish before God, who rode to the saint with great arrogance, and insolently ordered them to show him whether the holy saint was uncorrupted; but as soon as he saw the saint's body, he immediately went insane and roared savagely and ended miserably by an evil death. This is like what the faithful Pope Gregory[2] said in his treatise about the holy Lawrence who lies in Rome, that men, both good and evil, were forever wanting to see how he lay; but God stopped them, inasmuch as there once died seven men together in the looking; then the others left off looking at the martyr with human foolishness.

We have heard in common talk of many miracles concerning the holy Edmund, which we will not set down here in writing; but everyone knows of them. By this saint, and by others such, it is clear that Almighty God is able to raise man again at Judgement day, incorruptible from the earth, he who keeps Edmund whole in his body until the great day, although he came from the earth. The place was worthy of the venerable saint, in that men honoured it and supplied it well for Christ's service with pure servants of God, because the saint is more glorious than men might conceive.

The English nation is not deprived of the Lord's saints, since in England lie such saints as this saintly king, and the blessed Cuthbert,[3] and in Ely Audrey, and her sister also,[4] incorrupt in body, for the confirmation of the faith. There are also many other saints among the English who work many miracles – as is widely known – to the praise of the Almighty, in whom they believed. Through his glorious saints Christ makes clear to men that he who performs such miracles is Almighty God, even though the wretched Jews completely rejected him; wherefore they are damned, just as they wished for themselves.[5] There are no

[1] It is perhaps significant that Theodred of London should have played an important part in reforming the laws of Athelstan in this respect.

[2] PL., LXXVII 701–4. The story of Lawrence's martyrdom is told as one of Ælfric's Catholic Homilies.

[3] Bishop of Lindisfarne 685–7, whose life is told as one of Ælfric's Catholic Homilies.

[4] The story of St Æthelthrytha, abbess of Ely (ob. 680) and her sister Seaxburg is told elsewhere in Ælfric's Lives.

[5] Matthew, XXVII 25.

miracles performed at their graves, for they do not believe in the
living Christ; but Christ makes clear to men where the true faith
is, inasmuch as he performs such miracles through his saints
widely throughout this earth. Wherefore to him, with his
heavenly Father and the Holy Spirit, be glory for ever. Amen.

THE FESTIVAL OF ST AGATHA, VIRGIN

Agatha was one of several virgin martyrs venerated by the early Church. Her martyrdom was
commemorated on 5 February. She seems to have been killed at Catania in Sicily in 251, under
the Emperor Decius, during whose short rule the Church was persecuted with particular
severity. Several early Greek and Latin accounts of her martyrdom exist, although it is not
clear which was the immediate source used by Ælfric.

Only one complete copy of this work survives, occupying ff. 50–3 of the British Library MS.
edited by W. W. Skeat (see p. 158).

A Middle English verse account is found in the *Early South-English Legendary*, and another
was edited by C. Horstmann, *Sammlung Altenglischer Legenden*, Leipzig, 1881, pp. 45–8.

There was a certain blessed virgin, wise and faithful, called
Agatha, in the province of Sicily at the time when the murderous
persecutor Quintianus cruelly ruled that province under the
emperor. He was a greedy miser, and subject to his lust, a
wretched slave of the Devil, and hated the Lord. Then it came to
his ears concerning Agatha's manner of life, and he wondered
how he might get the virgin for himself. He commanded her to be
fetched, and gave her over to a foul woman called Aphrodosia,
obscene in habits (who had nine daughters, worthless and filthy),
so that for the space of a month she should learn her habits
and her mind should be changed through the enticements of
prostitutes.

So then Aphrodosia, the vilest woman, with her nine daughters,
vexed Agatha, sometimes flattering, sometimes frightening,
imagining that she could change her mind. Then said Agatha to
that evil family: 'Your words are like wind but they cannot beat
down my steadfast mind, which is fixed on a firm foundation.' She
said this with weeping, and wished to suffer the deadly torments
for Christ's name, just as the thirsty man in the heat of the sun
wishes for well-springs or the cooling of water. Then Aphrodosia
saw that she could not subdue the woman's spirit with her
shameful enticements, and went to Quintianus and spoke to him
thus: 'Stones might become soft and the hard iron like lead before

ever the faith in Agatha's breast might be quenched. Day and night I and my daughters have done nothing but constantly entice her to your submission, but we have had little success. I promised her jewels and apparel of gold and other honours, and a fine house, estates and retinue; and she scorned it all, like the dung that lies under foot.'

Then Quintianus became angry and commanded her to be fetched immediately, and at first questioned her about her birth. Then Agatha said: 'I am from a nobly-born family, as all my family can bear witness for me.' Then said the judge: 'Why do you behave yourself with low habits as if you were a maid-servant?' Agatha answered: 'I am God's hand-maiden, and for a man to be Christ's servant is a great nobility.' Quintianus said to the virgin of Christ: 'What then! Have we no nobility because we scorn the service of your Christ?' Agatha answered the wicked man, and said: 'Your nobility turns into such shameful thraldom, in that you are slaves of sin and of stones.' Quintianus, the murderous torturer, said: 'We can easily punish whatever slander you utter with insane mouth. But before you come to the aforesaid tortures, say why you scorn the worship of our gods.' Agatha answered the wicked man thus: 'You do not speak of gods, but of cruel devils, whose likeness you copy in bronze and stone, and all those graven images skilfully gild over.' Then Quintianus said that she must choose one of two things: either she should die with the condemned, foolishly, or she should sacrifice to the gods, like a noble and wise woman. Agatha answered him resolutely, and said: 'May your wife be such as Venus, your foul goddess, was, and may you be such as Jove, your shameful god, was, that both of you might be numbered amongst the gods.'[1] Then Quintianus ordered her to be struck repeatedly in the face with hands, so that she should not shout out. Then Agatha spoke the same words again. Quintianus said: 'In that you insult me repeatedly, you declare that you have chosen to suffer the tortures.' The virgin answered him: 'I greatly wonder that you, a wise man, should have stooped to such great folly that you esteem as gods such things as you are ashamed to resemble. If they are true gods, I wish you a god; if you abhor them, then the two of us speak alike. Call them so evil and so unclean, that if you would curse anyone you should wish him thus, that his life be like your hateful gods.'

---

[1] For the stories alluded to, see Wulfstan's sermon on false gods, pp. 186–7.

Quintianus said to her: 'Why do you talk so much folly? Sacrifice to the gods so that I do not cruelly destroy you.' Then, unafraid, Agatha answered the judge: 'If you will now set wild beasts on me, they shall immediately be tame enough to handle, through the Saviour's name. If you prepare a fire for me, there will quickly come to me through the angels of the Lord healing dews from heaven. If you threaten me with a flogging, I have the Holy Spirit, through whom I scorn all your flogging.' Then the judge shook his devilish head, and ordered her to be brought into a dark prison, and ordered that she should consider how she might escape the cruel tortures. Then said Agatha: 'You wretch, you consider how you might escape the everlasting torments!' Then she went cheerfully into the dark prison, as if she were invited to a good party, and committed her struggle to the benevolent Lord.

Well, then in the morning the wicked judge ordered Agatha to be brought into his hateful presence, and enquired what she had devised for her safety. Agatha said to him: 'Christ is my salvation.' The judge asked: 'How long do you want to protract this folly through confessing Christ, unhappy woman? Renounce your Christ and call upon the gods, lest you lose your life while young.' Agatha answered simply and said: 'You renounce your gods, which are stone and wood, and pray to your Maker who truly lives; if you reject him you will suffer in eternal torments.' Then the wicked man became incensed, and commanded her to be stretched on the rack and cruelly twisted like a rope, and said: 'Relinquish your obstinacy, so that your life might be saved.' On the rack Agatha answered thus: 'I rejoice in these hateful torments, just like he who sees one for whom he has longed, or he who finds many hoards of gold. My soul cannot be brought with bliss into heaven, unless my body be constrained in your bonds and gripped in your fetters by your executioners.' Then the cruel man became enraged, and commanded her to be tortured on the rack, in the breast, and afterwards commanded it to be cut off. Agatha said to him: 'Oh you most wicked man! Are you not ashamed to cut off that which you yourself have sucked? But I have my breast sound in my soul, with which I shall assuredly nurse my understanding.' Then Quintianus commanded her to be taken to prison, and commanded her to be deprived of food and drink, and said that no doctor should be allowed to treat her. Well, then at midnight a certain grey-haired man came into the prison, and his boy in front of him with a lamp in his hands, and wanted to treat the saint. The blessed Agatha said to the doctor: 'I have never cared about any doctoring in my life; I have my Saviour, who heals with his Word. He can, if he will, heal me mightily.' Then said the grey-haired man: 'He sent me to you; I am his apostle,[1] and even now you are made whole in his name.' And straightway he departed. Then Agatha knelt and thanked Christ that he had remembered her and had sent his famous apostle to her with such solace. After that prayer she looked at her breast, and the breast that had been cut off was restored through Christ, and all her wounds were healed. Then there shone a great light in the dark prison, so that the warders fled, seized with fear. Then the prisoners urged the holy virgin that she should go away and flee from the torments. Then Agatha, the noble virgin said: 'I do not wish to spoil my crown, nor get the warders into trouble, so I will remain here.'

Then on the fifth day the judge ordered her to be fetched, and said that she must sacrifice to the gods or be tortured with severe punishments. Then said Agatha: 'You wretched fool who want to call on stone and not on the true God, who for his name's sake has healed me of all the tortures which you cruelly inflicted on my body, and restored my breast which you, wicked man, cut off.' Then the idolater asked who had healed her. Agatha said: 'Christ the Son of God.' Quintianus said to the pure virgin: 'Do you still name Christ!' She said to him in answer: 'I confess Christ with my lips, and will always call on him with my heart.' Then said the servant of the Devil: 'Now I shall see whether Christ will heal you.' Then he commanded the floor to be strewn across with many burning coals and broken tiles, and commanded her to be rolled into the fire naked thus. Then in that very place there was a great earthquake, and the stone wall fell upon the foolish councillor so that he was completely crushed, and another attendant with him – very rightly so because they were councillors to the wicked judge in his evil deeds. Likewise, the city all shook because of the earthquake, and the citizens ran together to the wicked man demanding with a tumult why he had so cruelly tormented the virgin of God? Then Quintianus fled, frightened because of the tumult; and the earthquake greatly terrified him also. Nevertheless he ordered her to be brought into the prison. Well, then Agatha, with outstretched hands, cried inwardly to the

[1] St Peter, according to the Latin version, conventionally depicted in early medieval art as a grey-haired old man. Cf. Acts, XII 4 f.

Saviour thus: 'O my Lord, you who have created me in human form, and ever from childhood have shielded me until this; you who have deflected earthly love from me; you who caused me to overcome the executor's tortures, sharp iron, and fire and the lacerating claws; you who gave me patience in the pains, I pray you, Lord, that you will now take my soul to you, because it is now time that I should leave this world and might come to your gracious mercy, my dear Lord.' After this prayer within the prison, she gave up her spirit and went to God.

Then the citizens came and buried her body with great honour in a completely new tomb. Then there came an angel of God, walking like a man, at whose feet followed many fair youths, and set a marble stone within the tomb at the virgin's head, inscribed with these words: *Mentem sanctam spontaneam, honorem deo, et patrie liberationem*, that is in English: 'A mind spontaneously holy, an honour to the benevolent God, and the country's deliverance'. Then the angel went away with the youths; and there was no man in the province who had seen them before.

Well, then Quintianus, Christ's adversary, went in a ship across the Simeto, about Agatha's property, and wanted to take all her family prisoner also. But because of Christ he could not. As he lay in the ship, a horse seized him violently with its teeth and lifted him up; then another horse kicked out at him and sent him flying overboard, and afterwards his foul body was never found. Then no man dared to trouble her family but, terrified by God, honoured them all. In the same province of the land of Sicily is a burning mountain which they call Etna, kindled with *sulphur*, that is 'brimstone' in English. The mountain burns continually, as many others do. Then about twelve months after Agatha's passion it happened that Etna exploded with a very terrible fire, and it ran down the mountain like a flood, and the stones melted away and the earth burned up until it came to the city. Then the heathens ran to the saint's tomb and took up the veil from the saint's tomb against the fire which terrified them so much. Thereupon the fire was stilled and soon stopped because of the merits of Agatha, the noble woman. It burned for six days, and stopped on the anniversary of the blessed Agatha's departure to the eternal life, so that it might be made clear that the city was delivered from the danger of fire through Agatha's intercession, to the praise of the Saviour who so honours his saints. Wherefore to him be ever glory, world without end. Amen.

ÆLFRIC'S COLLOQUY

The colloquy, or set conversation-piece, between master and pupils formed a common method of instruction throughout medieval times. It was especially valuable as a device for teaching the grammar, vocabulary and correct pronunciation of Latin. Special attention was paid to this, as monks were expected to avoid the vernacular wherever possible; pupils from the monastic schools were required to read aloud in turn at meal-times, and faults were severely punished. This colloquy is ascribed to Ælfric by his sometime pupil Ælfric Bata, who was later to compose Latin colloquies of his own. Probably it was written for the pupils at Cerne Abbas, were Ælfric lived from about 987 to 1002, and where he may have been school-master.

Four eleventh-century copies of Ælfric's Latin colloquy survive, one of which (British Library MS. Cotton Tiberius A iii, ff. 60ᵛ–4ᵛ) is provided with a rough but more-or-less continuous interlinear gloss in a contemporary or near-contemporary hand. The most useful edition is that by G. N. Garmonsway, *Ælfric's Colloquy*, 2nd ed., Exeter, 1979.

Directions respecting the various characters assumed in the dialogue are found only towards the end of the text; for the sake of clarity these have been supplied throughout.

Pupils Oh master, we children beg that you will teach us to speak correctly, because we are unlearned and speak badly.

Master What do you want to talk about?

Pupils We don't care what we talk about, as long as it is accurate and useful conversation, and not frivolous or filthy.

Master Are you prepared to be beaten while learning?

Pupils We would rather be beaten for the sake of learning than be ignorant. But we know that you are kind and unwilling to inflict blows on us unless we compel you to.

Master I ask you (*indicating a particular pupil*), what do you say to me? What is your work?

'*Monk*' I am a professed monk, and every day I sing seven times with the brethren, and I am busy with reading and singing, but nevertheless, between-times I want to learn to speak the Latin language.

Master What do your friends do?

'*Monk*' Some are ploughmen, some shepherds, some oxherds; some again, huntsmen, some fishermen, some fowlers, some merchants, some shoe-makers, salters, bakers.

Master What do you say, ploughman? How do you carry out your work?

'*Ploughman*' Oh, I work very hard, dear lord. I go out at daybreak driving the oxen to the field, and yoke them to the plough; for fear of my lord, there is no winter so severe that I dare hide at home; but the oxen, having been yoked and the share and coulter fastened to the plough, I must plough a full acre or more every day.

Master Have you any companion?

'*Ploughman*' I have a lad driving the oxen with a goad, who is now also hoarse because of the cold and shouting.

Master What else do you do in the day?

'*Ploughman*' I do more than that, certainly. I have to fill the oxen's bins with hay, and water them, and carry their muck outside.

Master Oh, oh! It's hard work.

'*Ploughman*' It's hard work, sir, because I am not free.

Master What do you say shepherd? Do you have any work?

'*Shepherd*' I have indeed, sir. In the early morning I drive my sheep to their pasture, and in the heat and in cold, stand over them with dogs, lest wolves devour them; and I lead them back to their folds and milk them twice a day, and move their folds; and in addition I make cheese and butter; and I am loyal to my lord.

Master Oh, oxherd, what do you work at?

'*Oxherd*' Oh, I work hard, my lord. When the ploughman unyokes the oxen, I lead them to pasture, and I stand over them all night watching for thieves; and then in the early morning I hand them over to the ploughman well fed and watered.

Master Is this one of your companions?

'*Oxherd*' Indeed, he is.

Master Do you know how to do anything?

'*Huntsman*' I know one trade.

Master Which?

'*Huntsman*' I am a huntsman.

Master Whose?

'*Huntsman*' The king's.

Master How do you carry out your trade?

'*Huntsman*' I weave myself nets and set them in a suitable place, and urge on my dogs so that they chase the wild animals until they come into the nets unawares and are thus ensnared; and I kill them in the nets.

Master Don't you know how to hunt without nets?

'*Huntsman*' I can hunt without nets, certainly.

Master How?

'*Huntsman*' I hunt for wild animals with fast dogs.

Master Which animals do you mostly catch?

'*Huntsman*' I catch stags and wild boars and roe-buck and does, and sometimes hares.

Master Were you out hunting today?

'*Huntsman*' I wasn't, because it's Sunday; but I was out hunting yesterday.

Master What did you catch?

'*Huntsman*' Two stags and a boar.

Master How did you take them?

'*Huntsman*' I took the stags in nets, and the boar I killed.

Master How did you dare stick a boar?

'*Huntsman*' The dogs drove it towards me, and I stuck it quickly, standing there in its path.

Master You were very brave then.

'*Huntsman*' A huntsman mustn't be afraid, because all sorts of wild animals live in the woods.

Master What do you do with you game?

'*Huntsman*' Whatever I take I give to the king, since I am his huntsman.

Master What does he give you?

'*Huntsman*' He clothes and feeds me well, and sometimes gives me a horse or ring so that I follow my trade the more willingly.

Master (indicating another) What trade do you follow?

'*Fisherman*' I am a fisherman.

Master What do you gain from your trade?

'*Fisherman*' Food and clothing and money.

Master How do you catch the fish?

'*Fisherman*' I board my boat and cast my net into the river; and throw in a hook and bait and baskets; and whatever they catch I take.

Master What if the fishes are unclean?

'*Fisherman*' I throw the unclean ones away, and take the clean ones for food.

Master Where do you sell your fish?

'*Fisherman*' In the city.

Master Who buys them?

'*Fisherman*' The citizens. I can't catch as many as I can sell.

Master Which fish do you catch?

'*Fisherman*' Eels and pike, minnows and burbot, trout and lampreys and whatever swims in the water. Small fish.

Master Why don't you fish in the sea?

'*Fisherman*' Sometimes I do, but rarely, because it is a lot of rowing for me to the sea.

Master What do you catch in the sea?

'*Fisherman*' Herrings and salmon, porpoises and sturgeon,

oysters and crabs, mussels, winkles, cockles, plaice and flounders and lobsters, and many similar things.

Master Would you like to catch a whale?

'*Fisherman*' Not me!

Master Why?

'*Fisherman*' Because it is a risky business catching a whale. It's safer for me to go on the river with my boat, than to go hunting whales with many boats.

Master Why so?

'*Fisherman*' Because I prefer to catch a fish that I can kill, rather than a fish that can sink or kill not only me but also my companions with a single blow.

Master Nevertheless, many catch whales and escape danger, and make a great profit by it.

'*Fisherman*' You are right, but I dare not because of my timid spirit!

Master What do you say, fowler? How do you trap birds?

'*Fowler*' I trap birds in many ways: sometimes with nets, sometimes with snares, sometimes with lime, by whistling, with a hawk or with a trap.

Master Have you got a hawk?

'*Fowler*' I have.

Master Do you know how to tame them?

'*Fowler*' Yes, I know how. What good would they be to me unless I knew how to tame them?

'*Huntsman*' Give me a hawk.

'*Fowler*' I will give you one willingly, if you will give me a fast dog. Which hawk will you have, the bigger one or the smaller?

'*Huntsman*' Give me the bigger one.

Master How do you feed your hawks?

'*Fowler*' They feed themselves, and me, in winter; and in the spring I let them fly away to the woods; and in the autumn I take young birds and tame them.

Master And why do you let those you have tamed fly away from you?

'*Fowler*' Because I don't want to feed them in the summer, since they eat too much.

Master Yet many feed the tamed ones throughout the summer, in order to have them already again.

'*Fowler*' Yes, so they do. But I don't want to go to so much trouble over them, because I know how to catch others – not just one, but many more.

Master What do you say, merchant?

'*Merchant*' I say that I am useful both to king and ealdormen, and to the wealthy and to all people.

Master And how?

'*Merchant*' I board my ship with my cargo and sail to lands overseas, and sell my goods, and buy precious things which aren't produced in this country. And in great danger on the sea I bring them back to you here; and sometimes I suffer shipwreck with the loss of all my goods, scarcely escaping alive.

Master What things do you bring us?

'*Merchant*' Purple cloth and silks, precious jewels and gold, unusual clothes and spices, wine and oil, ivory and bronze, copper and tin, sulphur and glass and many similar things.

Master Do you want to sell your goods here for just what you paid for them there?

'*Merchant*' I don't want to. What would my labour benefit me then? I want to sell dearer here than I buy there so that I gain some profit, with which I may feed myself and my wife and my sons.

Master You, shoemaker, what do you work at for our use?

'*Shoemaker*' My trade is certainly very useful and necessary to you.

Master How so?

'*Shoemaker*' I buy hides and skins, and by my craft prepare them and make them into various kinds of footwear, slippers and shoes, leggings and leather bottles, reins and trappings, flasks and leather vessels, spur-straps and halters, bags and purses. And not one of you would want to pass the winter without my craft.

Master Salter, what good is your craft to us?

'*Salter*' My craft is very useful to all of you. Not one of you enjoys satisfaction in a meal or food, unless he entertain my craft.

Master How so?

'*Salter*' What man enjoys pleasant foods to the full without the flavour of salt? Who fills his pantry or storeroom without my craft? Indeed you will lose all butter and cheese-curd unless I am present with you as a preservative; you couldn't even use your herbs without me.

Master What do you say, baker? What is the use of your trade; or can we survive without you?

'*Baker*' You might live without my trade for a while, but neither for long nor very well. Truly, without my craft every table would seem empty; and without bread all food would turn distasteful. I make people's hearts strong; I am the stamina of men, and even the little ones are unwilling to pass me by.

Master What shall we say of the cook? Do we need his craft in any way?

The 'Cook' says: If you expel me from your society, you'll eat your vegetables raw and your meat uncooked; and you can't even have a good broth without my art.

Master We don't care about your art; it isn't necessary to us, because we can boil things that need boiling, and roast the things that need roasting, for ourselves.

The 'Cook' says: However, if you drive me out so as to do that, then you'll all be servants, and none of you will be lord. And without my craft you still won't be able to eat.

Master Oh monk, you who are speaking to me. Now, I have found that you have good and very necessary companions; and who are these I ask you?

'Monk' I have craftsmen: blacksmiths, a goldsmith, silversmith, coppersmith, carpenters and workers in many other different crafts.

Master Have you got any wise councillor?

'Monk' Certainly I have. How can our community be directed without a councillor?

Master What do you say, wise man? Which trade among these seems to you to be superior?

'Councillor' I tell you, to me the service of God seems to hold the first place among these crafts, just as it reads in the gospel: 'Seek first the kingdom of God and his righteousness, and all these things shall be added unto you.'[1]

Master And which among the secular arts seems to you to hold the first place?

'Councillor' Agriculture, because the ploughman feeds us all.

The 'Smith' says: Where does the ploughman get his ploughshare or coulter or goad, except by my craft? Where the fisherman his hook, or the shoemaker his awl, or the tailor his needle? Isn't it from my work?

The 'Councillor' answers: What you say is in fact true. But we would all prefer to live with you, ploughman, than with you,

---

[1] Matthew, VI 33.

because the ploughman gives us bread and drink. You, what do you give us in your smithy but iron sparks, and the noise of hammers beating and bellows blowing?

The 'Carpenter' says: Which of you doesn't make use of my craft, when I make houses and various vessels and boats for you all?

The 'Blacksmith'[1] answers: Oh, carpenter, why do you talk like that when you couldn't pierce even one hole without my craft?

The 'Councillor' says: Oh, friends and good workmen, let us bring these arguments to an end quickly, and let there be peace and concord between us, and let each one of us help the others by his craft. And let us always agree with the ploughman, where we find food for ourselves and fodder for our horses. And I give this advice to all workmen, that each one pursue his trade diligently; for he who abandons his craft will be abandoned by his craft. Whoever you are, whether priest or monk or peasant or soldier, exercise yourself in this, and be what you are; because it is a great disgrace and shame for a man not to want to be what he is, and what he has to be.

Master Oh, boys, how do you like this speech?

Pupil We like it well, but you talk very profoundly and use speech beyond our ability; but talk to us according to our comprehension, so that we can understand the things you say.

Master I ask you, why are you so eager to learn?

Pupil Because we don't want to be like stupid animals, who know nothing but grass and water.

Master And what do you want?

Pupil We want to be clever.

Master With what kind of cleverness? Do you want to be subtle or cunning in deceit, crafty in speech, artful, wily, speaking good and thinking evil, given to bland words, nourishing guile within, just like a sepulchre, painted outside and full of a stink inside?

Pupil We don't want to be clever like that, because he who deludes himself with pretence is not clever.

Master But how do you want to be?

Pupil We want to be sincere, without hypocrisy, and wise, so that we turn away from evil and do good. However, you are still questioning us more deeply than our years can take; so speak to us in our own way, not so deeply.

---

[1] MS. Goldsmith.

Master I will do just as you ask. You, boy, what did you do today?

Pupil I did lots of things. Last night when I heard the ringing of the bell I got up from my bed and went to church and sang matins with the brethren, after which we sang of all the saints and the morning hymns; after this the six o'clock service and the seven psalms with the litanies and the chapter-Eucharist. Then we sang the nine o'clock service and did the Eucharist for the day; after this we sang the midday service, and ate and drank and slept. And we got up again and sang the three o'clock service; and now we are here before you, ready to hear what you have to say to us!

Master When are you going to sing evensong and compline?

Pupil When it's time!

Master Have you been beaten today?

Pupil I haven't, because I behave myself carefully.

Master And how about your friends?

Pupil Why do you ask me about that? I dare not reveal our secrets to you. Each one of us knows if he was beaten or not.

Master What do you eat in the day?

Pupil I still enjoy meat, because I am a child living under instruction.

Master What else do you eat?

Pupil I eat vegetables and eggs, fish and cheese, butter and beans and all clean things, with much gratefulness.

Master You are very greedy if you eat everything that is in front of you.

Pupil I am not so great a glutton that I can eat all kinds of food at one meal.

Master Then how so?

Pupil Sometimes I partake of this food and sometimes that, in moderation as befits a monk, not with greed, because I am no glutton.

Master And what do you drink?

Pupil Ale if I have it, or water if I have no ale.

Master Don't you drink wine?

Pupil I'm not rich enough to buy myself wine; and wine isn't a drink for children or the foolish, but for the old and wise.

Master Where do you sleep?

Pupil In the dormitory with the brothers.

Pupil Who wakes you up for matins?

Pupil Sometimes I hear the ringing of the bell and get up; sometimes my teacher wakes me sternly with a cane.

Master Well, you boys and charming scholars, your teacher reminds you to be obedient to the commandments of God, and to behave yourselves properly everywhere. When you hear the church bells, go in an orderly fashion and go into the church and bow humbly towards the holy altars, and stand up properly, and sing in unison, and pray for your sins; and go out into the cloisters or to study without playing the fool.

WULFSTAN

THE SERMON OF 'WOLF' TO THE ENGLISH WHEN THE DANES PERSECUTED THEM MOST, WHICH WAS IN THE YEAR 1014 FROM THE INCARNATION OF OUR LORD JESUS CHRIST

'Wolf' (Lat. *Lupus*) was a pen-name used on several occasions by the great statesman-cleric Wulfstan, who was Bishop of London from 996 to 1002 and Archbishop of York from 1002 to 1023, which office he held in plurality with the see of Worcester until 1016. The author of at least twenty-one homilies, as well as such codes as *The Institutes of Polity* and the so-called *Canons of Edgar*, he was equally active in affairs of state, and responsible for much of the legislation of both Æthelred and the Danish King Cnut.

Wulfstan's life spanned a particularly troubled period of English history. Viking raids were once more a serious menace in the last decade of the tenth century, inflicting a series of humiliating military defeats, of which the poem on *The Battle of Maldon* is one literary reflection. Danegeld was levied, and some time after Christmas 1013 the incompetent King Æthelred was exiled into Normandy to allow the Danish King Swegn to succeed. Æthelred returned on Swegn's death the following year, but Danish depredations continued under the direction of Swegn's son Cnut; and upon Æthelred's death in 1016, Cnut assumed the throne.

This homily, no. XX (EI) in the collective edition by Dorothy Bethurum, *The Homilies of Wulfstan*, Oxford, 1957, pp. 267–75, exists in several MS. versions, the best of which is found in the early eleventh-century British Library MS. Cotton Nero A 1, ff. 110–15. Containing selections from *The Institutes of Polity*, copies of Æthelred's code of 1008 and other matters of interest to Wulfstan, this was very probably his own copy (see pp. 8, 187). Certain entries have been identified as being in the archbishop's own hand. There is a facsimile edition by H. R. Loyn, *A Wulfstan Manuscript*, EEMF., XVII, Copenhagen, 1971.

There is a convenient separate edition of this homily by Dorothy Whitelock, *Sermo Lupi ad Anglos*, 2nd ed., Exeter, 1976.

Beloved men, recognize what the truth is: this world is in haste and it is drawing near the end,[1] and therefore the longer it is the worse it will get in the world. And it needs must thus become very much worse as a result of the people's sins prior to the advent of Antichrist; and then, indeed, it will be terrible and cruel throughout the world. Understand properly also that for many years now the Devil has led this nation too far astray, and that there has been

[1] It was commonly believed that the world would come to an end a thousand years after either Christ's birth or his death, but in any case imminently. For the apocalyptic signs anticipated, see Blickling Homily 7, p. 126 f.

little loyalty among men although they spoke fair, and too many wrongs have prevailed in the land. And there were never many men who sought a remedy as diligently as they should; but daily they added one evil to another, and embarked on many wrongs and unlawful acts, all too commonly throughout this whole nation. And on that account, we have also suffered many injuries and insults. And if we are to expect any remedy then we must deserve better of God than we have done hitherto. Because we have earned the miseries which oppress us by great demerit, we must obtain the cure from God, if it is to improve henceforth by very great merit. Indeed, we know full well that a great breach requires a great repair and a great conflagration no little water if one is to quench the fire at all. And the necessity is great for every man henceforth to observe God's law diligently and pay God's dues properly.[1] Among heathen peoples one dare not withhold little or much of what is appointed for the worship of false gods, and we everywhere withhold God's dues all too frequently. And among heathen peoples one dare not diminish, inside or out, any of the things which are brought to the false gods and are made over as gifts, and we have completely despoiled the houses of God inside and out. And God's servants are everywhere deprived of respect and protection; and with the heathen peoples one dare not in any way abuse the ministers of false gods, as one now does the servants of God, too commonly where Christians ought to keep God's law and protect God's servants.[2] But it is true what I say; there is need of a remedy, because God's dues have for too long dwindled away in every region within this nation, and the laws of the people have deteriorated all too much, and sanctuaries are commonly violated, and the houses of God are completely despoiled of ancient rights, and stripped of everything decent inside. And widows are wrongfully forced to take a husband.[3] And too many are harassed and greatly humiliated, and poor men are painfully deceived and cruelly enslaved and, completely innocent, commonly sold out of this country into the power of foreigners,[4] and through cruel injustice children in the cradle are enslaved for petty theft commonly throughout this nation, and the rights of freemen are taken away and the rights of slaves

---

[1] See The Laws of Æthelred 11, p. 10.
[2] Cf. *Institutes of Polity* 19 (p. 200), of which several other echoes occur.
[3] See The Laws of Æthelred 21, p. 11.
[4] Now forbidden by law, see pp. 5, 9.

restricted, and the right to alms diminished; and, to be brief, God's laws are hated and his teachings scorned. And therefore, through God's anger, we are all frequently put to shame; let him realize it who can. And although one might not imagine so, the harm will become common to this entire nation, unless God defend us.

For it is clear and evident in us all that we have hitherto more often transgressed than we have atoned, and therefore many things fall upon this nation. For long now, nothing has prospered here or elsewhere, but in every region there has been devastation and famine, burning and bloodshed over and again. And stealing and slaughter, plague and pestilence, murrain and disease, slander and hatred, and the plundering of robbers have damaged us very severely; and excessive taxes have greatly oppressed us, and bad weather has very often caused us crop-failures; wherefore for many years now, so it seems, there have been in this country many injustices and unsteady loyalties among men everywhere. Now very often kinsman will not protect a kinsman any more than a stranger, nor a father his son, nor sometimes a son his own father, nor one brother another. Nor has any of us regulated his life just as he ought, neither clerics according to rule, nor laymen according to the law. But all too frequently, we have made lust a law to us, and have kept neither the teachings nor the laws of God or man just as we ought; nor has anyone intended loyally towards another as justly as he ought, but almost all men have betrayed and injured others by word and deed; and in any case, almost all men wrongfully stab others in the back with shameful attack; let him do more if he can. For there are here in the land great disloyalties towards God and towards the state, and there are also many here in the country who are betrayers of their lords in various ways. And the greatest betrayal in the world of one's lord is that a man betray his lord's soul; and it is also a very great betrayal of one's lord in the world, that a man should plot against his lord's life or, living, drive him from the land; and both have happened in this country. They plotted against Edward and then killed, and afterwards burnt him.[1] And they have destroyed too many godfathers and godchildren widely throughout this nation,

---

[1] Æthelred's half brother, the young King Edward, was killed at Corfe in Dorset in 978. According to some early accounts Edward's death was contrived by his stepmother, looking for her own son Æthelred to succeed. Recognized as a martyr-saint shortly afterwards, Æthelred enjoins that his festival be kept throughout the country (see p. 10). Some versions of the homily insert a sentence describing Æthelred's exile.

as well as too many other innocent people who have been all too commonly slain. And all too many religious foundations have commonly been undone because previously certain men have been placed there, as they should not have been if one wished to show respect to God's sanctuary; and too many Christian people have been sold out of this country all the time now. And all that is hateful to God, let him believe it who will. And it is shameful to speak of what has too commonly happened, and it is dreadful to know what many too often do, who practise that wretchedness that they club together and buy one woman in common as a joint purchase, and with the one commit filth one after another and each after the other just like dogs who do not care about filth; and then sell for a price out of the land into the power of enemies the creature of God and his own purchase that he dearly bought.

Also we know well where the wretchedness has occurred that father has sold son for a price, and son his mother, and one brother has sold another into the power of foreigners; and all these are grave and dreadful deeds, let him understand who will. And yet what is injuring this nation is greater and also more multifarious. Many are forsworn and greatly perjured, and pledges are broken over and again; and it is evident in this nation that the wrath of God violently oppresses us, let him realize it who can.

And indeed, how can more shame befall men through the wrath of God than frequently does us on account of our own deeds? If any slave escape from his lord, and, leaving Christendom, becomes a Viking, and after that it happens that an armed encounter occurs between thegn and slave; if the slave should slay the thegn outright he will lie without payment to any of his family; and if the thegn should slay outright the slave whom he previously owned, he will pay the price of a thegn.[1] Over-cowardly laws and shameful tributes are, through the wrath of God, common among us, understand it who can; and many misfortunes befall this nation over and again. For long now nothing has prospered, within or without, but there has been devastation and persecution in every part, over and again. And for long now the English have been entirely without victory and too much cowed because of the wrath of God, and the pirates so strong with God's consent, that

[1] The peace-treaty between Alfred and Guthrum had agreed equal rates of compensation between Vikings and English freemen, but this was intended specifically not to apply to runaway slaves (see p. 7).

in battle often one will put to flight ten, and sometimes less sometimes more, all because of our sins. And often ten or twelve, one after another, will disgracefully insult the thegn's wife, and sometimes his daughter or near kinswoman, while he who considered himself proud and powerful and brave enough before that happened, looks on. And often a slave will bind very fast the thegn who was previously his lord, and make him a slave through the wrath of God. Alas for the misery, and alas for the public disgrace which the English now bear, all because of the wrath of God! Often two pirates, or sometimes three, will drive herds of Christian men out through this people from sea to sea, huddled together as a public shame to us all, if we could in earnest properly feel any. But all the disgrace we often suffer we repay with honour to those who bring shame on us. We pay them continually, and they humiliate us daily. They ravage and they burn, plunder and rob, and carry away on board; and indeed, what else is there in all these events but the wrath of God clear and visible towards this nation?

And is it no wonder things go badly for us though. For we know full well that for many years now men have too often not cared what they did by word or deed; but this nation, so it seems, has become totally sinful through manifold sins and through many misdeeds: through deadly sins and through evil deeds, through avarice and through greed, through theft and through pillaging, through the selling of men and through heathen vices, through betrayals and through plots, through breaches of the law and through legal offences, through attacks on kinsmen and through manslaughters, through injury done to those in holy orders and through adulteries, through incest and through various fornications. And commonly also, as we said before, more than should be are ruined and perjured through the breaking of oaths and through the breaking of pledges and through various lies. And failure to observe festivals and the breaking of fasts[1] occurs commonly over and again. And here in the land also there are all too many degenerate apostates and malignant enemies of the Church and cruel tyrants; and those who scorn the divine laws and Christian customs are widespread; and everywhere in the nation are those who foolishly mock, most often those things which the messengers of God command, and especially those

---

[1] Cf. The Laws of Æthelred, p. 10.

things which always appertain to God's laws by right. And therefore it has now reached such an evil state of affairs far and wide, that men are now more ashamed of good deeds than of misdeeds; because too often they dismiss good deeds with derision, and God-fearing people are abused all too much, and especially reviled and treated with contempt are those who love justice and fear God in any action. And because they behave thus – that they blame all that they should praise, and hate too much what they should love – they bring all too many evil intentions and wicked deeds, so that they are not ashamed although they sin greatly and commit wrongs even against God himself. But because of idle calumny, they are ashamed to atone for their misdeeds as the books direct,[1] like those fools who because of their pride will not guard against injury, until they cannot even though they wish to.

Here, so it seems, too many in the land are grievously hurt with the injuries of sin. Here are slayers of men and slayers of kinsmen and killers of priests and enemies of the monasteries; and here are perjurers and murderers; and here are whores and those who kill children and many foul fornicating adulterers; and here are wizards and witches;[2] and here are plunderers and robbers and those who despoil; and, to be brief, countless numbers of all crimes and misdeeds. And we are not ashamed of it; but we are too ashamed to begin reparation as the books direct; and that is clear in this wretched nation, burdened with sin. Alas, many might easily recall much more in addition, which one man could not outline in a hurry, to indicate how wretchedly it has gone all the time now widely throughout this nation. And indeed, let each diligently examine himself, and not put it off all too long.

But look, in God's name, let us do as is necessary for us, defend ourselves as best we may, lest we all perish together. There was a historian in the time of the Britons called Gildas.[3] He wrote about their misdeeds, how by their sins they angered God so very excessively that finally he allowed the host of the English to

[1] Formal penitential lists compiled by the Church.
[2] Wulfstan uses the word *wælcyrie*, borrowed from the Viking word *valkyrja*, 'chooser of the slain'; for belief in this aspect of witchcraft, see p. 35.
[3] Sixth-century author of the *Liber querulus de excidio Britanniae*. In this instance Wulfstan's reference seems to have come indirectly through a favourite source: a letter by Alcuin of York, written shortly after he had heard of the destruction of Lindisfarne by the Danes in 793, and attributing the calamities of his own day to the sins of the English (*MGH. Epist.* IV 47).

conquer their land and to destroy the nobility of the Britons altogether. And as he said, that came about through robbery by the powerful and through the coveting of ill-gotten gains, through the lawlessness of the nation and through unjust judgements, through the laziness of bishops and through the base cowardice of God's heralds, who all too frequently refrained from telling the truth and mumbled with their jaws where they ought to have cried out. Likewise, through the foul extravagance of the people and through gluttony and manifold sins, they destroyed their country and they themselves perished. But let us do as is necessary for us – warn ourselves by such things. And it is true what I say; we know of worse deeds among the English than we have anywhere heard of among the Britons. And therefore it is very necessary that we reflect about ourselves and earnestly plead with God himself. And let us do as is necessary for us – bow to justice and in some part to leave off injustice, and to compensate very carefully for what we previously broke. And let us love God and follow God's laws, and very diligently practise what we promised when we received baptism – or those who were our sponsors at baptism. And let us order words and works aright, and earnestly cleanse our conscience, and carefully keep oath and pledge, and have some loyalty between us without deceit. And let us frequently consider the great Judgement to which we must all come, and carefully defend ourselves against the surging flame of hell-torment, and earn for ourselves those glories and those joys which God has prepared for them that work his will in the world. May God help us. Amen.

SERMON ON FALSE GODS

The re-working by Wulfstan of a small part of one of Ælfric's homilies (edited by J. C. Pope, *Homilies of Ælfric, A Supplementary Collection*, EETS., CCLX, London, 1968, pp. 676–712), which in turn drew on part of the tract 'De Correctione Rusticorum' by the sixth-century Visigothic Archbishop Martin of Braga (edited by C. P. Caspari, Christiana, 1883).

The equation of Classical and Germanic deities is a natural one, found as early as Caesar (*De Bello Gallico*, VI 17) and Tacitus (*Germania*, 3, 9). Compare the etymologies of French and English names for the days of the week. The idea that pagan gods originated as men was a medieval commonplace. The fifth-century Frankish Queen Clotilda is reported to have made the same accusation of her husband Clovis' gods, whom she calls by Classical names, and about whom she tells similar stories to those told by Wulfstan (*MGH. Scrip. Rer. Merov.*, II 74). Wulfstan's northern seat at York was at the heart of the Scandinavian settlement, and heathen worship must have been a constant preoccupation. He refers to it several times both in his sermons and in the legal codes for which he was responsible.

The sole copy of this sermon is found on ff. 58ᵛ–61 of the most important of the Wulfstan MSS.: Bodleian MS. Hatton 113–14, a two-volume collective homiliary compiled by the Worcester scribe Wulfgeat some time about 1070 for a later Bishop of Worcester, Wulfstan II. This contained some six dozen homilies altogether, including almost all of Wulfstan's known sermons and several of Ælfric's Catholic Homilies. The text of this sermon is printed as no. XII in Dorothy Bethurum's edition of *The Homilies of Wulfstan*, Oxford, 1957, pp. 221–4.

Now, it was long ago that, because of the Devil, many things went wrong and that mankind disobeyed God too much, and that paganism all too widely inflicted damage – and widely inflicts damage still. We do not read anywhere in books, though, that they set up any idolatry anywhere in the world during all the time which was before Noah's flood. But then it happened that after Noah's flood, Nimrod and the giants wrought the marvellous tower; and as the book tells, it came to pass that there were as many languages as there were workmen.[1] Then afterwards they dispersed into distant lands, and then mankind soon greatly increased. And then at last they were deceived by the old Devil who had long before betrayed Adam, so that they perversely and heretically made pagan gods for themselves and scorned the true God and their own Creator who created and fashioned them as men.

Moreover, through the teaching of the Devil, they took it for wisdom to worship the sun and the moon as gods on account of their shining brightness; and then at last, through the teaching of the Devil, offered them sacrifices and forsook their Lord who had created and fashioned them. Some men also said that the shining stars were gods, and began to worship them earnestly; and some believed in fire on account of its sudden heat, some also in water, and some believed in the earth because it nourished all things. But they might have readily discerned, if they had the power of reason, that he is the true God who created all things for the enjoyment and use of us men, which he granted mankind because of his great goodness. Moreover, these created things act entirely as their own Creator ordained for them, and can do nothing except by our Lord's consent, for there is no other Creator but the one true God in whom we believe. And with sure faith we love and worship him alone over all other things, saying with our mouths and with conviction of heart, that he alone is the true God, who has created and fashioned all things.

[1] Genesis, X 8–11, XI 1–9. Cf. Ælfric's *Treatise on the Old and New Testament*, ed. S. J. Crawford, EETS., OS., CLX, London, 1922, p. 25.

Yet the heathen would not be satisfied with as few gods as they had previously, but in the end took to worshipping various giants and violent men of the earth who became strong in worldly power and were awe-inspiring while they lived, and foully followed their own lusts. In former days there was a certain man living in the island called Crete who was called Saturn, and who was so savage that he destroyed his own sons – all but one – and unlike a father destroyed them early in childhood. Reluctantly he left one alive however, although he had destroyed all the brothers otherwise; and he was called Jove, and he became a malignant enemy. He afterwards drove his own father out of that same aforesaid island called Crete and would readily have killed him if he could. And this Jove was so very lecherous that he took to wife his own sister, who was named Juno; and she became a very important goddess according to pagan reckoning. Their two daughters were Minerva and Venus. These wicked men about whom we speak were reckoned the greatest gods in those days, and through the teaching of the Devil the heathen greatly honoured them. But the son, though, was more worshipped in paganism than the father was, and he is also reckoned the most honourable of all those whom the heathen in their error, took for gods in those days. And he whom the Danish people love most, and in their error most earnestly worship, was called by the other name Thor among certain nations. His son was called Mars, who always brought about strife and contention; and he frequently stirred up conflict and enmity. After his death the heathen also honoured this wretch as an important god. And as often as they went to war or intended to do battle, then they offered their sacrifices beforehand in honour of this false god; and they believed that he could assist them in battle because he loved battle and conflict when alive. There was also a certain man called Mercury in life, who was very crafty and, although very clever in speech, deceitful in his actions and in trickeries. Him also the heathen made for themselves a great god according to their reckoning, and over and again, through the teaching of the devil, offered him sacrifices at crossroads and often brought him various sacrifices of praise on the high hills. This false god also was venerated among all the heathen in those days, and in the Danish manner he is called by the other name Odin. Now some of those Danish men say in their error that Jove, whom they call Thor, was the son of Mercury, whom they name Odin; but they are not right because we read in books, both pagan and Christian,[1] that the malignant Jove is in fact Saturn's son.[2] And a certain woman called Venus was the daughter of Jove, and she was so foul and so abandoned in lechery that through the teaching of the Devil, her own brother copulated with her so they said. And the heathen also worship that evil creature as an exalted woman.

Many other heathen gods also were devised in various ways, and heathen goddesses likewise held in great honour throughout the world to the ruin of mankind; but these, though, are reckoned the most important in paganism, although they lived foully in the world. And the scheming Devil, who always deceives mankind, brought those heathen men into profound error so that they chose as gods for themselves such vile men who had made their vile lust a law for themselves and for as long as they lived spent all their lives in uncleanness. But blessed is he who completely scorns such affairs and loves and honours the true God who created and fashioned all things. Almighty God is one in three persons, that is Father and Son and Holy Spirit. All three names encompass one divine power and one eternal God, ruler and maker of all creation. To him for ever be praise and honour in all worlds, world without end. Amen.

THE INSTITUTES OF POLITY

Written probably towards the end of his career, *The Institutes of Polity* represent the summary of Archbishop Wulfstan's experience as a jurist. There are constant echoes both of his homilies and the legal codes for which he was responsible (cf. p. 179). There is some evidence for continuing revision, and possibly it remained incomplete at his death in 1023.

An incomplete and somewhat disordered draft of the Institutes is found in Wulfstan's own hand-book, British Library MS. Cotton Nero A1 (see p. 178), and there is a related collection of extracts in that mid-eleventh-century manuscript which contains the Old English Apollonius of Tyre (see p. 234). A fuller form of the text, albeit incorporating some extraneous homiletic and canon material, is found in Bodleian MS. Junius 121, ff. 9–59 *passim*. Written by the scribe Wulfgeat of Worcester as a companion volume to his two-volume homiliary (see p. 185), this manuscript also includes the so-called Canons of Edgar, homilies and other matters of interest to Wulfstan.

The greater part of the Junius text was printed by B. Thorpe, *Ancient Laws and Institutes of England*, London, 1840, II, pp. 304–40, and there is a critical edition by Karl Jost, *Die 'Institutes of Polity, Civil and Ecclesiastical'*, Bern, 1959. The translation follows Jost's

[1] Of several early medieval accounts, the essay 'De Diis Gentis' by the ninth-century Abbot of Fulda, Hrabanus Maurus (*PL*., CXI 426–36) was perhaps best known at this time.
[2] The twelfth-century Danish writer Saxo Grammaticus rightly attributes this confusion to an over-elaborate equation of the Classical and Germanic gods (*Gesta Danorum*, ed. A. Holder, Strassburg, 1886, pp. 183–4).

ordering of sections. Thorpe's numbering of the sections is added in brackets where this differs.

1 Concerning the Heavenly King

In nomine domini. There is one eternal King, ruler and maker of all creation. He is rightly King and the glory of kings, and the best of all kings who ever were or are to be. To him be ever praise and glory and eternal honour, world without end. Amen.

2 Concerning the Earthly King

It behoves the Christian king in a Christian nation to be, as is right, the people's comfort and a righteous shepherd over the Christian flock. And it behoves him to raise up the Christian faith with all his power and zealously advance and protect God's Church everywhere, and with just law to bring peace and reconciliation to all Christian people, as diligently as he can, and in everything cherish righteousness in the sight of God and the world. For if he cherish justice in the sight of God and the world, through that he himself foremost shall prosper and his subjects similarly. And it behoves him diligently to support those who desire righteousness, and strictly punish those who desire perversity. He must severely correct wicked men with worldly punishment, and he must loathe and suppress robbers and plunderers and despoilers of the world's goods, and sternly resist all God's foes. And with justice he must be both merciful and austere: merciful to the good and stern to the evil. That is the king's right and a kingly custom, and that shall accomplish most in the nation.

Indeed, by what means shall peace and comfort come to God's servants and God's poor, but through Christ and through a Christian king? Through an unwise king, the people will be made wretched not once but very often, because of his misdirection. Through the king's wisdom the people will become prosperous and successful and victorious. And therefore the wise king must extol and exalt the Christian faith and kingship, and he must always repress and condemn heathenism. He must very earnestly attend to book-learning, and carefully keep God's commands and frequently seek out wisdom with the council, if he wish to obey God aright. And if anywhere in the nation anyone be so violent that he will keep no law as he should, but violates the law of God or hinders the law of the people, then it is to be made known to the king, if it is necessary; and then he is immediately to take counsel concerning the compensation and diligently subject him to that which is his duty, even by compulsion if he cannot otherwise. And he is to do what is needful for him if he wish to merit the mercy of God; purify his nation in the sight of God and the world, and frequently meditate what he is to do and what not to do according to God's law. And thus both in life and after life he shall in particular always gain reputation and respect to the extent that he love God's law and abhor injustice, and for his own good willingly attend to divine teaching over and again. For he who takes little bodily nourishment soon weakens, and he who rarely takes spiritual nourishment will soon severely injure his soul. But he who most often obeys the divine teaching and most diligently keeps it will be blessed.

3 Concerning Kingship

There are eight columns which firmly support lawful kingship: truth, patience, liberality, good counsel (*veritas, patientia, largitas, persuasibilitas*): formidableness, helpfulness, moderation, righteousness (*correctio malorum, exultatio bonorum, levitas tributi, equitas iudicii*). And seven things befit a righteous king: first that he have a very great awe of God; and second that he always cherish righteousness; and third that he be humble before God; and fourth that he be resolute against evil; and fifth that he comfort and feed God's poor; and sixth that he advance and protect the Church of God; and seventh that he order correct judgement for friend and stranger alike.

4 Concerning the Throne

Every lawful throne which stands perfectly upright, stands on three pillars: one is *oratores*, and the second is *laboratores* and the third is *bellatores*. 'Oratores' are prayer-men, who must serve God and earnestly intercede both day and night for the entire nation. 'Laboratores' are workmen, who must supply that by which the entire nation shall live. 'Bellatores' are soldiers, who must defend the land by fighting with weapons. Every throne in a Christian nation must stand upright on these three pillars. And should any of them weaken, the throne will immediately totter; and should any of them shatter, then the throne will tumble down, and that is entirely to the nation's detriment. But let them be diligently fixed and strengthened and made firm with the wise teaching of God and with worldly justice; that will be to the lasting benefit of the nation. And it is true what I say: should the Christian faith weaken, the kingship will immediately totter; and should bad laws arise anywhere in the land, or vicious habits be too greatly cherished anywhere, that will be entirely to the nation's detriment. But let there be done what is necessary, injustice put down and God's law raised up; that may be of advantage in the sight of God and the world. Amen.

5 Concerning the Nation's Councillors

It rightly befits kings and bishops, earls and generals, reeves and judges, scholars and lawyers, that they be in agreement in the sight of God and the world, and cherish God's law. And bishops are heralds and teachers of God's law, and they must preach justice and forbid injustice; and he who scorns to listen to them, let him settle that with God himself. And if bishops neglect to punish sins or forbid injustice, nor make known God's law, but mumble with their jaws where they ought to cry out, woe to them for that silence! The prophet spoke concerning them and said angrily thus: *Haec dicit dominus: Si non adnuntiaveris iniquo iniquitatem suam, sanguinem eius de manu tua requiram.*[1] 'If', said our Lord, 'you will not punish the sins of the sinful and forbid injustice, and make known the wickednesses of the wicked, you must pay bitterly for the soul.' This may be a concern to the heart of every bishop; let him earnestly consider it as he will. And he who will not obey God's preachers aright, nor care for divine teaching as he should, he must obey foes if he will not friends. For he who scorns God's preacher is a scorner of God; just as Christ himself clearly said in his Gospel, when he spoke thus: *Qui vos audit, me audit, et qui vos spernit, me spernit.*[2] He said: 'He who hears you hears me, and he who despises you, despises me.' Alas, grievous is the burden which God's herald must bear if he will not earnestly forbid injustice. For although he himself do good, and another man do ill, it shall injure him if he will not punish it. And although God's herald do ill, one is not to pay attention to that, but if he teach what is good take heed of his teaching; just as

[1] Ezekiel, III 18.
[2] Luke, X 16.

Christ taught that one should do, when in his Gospel he clearly said thus: *Quae hi dicunt, facite; quae autem faciunt, facere nolite.*[1] He said: 'Follow their teachings and not their sins.' No man ought ever to neglect himself because of a bishop's sins, but follow his teaching if he teach well. And so, beloved men, do as I ask, without anger. Listen to what I say. I very well know myself to be all too greatly sinful in word and deed; but for fear of God I dare not keep altogether silent about those many things that injure this nation.

6 *Likewise, concerning Bishops*[2]

Bishops must attend to books and prayers, and over and again call on Christ by day and night and diligently intercede for all Christian people. And they must learn and teach correctly, and diligently enquire about the deeds of the people. And they must preach and carefully give an example of the spiritual duty of a Christian nation. And they must not willingly consent to any injustice, but diligently support every righteousness. They must bear in mind the fear of God and not be all too slothful for fear of the world. But let him who will, always take care diligently to preach God's law and forbid unrighteousness. For the shepherd will be found weak for the flock, who will not defend the flock which he must keep, at least with a cry, if he can do nothing else, if any despoiler of the people begin to ravage. There is no spoiler so evil as is the Devil himself. He is forever concerned with one thing – how he can most ravage men's souls. So those shepherds who have to shield the people against the despoiler of the nation must be very watchful and earnestly crying out. Those are bishops and priests who must protect and defend the spiritual flock with wise teaching, so that the ravening werewolf do not too greatly rend nor devour too many of the spiritual flock. And he who scorns to listen to them, let him settle that with God himself.

Alas, there are nevertheless many of those who care little and pay scant heed to the precepts of books or the teachings of bishops, and moreover lightly dismiss blessings or curses and do not understand as they should, what Christ clearly said in his Gospel when he spoke thus: *Qui nos audit,* et reliqua.[3] And likewise: *Quodcumque ligaveratis,* et cetera.[4] And likewise:

---

[1] Matthew, XXIII 3.
[2] This heading is in Latin.
[3] Luke, X 16.
[4] Matthew, XVI 19.

Quorum remiseritis peccata, remittuntur eis, et cetera.[1] *Alibi etiam scriptum est: Quodcumque benedixeritis*, et cetera.[2] *Et psalmista terribiliter loquitur dicens: Qui noluit benedictionem, prolongabitur ab eo.*[3] Such a thing is to be borne in mind, and the wrath of God continually to be guarded against. Now we also earnestly instruct every man to follow God's teaching and his laws; then will he merit eternal joy.

7 (8) Likewise

The daily work of a bishop is rightly: his prayers first and then his book-work, reading or writing, teaching or learning, and his Church hours at the correct time, always together with those things which pertain to it, and washing the feet of the poor and his distribution of alms and the direction of works where it be necessary. Good manual crafts befit him also, and that those in his household cultivate crafts, so that at any rate no one too idle dwell there. And it also befits him well that in a meeting he over and again disseminate divine teaching to the people with whom he then is.

8 (9) Likewise

Wisdom and prudence always befit bishops, and that those that attend them have honourable ways, and that they practise some special craft also. Nothing useless ever befits bishops: not folly nor stupidity, nor too much drinking, nor childishness in speech, nor idle buffoonery of any kind, not at home nor on a journey, nor in any place. But wisdom and prudence are appropriate to their rank, and gravity befits those that attend them.

9 (11) Concerning Earls

It is necessary for earls and generals and such judges of the world, and similarly reeves, to cherish justice in the sight of God and the world, and nowhere neglect their wisdom through bad judgement, for money or for friendship, so that they turn injustice to justice or decree bad judgement to the injury of the poor. But above all other things, they must honour and defend the Church, and must comfort the widow and the orphan, help the poor and

1 John, XX 23.
2 Cf. Numbers, XXIV 9.
3 Psalm CVIII 18.

protect wretched slaves, if they wish to work God's will aright. And they must hate thieves and despoilers of the people and they must condemn robbers and plunderers, unless they desist. And they must always severely shun injustice. For it is true what I say, believe it who will. Woe to him who practises perversity all too long, unless he desist. He must assuredly plunge into the dim and deep abyss of hell-torment, deprived of help. But there are too few of those who understand that as one should; but may God amend it. But every friend is to do what is needful, earnestly take warning and defend himself, so that he do not anger God all too greatly, but propitiate his Lord with righteous action.

10 (12) Concerning the Reeve

It is right that reeves work diligently and always provide for their lords aright. But now it has happened all too greatly that since Edgar died,[1] even as God willed, there are more robbers than righteous men; and it is a wretched thing that those who should be shepherds of Christian people are robbers. At times they rob the blameless poor and abuse the flock they should guard, and betray poor men with evil slanders, and give rise to unjust laws in all sorts of ways to the injury of the poor, and rob widows over and again. But at one time in the nation those men were chosen wisely as shepherds for the people, who would not for shame in the world, nor dare not for fear of God, practise deceit in anything, nor acquire anything wrongly, but acquired things rightly. And since, it has been done most diligently of all by those who knew how to cheat and deceive most oppressively and to injure wretched men with falsehood and how most quickly to obtain money from the innocent. Since then, one has greatly angered God over and again. And woe to him who has acquired most of his riches through injustice, unless he desist, and the more deeply atone in the sight of God and the world.

11 (19) Concerning Priests

In their parishes priests wisely and prudently lead and instruct those spiritual flocks that they must guard. They must both preach well and set a good example to other men. And at God's Judgement they must pay at God's hand the reckoning both of

---

[1] King of all England, 959–75.

their own deeds and of all the people that they must guard. And if they shall have done anything, they may not hesitate, neither for fear nor for love of any man, to preach righteousness and forbid unrighteousness. The shepherd will be useless to the fold who will not defend the flock which he must guard with an outcry if he can do nothing else, if any despoiler of the people begin to ravage. There is no spoiler so evil as is the Devil himself; he is forever concerned with one thing – how he can most ravage men's souls. So those shepherds who have to shield the people against the despoiler of the nation ought to be very watchful and earnestly crying out. Those are the bishops and priests who must protect and defend the spiritual flock with wise teaching. If he will defend himself therefore, he may not hesitate neither for love nor for fear to say to men what is most righteous. Nor may he hesitate either before the humble or before the powerful; for should he be afraid or be ashamed to say what is right, he does wrong. He will fare wretchedly if as a result of his softness the flock which he has to guard should perish, and he himself along with it. If any of our shepherds neglect a single sheep, we desire that he should pay for it. And how, then, shall those shepherds fare at God's awful Judgement who cannot guard those sacred flocks that Christ bought with his own life, and which they must guard, if they are able, but through lack of learning can neither lead, nor teach, nor cure them aright? With what do we expect them to pay for them then? Woe, then, to them that they ever received what they could not guard. Indeed, how can a blind man lead another? How can an untaught judge teach another? Woe certainly to them who receive a sacred flock and can take care neither of themselves nor the flock that they have to guard; and worse, those who can and will not. Alas, alas, there are many of those, so it seems, who desire the priesthood unrighteously, mostly for vain-glory and for greed of worldly riches, and do not know what they ought to know. Concerning them the prophet spoke and said thus: *Ve sacerdotibus qui comedunt peccata populi*, et reliqua.[1] 'Woe to those priests', he said, 'who devour and swallow up the people's sins.' Those are they who will not, or cannot, or dare not warn the people against sins and punish sins; but nevertheless want their monies for tithes and for all Church dues; and neither lead them well with examples, nor teach them well with preaching, nor cure

[1] Hosea, IV 8.

them well with penances, nor intercede for them with prayer, but seize whatever they can grasp of men's possessions, just as voracious ravens do from a carcass wherever they can get to it. It is all the worse after they have got it all; then they do not employ it as they should, but adorn their women with that with which they should adorn altars, and turn to their own worldly pride and empty vanity all that they should do for the worship of God in Church matters, or to the benefit of poor men, or in buying prisoners-of-war, or in some matters which might be of lasting benefit both to themselves and also to those who give them their goods in God's grace. It is, then, very necessary that he who before this did ill, diligently amend it henceforth. For let him understand who can: what a priest has to do for the benefit of the people is great and wonderful, if he wish to propitiate his Lord aright. Great is the exorcism and wonderful the consecration which drives away devils and puts them to flight as often as baptism is performed or the Eucharist consecrated. And angels hover there and protect those deeds, and through the power of God assist the priests as often as they serve Christ aright. And so they always do, as often as they earnestly call on Christ with inmost heart and diligently intercede for the people's needs. And for fear of God therefore, one must feel respect for those in orders, with discernment.

Well beloved, we are solemnly commanded that we should earnestly admonish and teach that every man incline to God and turn away from sins. The saying which God spoke through the prophet concerning those who should preach righteousness to God's people, that is bishops and priests, is very terrible. He said concerning them: *Clama, ne cesses; quasi tuba*, et reliqua.[1] 'Cry aloud and raise up your voices as loud as a trumpet, and proclaim to my people so that they turn away from sins.' So if you do not do that but pass it over in silence, and will not proclaim to the people its duty, then at Judgement Day you must pay the reckoning of all those souls which perish because they have not the teaching and the admonition which they need. May this saying[2] be very memorable to all those who are appointed that they should preach righteousness to God's people. And people have also a great need to be observant of the saying which is said after that. He, the prophet, after that said: 'If you preach righteousness to

---

[1] Isaiah, LVIII 1.
[2] Apparently an allusion to Ezekiel, III 17–18.

the people and you cannot turn them to righteousness, you will nevertheless save your own soul.'[1] And he who pursues evil and will not desist, he must endure eternal torment; that is, they must then go to hell with soul and with body and dwell with the Devil in hell-torments. Woe to that one who must dwell there in torments. It were better for him never to have become a man in the world, than to have become one. There is no man living who can recount all the miseries which he who falls completely into those torments must endure; and it is all the worse that there will never come an end to it for eternity.

12 (23) Concerning Men in Orders

Every chastity befits men in orders, since they must forbid every unchastity to all other men. And if they act rightly, they must themselves most diligently set an example in every chastity. So it is very terrible that some of those who should preach righteousness to all Christian men, and moreover set an example, have become an example for perdition rather than for benefit. That is, those adulterers who through holy orders have entered into an ecclesiastical marriage and afterwards violated it. It is allowed to no minister of the altar that he take a wife; but it is forbidden to each. Nevertheless there are now all too many who commit, and have committed, adultery. But for love of God, I pray and moreover strictly command that they desist from this. To a layman every woman is forbidden except his legitimate spouse; some of those in orders are so deceived by the Devil that they take a wife wrongfully and ruin themselves through the adultery in which they dwell. But I earnestly pray that henceforth they willingly desist from this deadly sin. The Church is the priest's spouse, and he has not rightly any other; for neither a wife nor the warfare of this world in any way befits a priest, if he wants to obey God aright and keep God's law as rightly becomes his rank.

The illustrious Emperor Constantine summoned a very great synod in the city of Nicaea for confirmation of the true faith. At that synod there were gathered three hundred and eighteen bishops from many nations; and there they declared the true faith and in declaration thereof established then the mass-creed, which is widely sung; and they put the church services in order appropriately, and many other things both concerning God's

[1] Ezekiel, III 19.

servants and God himself. There they said quite unanimously that it were right, if a minister of the altar, that is bishop or priest or deacon, take a wife, that he should have forfeited his order for ever and should be excommunicated, unless he desist and the more deeply atone. Four synods[1] were summoned in respect of the true faith about the Holy Trinity and about Christ's humanity. The first was at Nicaea; and afterwards the second was at Constantinople, where there were a hundred and fifty bishops. The third was at Ephesus, of two hundred bishops, and the fourth was at Chalcedon, of many bishops altogether. And they were all unanimous concerning those things which were first established at Nicaea, and they all forbade every intercourse with women to ministers of the altar forever. Let those who are so presumptuous that they scorn God and the decree of so many holy men as were assembled at these synods and everywhere since, reflect what reward they may imagine for themselves; and moreover need not imagine but know for certain that they must have evil reward and the wrath of God terribly since they so anger God in that they live all their lives in filth. I beseech ministers of the altar that they reflect upon themselves and desist from every filthiness. And let those who before this had the evil habit of adorning their women as they should altars, desist from this evil habit, and adorn their churches as best they can, so they command for themselves both godly counsel and earthly honour. A priest's mistress is nothing other than a snare of the Devil, and he who is snared thereby thenceforth until his end, will be seized fast by the Devil, and moreover he must afterwards pass into the power of fiends and totally perish. But let everyone diligently help himself while he may and is able, and every man turn from unrighteousness to righteousness; then they will be safe from eternal torment. And moreover, he who continues in good deeds thenceforth until his end, shall have for that eternal reward. Now the truth is told to you; understand yourselves by that, you who will. May God strengthen you for your own benefit, and keep us all as his will may be. Amen.

13 Concerning Abbots

It is right that abbots and especially abbesses constantly dwell fast in the monasteries and always diligently take care of their flocks

---

[1] In 325, 381, 431 and 451 respectively.

and ever set them a good example and preach properly, and never care too greatly or all too frequently about the cares of the world in vain pride, but concern themselves most often with sacred needs. So it befits abbots and men in monastic orders.

14 *Concerning Monks*

It is right that monks ever think on God by day and night in the inward heart and earnestly call on him, and live according to rule with all humility, and always separate themselves from worldly concerns as carefully as they can, and do what is their duty: ever care how they may best propitiate God and practise all that which they promised when they received orders; to attend diligently to their books and prayers, to learn and to teach as best they can, and completely scorn every pride and empty vanity and separate property and profitless action and unreasonable talk. So it befits monks. But as may be supposed, it is truly an evil that some are too proud and all too vain, and too given to wandering, and too profitless, and all too empty of every good deed, and too wicked in secret lustfulness: inwardly worthless and outwardly indignant. And some who should, if they would, be champions of God within their monasteries are apostates. That is, those wretches who have cast off orders and dwell in sin among worldly affairs. All too widely everything is going badly. So much is it worsening widely among men, that those in orders who through fear of God were at one time the most profitable and most laborious in divine ministry and in scholarship, are now everywhere well nigh the most useless, and never labour much at any needful matter on behalf of God nor on behalf of the world, but do all for pleasure and for ease, and love gluttony and vain joy, stroll about and wander and play the fool all day, chatter and sport and do nothing of any use. That is a detestable life that they live thus; it is the worse that the superiors do not amend it moreover; nor some of them conduct themselves as well as they should. But we need to amend it as earnestly as we can, and to be steadfast for the common good in the sight of God and the world.

15 *Concerning Women in Orders*

It is right that, just as we said before about monks, women in orders behave monastically, and not associate with secular men nor have all too much intimacy with them, but ever live according to rule and always separate themselves from worldly concerns as diligently as they can.

16 Concerning Priests and Nuns

It is right that priests, and equally nuns as well, live according to rule and maintain their chastity if they wish to dwell in a monastery or command respect in the sight of the world.

17 (22) Concerning Laymen

It is right that men in orders direct the lay how they should most correctly keep their conjugal state. It is a proper life, that a bachelor should remain in his bachelor state until he lawfully take a maiden in marriage, and afterwards have her and no other for as long as she should live. If then her death come about, then it is most proper that he henceforth remain a widower. By permission of the Apostle,[1] however, a layman may at need marry a second time. But the canons forbid to it the blessings which are appointed for a first marriage. And in addition a penance is appointed for such men to perform. And where a man marries again, the priest is forbidden to attend the marriage ceremony in the way he did before, or to give the blessing which pertains to a first marriage. By that it may be known that it is not altogether right that a man take a wife or a woman take a husband more than once. And it is certainly too much should it happen a third time, and completely wrong should it happen more often. And although a wife be allowed to laymen, nevertheless they have a duty to understand how it is allowed. Laymen may not have the society of a woman in carnal intercourse at times of festivals and times of fasts, any more than men in orders may have that thing at any time.

18 (17) Concerning the Widow

It is right that widows should earnestly follow the example of Anna.[2] She was in the temple day and night diligently serving. She fasted greatly and attended to prayers and called on Christ with mourning spirit, and distributed alms over and again, and ever propitiated God as far as she could by word and deed, and has now heavenly bliss for a reward. So shall a good widow obey her Lord.

[1] I Corinthians, VII 8–9.
[2] Cf. Luke, II 36–7.

19 (25) Concerning the Church

It is right that Christian men earnestly keep the Christian faith aright and diligently honour and protect the Church of Christ everywhere. We all have one heavenly Father and one spiritual Mother that is named *Ecclesia*, that is the Church of God; and we must ever love and honour that. And it is right that each church be under the protection of God and of all Christian people; and that the sanctuary of the church exist everywhere within the walls, and be equally inviolate with that offered personally by a consecrated king. For every church-sanctuary is Christ's own sanctuary, and every Christian man has an important duty to show great respect for that sanctuary. For it is the need of every Christian man that he earnestly love and honour God's Church and frequently and diligently seek it out for his own good. And those in orders especially must serve and minister there very often; and earnestly intercede for all Christian people. Ministers of the altar then, have always to consider that they, at least, order their lives rightly as befits the Church. The priest's lawful wife is rightly the Church, and hence nobody who cares for God's law should have anything to do with him who is ordained to the Church, without he completely ruin himself by deadly sin. And then the regional administrator of Christ must take note of it, and dispose and judge about it as the books direct. And nobody should ever injure or threaten any wrong to a church in any way. But nonetheless churches are now far and wide feebly protected, and quite bereft of ancient rights, and stripped of everything decent inside. And servants of the Church are everywhere deprived of respect and protection. And woe to him who is the cause of this, though he should not imagine so. For every one of those who is an enemy of God's churches and who diminishes or injures the rights of God's churches is assuredly the enemy of God himself; as it is written: *Inimicus enim Christi efficitur omnis, qui ecclesiasticas res usurpare iniuste conatur*, et reliqua.[1] And St Gregory spoke awfully concerning them also, when he said thus: *Si quis ecclesiam Christi denudaverit vel sanctimonia violaverit, anathema sit. Ad quod respondentes omnes dixerunt: amen.*[2] The

---

[1] From the tract 'De pressuris ecclesiasticis' by Atto, Bishop of Vercelli (*ob.* 961), *PL.*, CXXXIV, 88.

[2] The source of this quotation is now lost, although it was ascribed to Gregory by other late Anglo-Saxon authorities (cf. D. Wilkins, *Concilia Magnae Britanniae et Hiberniae*, London, 1737, I, 212).

need that every man should diligently defend himself against these things is great; and every friend of God is constantly to take care himself that he do not too greatly abuse the bride of Christ. We must all love and honour one God and diligently keep one Christian faith, and cast out every heathen practice with all our might. And let us loyally support one royal lord; and let each friend support the other with true fidelity.

20 (24) *Concerning all Christian Men*

It is right that all Christian men keep their Christian faith aright and live that life which befits them, according to God's law and according to earthly propriety, and diligently order all their ways by the directions of those who are able to direct them wisely and prudently. And that, then, is the foremost of counsels, that before all other things every man love one God and steadfastly have one faith in him who first made us all, and again bought us with a costly price. And also we have need earnestly to consider how we may always most righteously keep God's own commandments, and fulfil all that which we promised when we received baptism – or those who were our sponsors at our baptism. That is first then, that one promises when one desires baptism, that one will ever shun the Devil and diligently eschew his evil teaching, and continually cast off all his unrighteousness and eternally withstand all his company. And immediately thereafter, many times one truly declares with proper faith that always henceforth one will ever believe in one God and always love him before all other things, and earnestly ever follow his teachings and righteously keep his own commandments. And then that baptism will be, as it were, a pledge of all those words and all that promise, keep it who will. And it is true what I say: thenceforth angels continually watch over every man, how after his baptism he should fulfil what he previously promised when he desired baptism. Let us over and again think of that, and diligently fulfil what we promised when we received baptism, as our duty is. And let us order words and works aright, and earnestly cleanse our conscience, and carefully keep oath and pledge, and frequently consider the great Judgement to which we all must come; and carefully defend ourselves against the surging flame of hell-torment, and earn for ourselves those glories and those joys which God has prepared for those who do his will in the world. Amen.

TROUBLE AT SANDWICH

Sandwich, one of the later 'cinque ports', lay on the tidal estuary of the River Stour which divided the Isle of Thanet from mainland Kent. An exceptionally important trading-post with the Low Countries, with potentially valuable harbour-dues, it figures prominently as a port-of-call in the later Anglo-Saxon Chronicle. Its rights and privileges were transferred by Cnut to the Cathedral of Christ Church, Canterbury in 1023. The Anglo-Saxon Chronicle, ascribing this gift to 1031, the year of Cnut's return from Rome, says that the king did this 'immediately he arrived in England'; if so, the Canterbury enactment almost certainly took place shortly after he had passed through Sandwich itself, his most likely point of entry. About fifteen years later, rights over the port were abrogated by Cnut's alleged son and successor, Harold Harefoot, but apparently rescinded as an act of death-bed penitence.

A near-contemporary copy of Cnut's endowment is bound into the 'Red Book of Canterbury', Canterbury Cathedral MS. Chart. Ant. S260, where it is bracketed by Latin versions of the same charter (S259 and S261). A Middle English version is given in two Cathedral Registers: A, f. 144 and E, ff. 44'–5. The terms of the charter are unusual, perhaps pointing to Scandinavian customs; several of the signatories have Anglicized Scandinavian names. The account of Harold's two-year abrogation of Canterbury's rights is found in another near-contemporary parchment: British Library MS. Cotton Augustus II, 90, which a thirteenth-century endorsement attributes to the year 1038. The texts were edited by J. M. Kemble, *Codex Diplomaticus Aevi Saxonici*, London, 1839–48, IV, pp. 23–5, 56–8; and by A. J. Robertson, *Anglo-Saxon Charters*, Cambridge, 1939, pp. 158–61. The MSS. are reproduced respectively by: W. B. Sanders, *Facsimiles of Anglo-Saxon Manuscripts*, Southampton, 1878–84, I, no. 19; and E. A. Bond, *Facsimiles of Ancient Charters in the British Museum*, London, 1873–8, IV, no. 20.

Grant by King Cnut to Christ Church, Canterbury 1023

+ In the name of the highest God and of our Lord Saviour Christ. Our holy and our righteous fathers with very clear assurance and with frequent exhortation remind us to dread and to love untiringly, with inward joyfulness in our hearts and with eagerness in good works, the Almighty God whom we love and we believe, because he shall pay recompense for all our works at Judgement Day according to each man's deserts. So therefore let us strive with the highest endeavour of our heart's labour to follow him. Although we be laden with the burden of this mortal life, and be defiled with the transitory possessions of this world, nevertheless we may purchase the eternal reward of the heavenly life with these decaying riches. And therefore I, Cnut, through God's grace king of England and of all the islands that lie about, lay upon Christ's altar in Canterbury the royal crown from my head with my own hands, for the benefit of that same monastery. And I grant to that same monastery for the support of the monks, the port of Sandwich and all the landing-places and the dues from that same water from both sides of the river – whoever owns the land – from Piper's Promontory to the boundary inlet, so that when it is high tide and a ship is afloat, the stewards of Christ Church receive the dues from as far inland as a 'tapor-axe'[1] can be thrown out of the ship up onto the land. Nobody shall ever in any kind of way have any control in that same port except the monks of Christ Church, and theirs shall be the ship and the ferrying across the port, and shall be the toll of every ship that comes to that same port at Sandwich, whatever it be and whence-so-ever it come. And if there is anything in the open sea outside the port, for as far as the sea furthest recedes – and in addition the distance a man who holds a pole in his hand and stretches it as far as he can reach into the sea – that is the monks'; and all that is found on this side of the central channel and brought to Sandwich, be it clothing, be it net, or weapon, or iron, gold or silver – the half part shall be for the monks and the other part shall stay with those who find it.

And henceforth if any other document is produced which was made heretofore which in any kind of way seems to gainsay this our guarantee, that document shall be thrown away for mice to gnaw, or into the fire to burn up; and he who produces it, whatever rank he be, shall be regarded as the sweepings of ashes, and be he disgraced with the most ignominious shame, and be he shunned with one mind by all men who are present.

And the firm guarantee of this land-charter forever henceforth be affirmed; and both with Almighty God's authority and mine, and with the guarantee of all my thegns it shall be guaranteed with continuing legality, steadfast and immovable in perpetuity against all attempts to gainsay it. And if there is anyone who, with swollen pride, wants either to violate or to diminish this our guarantee, know he himself (to be) anathematized by God and by all his saints, unless before death he make reparation, with worthy repentance, for that which he unrighteously committed.

This land-charter was written in the one-thousand-and-twenty-third year after our Lord Saviour Christ's birth, with the assent of those men whose names are written hereafter:

---

[1] A pleonastic Viking composite: Russo-English 'axe-axe'.

+ I Cnut, the King of England, immovably guarantee the guarantee of this document.

+ I Ægelnoth, Archbishop of Canterbury, confirm this privilege with the holy sign.

+ I Ælfric, the Archbishop of York, the same king's good intention guarantee with the sign of the holy cross.

+ I Ælfwine,[1] the Bishop of London, assent. + I Ælfwine,[2] Bishop of Winchester, gave assent. + I Brih(t)wald, Bishop of the Church of Cornwall, assented. + I Ægelric, Bishop of Dorsetshire, guaranteed. + I Ælmer, bishop. + I Godwine, bishop. + I Brihtwine, bishop. + I Æthelstan, bishop. + I Ælmær, abbot. + I Brihtmær, abbot. + I Brihtwine, abbot. + I Wulfnoth, abbot. + I Godwine, earl. + I Ægelaf, earl. + I Thrim, earl. + I Yric, earl. + I Thord, minister. + I Agemund, minister. + I Ægelric, minister. + I Ælfwine, minister. + I Brihtric, minister. + I Leofric, minister. + I Siræd, minister. + I Godwine, minister. + I Eadmær, minister.

Harold Harefoot seizes Sandwich

Here it makes known in this document that King Harold had Sandwich seized from Christ Church into his own hands, and had it himself for well-nigh twelve months – and in any case, fully two herring-seasons – entirely against the will of God and against all the saints who rest within Christ Church, just as it afterwards grievously turned out for him thereafter. And about the time of these events Ælfstan became abbot at St Augustine's,[3] and with his sharp tricks and with his gold and silver, he obtained very secretly from Steorra, who then was the king's adviser, that he be entitled to the third penny of the toll at Sandwich. Then, when he knew this, Archbishop Eadsige and all the community at Christ Church, decided that between them they send Ælfgar, a monk of Christ Church, to King Harold. And the king was then in Oxford, having fallen very sick, so that he lay in despair of his life. Lyfing, Bishop of Devonshire, was with the king then, and the monk Thancred with him. Then Christ Church's messenger came to the bishop. And he then went to the king, and Ælfgar the monk with him, and Oswerd of Harrietsham, and Thancred, and they said to the king that he had greatly sinned against Christ in that he should ever take from Christ Church anything which his predecessors had

---

[1] Properly Ælfwig.
[2] Properly Ælfsige.
[3] An ancient Benedictine abbey, close neighbour to the cathedral.

assigned to that place. Then they spoke to the king about the seizure of Sandwich into his own hands. Then the king lay and darkened with what they were saying, and afterwards swore by Almighty God and by all the saints that it was never by his advice nor his deed that anyone should ever take Sandwich from Christ Church. Then it was clearly evident that it was not King Harold's but other men's contrivance; and clearly Abbot Ælfstan's advice was with the men who had advised [taking] it from Christ Church. Then King Harold sent the monk Ælfgar back to Archbishop Eadsige and to all Christ Church's monks, and greeted them all with God's greeting, and his, and ordered that they should have Sandwich for Christ Church as fully and as completely as ever they had it in any king's day, both in rent and in water, both in shore and in fines,[1] and in all those things, as fully as any king had ever had it before him. Then, when Abbot Ælfstan found out about this, he came to Archbishop Eadsige and requested his support within the community respecting the third penny. And they both then approached all the brethren and requested the community that Abbot Ælfstan might give the community 10 pounds and be entitled to the third penny of the toll. But they refused, all of them together equally, that he should ever continue it – and that was even though Archbishop Eadsige supported him rather than the community. And then, when he could not proceed with this, he begged that he might make a wharf opposite Mildred's acre[2] as a protection against the flood. But all the community completely refused him that way of going about. And Archbishop Eadsige left it entirely to their own counsel. Then Abbot Ælfstan came there with a lot of help and had a great dyke dug at Ebbsfleet,[3] and intended a ship-canal to run through it, just like they had at Sandwich. But he did not succeed in that, for he labours in vain who labours against the will of Christ. And the abbot left it all thus, and the community took possession of their own, in the sight of God and of St Mary and of all the saints who rest within Christ Church and at St Augustine's. This is all true, believe it who will. Abbot Ælfstan never looked for

---

[1] For this sort of formula cf. Edward the Confessor's Writ, above, p. 44.

[2] In c. 1030 Cnut had given St Augustine's the relics and estates of St Mildred, a seventh-century Kentish princess, and abbess of Minster-in-Thanet just across the River Stour, that convent being deserted after repeated Viking depredations.

[3] In the sands at the very mouth of the Stour – the point of arrival of Hengest and Horsa in 449 and, traditionally, of Augustine in 597.

the third penny from Sandwich in any other way. May God's blessing be with us all for ever in perpetuity. Amen.

THE GOSPEL OF NICODEMUS

The Gospel of Nicodemus was perhaps the most influential of the various apocryphal New Testament writings extant in the early Middle Ages. It purports to have been written by the follower of Jesus who, together with Joseph of Arimathea, had taken and embalmed the body of Jesus for burial (John, III 1–21, XIX 19). Early Greek and Latin versions are printed by C. Tischendorf, *Evangelia Apocrypha*, Leipzig, 1876. However, it seems substantially to have been compiled in the fourth or fifth centuries.

The Old English version is found in two copies, both incomplete. One occurs in an eleventh-century manuscript: Cambridge University Library MS. Ii.2.11, ff. 173ᵛ–93, where it follows the late West Saxon translation of the four canonical Gospels and is followed in turn by another apocryphal work, the Old English Legend of Veronica. This was one of the books bequeathed to Exeter Cathedral library by Bishop Leofric in 1072, and was probably written for his use. A second, less complete copy, is included in a twelfth-century collection of homilies now bound up with the *Beowulf* manuscript, British Library MS. Cotton Vitellius A XV, ff. 60–86ᵛ. Extracts from the Gospel were occasionally incorporated in Old English homilies, like that included in another of Leofric's books, his copy of the Alfredian translation of Bede's *Historia Ecclesiastica*, Corpus Christi College, Cambridge, MS. 41, where it follows the Old English version of another apocryphal work, the so-called Apocalypse of Thomas.

The text was printed by W. H. Hulme, *Publications of the Modern Language Association of America*, 13 (1898), 457–542, and separately by S. J. Crawford, *The Gospel of Nicodemus*, Edinburgh, 1927.

The Gospel falls into two originally independent parts. The first furnishes a dramatic account of Christ's trial before Pilate. The second deals with the so-called 'Harrowing of Hell' (Old English *hergian*, 'to harry, despoil'). The idea that after his death Christ descended into Hell to deliver the righteous from the power of Satan, derives from such biblical references as Psalm CVII 10–20, and Ephesians, IV 8–9. It proved an attractive subject for artistic treatment, and is depicted in sculptures and manuscript illuminations of Anglo-Saxon and later times, and in the medieval drama to which its extensive dialogue sequences were naturally suited. Old English poems which deal with the subject include the Exeter Book *Descent into Hell* and *Christ III*, and *Christ and Satan*. And it is the subject of several Old English sermons (cf. *Blickling Homily* 7, pp. 123–6). See also the Old English Church Calendar, above, pp. 77–8. A Middle English version was edited by W. H. Hulme, EETS., ES., C, London, 1907.

In the name of the Holy Trinity. Here begin the acts which were performed by our Saviour, just as Theodosius,[1] the famous emperor, found it in Jerusalem in the judgement hall of Pontius Pilate, just as Nicodemus wrote it, entirely written in Hebrew characters thus.

---

[1] Apparently Theodosius I, last emperor of both East and West, 383–95.

I   The Acts of Pilate

1. It happened in fact in the nineteenth year in which Tiberius the great emperor ruled over all the kingdom of the Romans, his under-king being Herod, the son of the Galilean king who was called Herod. So it was in the nineteenth year of their rule, on the 8th of the kalends of April, that is the 25th March, that calamity came upon the Jewish people when they took the Saviour and hung him on a cross, just as Judas, his own follower, betrayed him. The elders of the Jews who were there were named thus: Annas and Caiaphas, Summas and Dathan, Gamaliel and Judas, Levi and Nepthalim, Alexander and Cyrus. And very many others went to Pilate and accused the Saviour and charged him with many evil deeds. And he had never done any of them. And nevertheless they said thus: 'We know this young man, and we are aware that he was the son of Joseph the carpenter and Mary. Now he says that he would be the son of God. And he says also that he himself would be king; and also profanes each sabbath and destroys the law of our fathers.'

Pilate answered them and said: 'What is it that he does, that might destroy the law?' Then the Jews answered him and said: 'It is forbidden in our law that a man should heal anything on the sabbath, even though it be lame. Now this man heals both the halt, the blind, the deaf, the dumb, the deformed-lame and those possessed by devils. He does such evil deeds and he casts out devils by the prince Beelzebub.' Pilate answered them and said: 'It is not by an unclean spirit that he casts out devils, but by the power of God.' Then the Jews said to him: 'Well, we ask you that of your majesty you should order him to come here before your judge-ment seat, and listen to his words.'

Then Pilate did so, ordered one of his couriers to be called, and said to him: 'Go discreetly and call here to me him who is named Jesus.' Whereupon the courier did so, and went out with great haste and found the Saviour and humbled himself before him. And forthwith he stretched out on the earth what he carried in his hands – which was a piece of clothing – and himself fell stretched out on the earth, and said: 'Behold, Lord, the judge ordered you to be summoned, so that you should go into him.' But the Saviour did not yet answer him. And moreover the Jews saw how the courier had humbled himself before the Saviour, and called out to Pilate and said: 'Did you order your messenger and your courier to come up to him and thus humble himself before him?' And they forthwith told all that they had seen the courier do.

Pilate then ordered the courier to be called to him, and immediately asked why he had done so. The courier answered him and said: 'When you sent me to Jerusalem to King Alexander, then I saw how the Saviour had sat upon an ass, and the Hebrew children held palm branches in their hands, and some their garments. And they laid out those garments and strewed those palm branches on the earth in front of the Saviour, and all cried with one voice: *Hosanna, benedictus qui venit in nomine Domini.*'[1]

The Jews then said to the courier: 'The children were Hebrew, moreover they spoke in Hebrew; and how is it that you should speak in Hebrew when you yourself are Greek?' The courier answered them and said: 'I asked one of the Hebrews what they said, and straightaway he interpreted it all for me.' Then said Pilate: 'What did they call out, and what does the Hebrew mean?' The courier answered him and said: 'All hail Lord, and blessed is he who comes in the name of the Lord, and save us, you who are on high.' Then said Pilate to the Jews: 'Now you also may bear witness to what the children said. In what way has this courier sinned?' They were silent and could give no answer.

Then the judge again said to the courier: 'Go out, and wherever you find him, bring him in to me.' Then the courier immediately did so, going out and finding the Saviour. And there he did just what he had done previously, humbling himself before the Saviour and saying to him: 'Behold, dear Lord, the judge orders you to be summoned in.' The courier earnestly entreated him to walk in over his garment. And the dear Lord humbled himself before him. But among those where he entered, many men humbled themselves before him, bowing their heads to him.

2. But Pilate, when he saw that, was very afraid; and getting up, went out. But his wife, whose name was Procula, sent to him saying to him thus: 'Have nothing to do with this righteous man, for this night I have heard many things concerning him.' Then when the Jews heard that, they said to Pilate: 'Now you can understand yourself that he is the author of every evil, now that he has afflicted your wife in her sleep so that she is deceived.' Then Pilate ordered the Saviour to be summoned to him, and said to

---

[1] Cf. Mark, XI 9.

him: 'Do you not hear the many things these people say against you?' The Saviour answered him and said: 'If they had not had power they would have spoken nothing: but each man may speak with his mouth evil or good!' The elders of the Jews then answered and said to the Saviour: 'We ourselves saw and we know first, that you were born of fornication; and second, that your birth in Bethlehem is very disputable; and third, that Joseph your father and Mary your mother fled into Egypt because they had no faith in anybody.'

Then said certain of those that stood near, who were simple and good men among the Jews: 'We do not say that he was born of fornication; but we know that Mary was betrothed to Joseph, and thus he was not born of fornication.' Then Pilate said to the people who said he was born of fornication: 'This statement that you make is not true, for there was a betrothal, just as your own people say.' Then those two cruel blasphemers Annas and Caiaphas answered Pilate: 'Behold, dear judge, all this multitude cries out and says that he was born of fornication, and is an evil-doer. He is lying, himself and his followers likewise.' Then Pilate called Annas and Caiaphas to him and said to them: 'Who are these men that speak with him?' They said: 'They are sons of heathen men, and have become Jews, and say falsely like him that he be not born of fornication.' Then those who knew the truth, that is Lazarus and Asterius, Antonius and Jacob, Zeras and Samuel, Isaac and Phineas, Crispus and Agrippa, Annas and Judas, answered the Jews, and said: 'We are neither heathen-born nor become a lie, but we are sons of Jewish men and we speak the truth, listen who will.'

Then Pilate called to him those twelve followers who spoke with the Saviour, and said to them: 'By the protection of Caesar, I adjure you to tell me whether he be born of fornication.' Then they said to Pilate: 'It is not allowed by our law to swear; but nevertheless, as we may have the protection of Caesar and as we are not deserving of death, he is not born of fornication.' Then Annas and Caiaphas said to Pilate: 'Behold, these men quite believe that he was not born of fornication and that he is not an evil-doer. Nevertheless, we ourselves know that he says that he is himself the son of God and king; but we do not believe it.' Pilate then ordered all the people to leave except for the twelve followers who said that he was not born of fornication, and ordered the Saviour to be led apart, and questioned the followers why the people were so evilly disposed towards the Saviour. They answered Pilate and said: 'Because of the malice they bear towards him, since he heals wretched people on the sabbath.' Pilate said to them: 'What, do they want to put him to death for good work?' They answered and said: 'Yes, kind sir.'

3. Pilate then became angry, and went out and said to the people: 'I now know for myself that I can find no fault in this man.' Then answered the Jews and said to Pilate: 'If he were not an evil-doer, we would never have delivered him to you.' Pilate said to them: 'Nevertheless, take him and judge him according to your law.' Then said they to Pilate: 'We are not allowed to put any man to death.'

Pilate again entered his judgement hall and called the Saviour himself to him, and said: 'Are you King of the Jews?' The Saviour answered him and said: 'Do you say that of yourself, or did other men say it to you about me?' Pilate then answered the Saviour and said: 'Do you not know that all Jewry and your nation and the chief priests have delivered you to me? So tell me, what have you done?' The Saviour answered him and said: 'My kingdom is not of this world; if my kingdom were of this world, my servants would have resisted, so that I should not be delivered to these Jews.' Pilate said to him: 'Are you really a king?' The Saviour answered him and said: 'You say that I am a king.' He, the Saviour said again to Pilate: 'But I am come into this world so that anyone of those that love the truth should hear my voice.' Pilate said to him: 'What is truth?' The Saviour answered him and said: 'Truth is of heaven.' Then said Pilate: 'Is there no truth on earth?' The Saviour answered him and said: 'Observe and see what just judgements they pass who are in the earth and have authority!'

4. Then Pilate ordered the Saviour to go outside his judgement hall, and said to the Jews: 'I can find no fault in this man.' Then said the Jews to Pilate: 'Oh yes! Yet he says more, that he can destroy this temple and raise it up again within the space of three days.' Then said Pilate: 'Which temple?' They said: 'The temple that Solomon built in seventy-six years; he can destroy that, he says, and build it up again within the space of three days.' Then said Pilate: 'I will act so that you will all see that I want to be guiltless of this man's blood.' Then said the Jews: 'Let his blood be on us and on our children.'

Then Pilate called the elders and the priests and the deacons to him and said to them secretly: 'Do not so, for I have found nothing in him that he should be deserving of death, neither in healing nor in profaning the sabbath.' Then said the elders and the priests to Pilate: 'Oh yes! Whatever man blasphemes the emperor, he is deserving of death.' Pilate again ordered the Jews to go out of the judgement hall, and crying out at the Saviour, said: 'What can I do with you now?' Whereupon the Saviour said to Pilate: 'It is sufficient; now it is sufficient.' Then said the Saviour: 'Thus Moses and many other prophets foretold about this very suffering, and about my resurrection.' Then when they heard of that, the Jews said to Pilate: 'What more do you want from him, or to hear of his blasphemy?' Then said Pilate to the Jews: 'If this statement that he makes is blasphemy, take him and lead him to your assembly and judge him according to your law.' Then said the Jews to Pilate: 'We wish him to be crucified.' Then said Pilate to the Jews: 'What has he done that he ought to die?' They said: 'Only because he said that he was the son of God, and himself a king!'

5. Then there stood before the judge a certain Jewish man whose name was Nicodemus, and said to the judge: 'Behold, kind sir, I pray you of your mercy that you allow me to say a few words.' Then said Pilate: 'Yes, speak.' Then said Nicodemus: 'I speak to you elders and priests and deacons, and all this multitude of Jews who are here in company. I ask you, what do you want from this man?' He uttered such words there as no other before dare . . .

> Although no pages are missing from either MS. at this point, some part of the text is absent. The outline may be reconstructed from the Latin versions, thus. Those whom Jesus had healed come forward to bear witness on his behalf. Pilate offers to release Jesus under a special dispensation, but the mob demands Barabbas instead. The Jews, says Pilate, are notoriously seditious and impious. But this is he whom Herod had sought at his birth. Pilate capitulates. Thereafter the story proceeds rapidly to the point of the crucifixion and death of Christ with little narrative diversion from the canonical account, save that the two thieves are named as Dysmas and Gestas. At this point the Old English text resumes.

11. . . . Then standing near him there was a certain man who was named Joseph. He was a good and righteous man, and it was never his wish that they should accuse the Saviour before any assembly. He was from the city which is called Arimathea, and until Christ was crucified, he was seeking the kingdom of God.[1]

[1] Cf. Luke, XXIII 51.

And he begged the body of Christ from Pilate, and took it from the cross, and folded it in a clean cloth and laid it in his new tomb in which no other man had previously lain before.

12. When the Jews heard that Joseph had asked for the Saviour's body, then they looked for him and the twelve followers who said that he was not born of fornication and Nicodemus and many others who formerly spoke with the Saviour and made his good works known. But they all hid themselves wherever they could, except Nicodemus himself, because he was an elder of the Jewish people. Then he came to them where they were assembled, and said to them: 'How did you come to this assembly, when I did not know of it earlier?' Then the Jews answered and said: 'But how are you so bold that you dare come into our assembly, you who agreed and spoke with the Saviour? But may you be always together here, and in the world to come also!' Then he answered and said: 'Amen, amen.' After that, Joseph showed himself and came to them likewise and spoke thus: 'Why are you so displeased with me? Is it because I asked for the Saviour's body from Pilate? It is true that I asked for it, and folded it in a clean cloth and laid it in my tomb, and rolled a great stone there in front of the cave. And I say truly, that you have not done well by the righteous one, in that you hung him on a cross and pierced him with a spear.'

Then when the Jews heard that, they seized him and ordered him to be shut up close in prison, and said to him: 'Know now and realize that what you thought will avail you little. We will see to it that you will never come to be buried. But we shall give your flesh to the birds of the air and to the wild beasts of the earth.' Then the Jews brought him into the prison and locked the door fast. And Annas and Caiaphas sealed the lock and set guards on it, and took council with the priests and with the deacons by what death they would slay Joseph. But it was the sabbath that day, and they wished to wait until the next day; and they afterwards assembled and discussed for a time how they might most shamefully treat him. But then it happened that after the sabbath they assembled the elders and the priests, and Annas and Caiaphas went along to the prison where they had shut Joseph up, and unsealed the lock and opened the door with the key. But Joseph was not found there. Then when the people heard that, they marvelled and were afraid.

13. But while they spoke about it and marvelled at it, one of the soldiers who had to guard the Saviour's tomb stood there and

straightaway said: 'I know that when we guarded the Saviour's tomb there came a great earthquake and we saw the angel of God, how he rolled the stone from the tomb and sat upon the stone; and I know that his face was like lightning and his garments were like snow, so that we were afraid, so that we lay there as if we were dead. And we listened. And we heard the angel speaking to the women who came to the Saviour's tomb. He said: "Fear not, for I know that you seek the Saviour who was crucified. But he is not here; he is risen, just as he previously foretold. But come and see the place where he was laid, and go quickly and tell his disciples that their Lord is risen from death and is gone before them into Galilee, where they may see him, just as he previously foretold to them." '[1]

The Jews, when they heard that, all cried out at the soldiers who guarded the Saviour's tomb, and said to them: 'Who were the women with whom the angel spoke, and why did you not take them into custody?' The soldiers answered them and said: 'We did not know who the women were, nor might we know it, nor could we; because, for fear of the angel and because of the sight that we saw there, we had become as though we were dead, and therefore we could not seize the women.' Then said the Jews: 'As our Lord lives, we do not believe you.' Then the soldiers answered and said to the Jews: 'Behold, for as many miracles as the Saviour wrought and you saw and heard, why as our Lord lives, will you not believe in him in whom you must believe? And nevertheless you spoke rightly just now when you said: "As our Lord lives", though you did not know what it meant. It is true that the same and truest Lord lives, whom you hung on a cross. And we heard tell that Joseph, who buried the Saviour's body, you shut up in a very secure prison and sealed the lock with a seal; and then when you came back you did not find him! But seriously, you give us Joseph whom you shut up in prison, and we will give you the Saviour, whom we had to guard in the tomb.' Then the Jews answered and said: 'Joseph we can find, because Joseph is in his city of Arimathea.' The soldiers answered them and said: 'If Joseph is in the city of Arimathea, then we say to you that the Saviour is in Galilee, just as we heard the angel say to the women.'

Then, when the Jews had heard all this, they were afraid and said among themselves: 'If this report spreads too widely, all too many will believe in the Saviour.' But I know that the Jews then

---

[1] Cf. Matthew, XXVIII 2–7.

collected a great deal of money and gave it to the soldiers, and spoke thus: 'We entreat you, dear friends, that you say thus: that his followers came in the night and stole the body while you were sleeping. And if it becomes known to the judge Pilate, we will take your part and ensure your safety.' Then the soldiers took the money and said just as they were instructed by the Jews. But all their report was made known and spread abroad.

14. And then it happened that recently there had come from Galilee to Jerusalem three famous men. The eldest was a priest, and his name was Phineas. And his friends were called one of them Egius, the other Adda, a teacher. When they came to the synod of the Jews, they said to the elders and to the priests and to all the assembly, that they had seen the crucified Saviour and he spoke with his disciples and sat among them on Mount Olivet, saying to them: 'Go out into all the world and preach to all nations, so that they be baptized in the name of the Father and the Son and the Holy Spirit. And whosoever believes and is baptized will be made whole forever in eternity.'[1] 'And when he had said this to his disciples, we saw how he ascended to heaven. And if we conceal the fact which we saw and heard concerning the Saviour, we know that we sin.'

Then the elders and the priests stood up and sternly adjured them by the old law, and spoke thus: 'We wish to make you a request, and will give you money if you will conceal all the report which you have made concerning the Saviour.' Then the three men answered them and said that they would do so. And the Jews found them three companions, who should bring them out of the kingdom, so that they might not remain in Jerusalem any length of time. And all the Jews then came together and were assembled, and pondered and talked about what that sign might be that had come to pass in the land of Israel. Annas and Caiaphas then said: 'It is never true that we must believe the soldiers who had to guard the Saviour's tomb; but it is more likely that his disciples came and gave them money and took the Saviour's body away.'

15. Then Nicodemus stood up, and spoke thus: 'Know that you speak truly concerning the children of Israel. You heard well what the three men said who came out of Galilee, when they said that they saw the Saviour on Mount Olivet speaking with his disciples, and saw where he ascended into heaven.' Then the Jews enquired where the prophet Elias was, and said thus: 'Where is

[1] Mark, XVI 15–16.

our father Elias?' Eliseus answered them and said: 'He is taken
above.' Then said some of those who stood there among the
people, who were sons of the prophets: 'But the chances are that
he is taken up in spirit and set upon the mountains of Israel. So let
us choose men and go throughout the mountains; perhaps we
may find him.' The people then asked Eliseus and the very men
who had spoken thus to do. so. And they forthwith travelled
throughout the mountains for the space of three days, but they
could not find him anywhere. Then said Nicodemus: 'Now
beloved, you children of Israel, listen to me; and let us again send
into the mountains of Israel; perhaps the spirit has caught up the
Saviour, and we might find him and humble ourselves before
him.' All the people liked Nicodemus' idea and they sent out many
men and sought the Saviour, and seeking, found him nowhere.
And turning, they came back again and spoke thus: 'Journeying
throughout the land of Israel, we could not find the Saviour
anywhere; but we found Joseph in Arimathea, his own city.'

Then when the elders and priests and all the people heard this,
they rejoiced and glorified the God of Israel that Joseph, whom
they had shut up in prison, was met with and found. The people
then formed a great assembly, and the elders and the priests said
among themselves: 'Well, how can we summon Joseph to us and
speak with him?' However, then they thought that they would
choose seven men who were friends of Joseph, and send them to
him and with them a letter which was written thus: 'Peace be with
you, Joseph, and with all who are with you. We know that we
have sinned both against God and against you, but we earnestly
beseech that you condescend to come to your fathers and to your
sons, for all marvel at your exaltation. We know that we
harboured wicked intentions towards you; but the Lord took you
and delivered you from our wicked intention. So peace be with
you, Joseph, and be honoured among all people.'

The messengers then went and came to Joseph, and greeted him
in a friendly manner, and gave their letter into his hand. And when
Joseph had read the letter, then said he: 'Blessed be the Lord God
who delivered me and would not shed my blood, and blessed be he
who has shieldeˇd me under his wings.' Joseph then stood up, and
kissed the men, and received them honourably. Then the next day
Joseph travelled to Jerusalem with the messengers, all mounted on
their asses. And the Jews, when they heard that, all ran towards
him crying out and saying: 'Well, father Joseph, peace attend your

coming.' Joseph answered and said: 'Peace be with all God's people.' And then they drew near him and kissed him. And Nicodemus took him home to his house with honour.

On the following day Annas and Caiaphas and Nicodemus said to Joseph: 'Now, we entreat you to make a confession to the true God and reveal to us all those things which we ask you. And tell us first, you who buried the Saviour's body, how you whom we had shut up, got out of prison. For we marvelled greatly at that, and fear gripped us when we wanted you and did not find you. And disclose to us how it all came to pass concerning you.' Joseph answered them and said: 'I will indeed. It was on the day when you shut me up. It happened that in the evening I fell to my prayers and sang diligently until it came to mid-night. Then the building was lifted up by the four corners, and I beheld the Saviour just as if it were lightning. And I fell down on the earth for fear. And he held me by the hand and lifted me up, and kissed me and said to me: "Do not be afraid; look at me, and recognize that it is I." Then I looked, and said: "Are you Elias, oh master?" Then said he to me: "I am not Elias, but I am the Saviour whose body you buried." Then said I to him: "Show me the tomb where I laid you." Thereupon the Saviour took me by the right hand and led me out into Arimathea to my own house, and said to me: "Peace be with you, Joseph; and do not go out of your house before the fortieth day. I wish to go to my disciples." ' Then when the Jews heard all this they were afraid and some fell down, and said among themselves: 'What can this sign be that has come to pass in the land of Israel? We know both the father and mother of the Saviour.'

II Christ's Descent into Hell

1. Then Joseph stood up and said to Annas and Caiaphas: 'In truth, it is right to marvel at what you have heard of the Saviour: that he rose up from death, and living ascended into heaven; and not only that he should rise up from death, but awoke many men from death and raised them up from their graves. And now listen to me. We all knew the blessed Simeon, and the famous priest who first carried the Saviour in his arms into the holy temple; and we all know that he had two sons, who were called one Carinus, and the other Leuticus; and we attended their burial. Let us also now go and we might find their graves open; and they are in the city of

Arimathea praying together, waiting and talking to nobody, and keeping such silence that they will talk to nobody. But let us go and visit them with all honour and bring them to us and earnestly adjure them to speak with us and tell us all the mysteries which came to pass concerning their resurrection.'

Then when Joseph had thus spoken all this, the people rejoiced and journeyed to the city of Arimathea and there wanted to know if what Joseph had said were true. But when they came there, then Annas and Caiaphas and Nicodemus and Joseph and Gamaliel went to the tomb; but they found no one in it. Then walking around the city, they found them given up to prayer on bended knees. And straightaway they kissed them, and with all reverence and in the fear of God they brought them to Jerusalem unto their assembly. And having locked the gates there, they took the book in which the divine law was written, and put it in their hands, and said thus: 'We adjure you by the heavenly God and by the divine law which you have in your hands, that if you believe in the same one who awoke you from death, tell us how you were raised up from death.' Carinus and Leuticus answered them and said: 'We will too! Moreover give us paper so that we may write down what we have heard and also seen.' Then the elders and the priests found them paper and brought it all there. Carinus and Leuticus were then provided with papers, one for each of them, and spoke thus:

2. 'Indeed, Lord Saviour Christ, you are the life and resurrection of all the dead. We beseech you to allow us to reveal the divine mysteries which came to pass through your death and through your resurrection. Oh most merciful Lord, you who forbade your servants to reveal the divine glory of your secret majesty, allow it to us.' Then a voice from heaven came to them, saying thus: 'Write and reveal it.'

Then they did so. Carinus and Leuticus wrote about it thus, and said: 'Behold, when we were with all our fathers in the depths of Hell, there came a brightness into that murky gloom, so that we were all illuminated and rejoiced. It suddenly came to pass, as if the golden sun were kindled in our sight there and shone over us all. And then Satan and all that cruel host were afraid, and said thus: "What is this light that shines on us here so suddenly?" Thereupon all the human race, our father Adam with all the patriarchs and with all the prophets, immediately rejoiced because of the great brightness. And they spoke thus: "This light is the Prince of light eternal, just as the Lord promised us that he would send us that light eternal." Then the prophet Isaiah cried out and said: "This is the light proceeding from the Father; and it is the Son of God, just as I foretold when I was on earth, when I spoke and prophesied that the land of Zebulun and the land of Naphtali with the river Jordan and the people that sat in darkness should see a great light; and I prophesied that those who dwelt in the kingdom of darkness should receive light.[1] And now it has come, and shines on us who formerly sat in the shadow of death. so let us all bless the light." '

Then the prophet Simeon said to them all as they rejoiced: 'Glorify the Lord Christ, Son of God, whom I carried into the temple in my arms, when I spoke thus: "You are a light and a comfort to all nations, and you are a glory and honour to all the people of Israel." '[2] When Simeon had spoken thus, all that company of saints greatly rejoiced. And thereafter there came, as it were, a clap of thunder, and all the saints cried out at it and said: 'Who are you?' The voice answered them and said: 'I am John, the prophet of the Most High, and I am come before him that I may prepare his ways and furnish the salvation of his people.'[3]

3. Then Adam, hearing this and speaking to his son who was named Seth, said: 'Relate to your children and to these patriarchs all those things which you heard from the archangel Michael when I sent you to the gate of Paradise to ask the Lord to send his angel with you to give you the oil from the tree of mercy, so that you might anoint my body with it when I was so sick.' Then Adam's son Seth, drawing near to the holy patriarchs and the prophets, said: 'Well, while I was praying to the Lord at the gate of Paradise, the archangel Michael appeared to me and said to me: "I am sent to you from the Lord, and I am appointed over all human bodies. Now I say to you Seth, there is no need to labour in prayer nor shed tears, to ask for the oil from the tree of mercy in order that with it you may anoint your father Adam for his body's pain, because the five thousand and five hundred years which must pass away before he is healed are not yet fulfilled. But then the most merciful Christ, the Son of God, will come and lead your father Adam into Paradise to the tree of mercy." ' Then when they all heard this, all the patriarchs and the prophets and all the saints

---

[1] Isaiah, IX 1–2.
[2] Cf. Luke, II 32.
[3] Cf. Luke, I 76–7.

who were there in that place of living torment, rejoiced, greatly glorifying God.

4. It was very terrible then, when Satan, the prince of hell and the general of death, said to Hell: 'Prepare yourself, that you may receive Christ, who has glorified himself, and is God's son and also man, and feared even by death. And my soul is so sorrowful that I think that I may not live; for he is a great adversary and evil-doer against me, and many whom I had in my power and drew to me: the blind and halt, the crippled and the leper, he will completely take away from you.' Then Hell, very grim and very dreadful, answered Satan, the ancient devil, and said: 'If he is a man, who is he, who is so strong and so powerful, that he be not afraid of death, whom we two have long imprisoned? For by your power you have dragged to me all who had power on earth, and I hold them fast. And if you are as powerful as you formerly were, who is the man and Saviour who fears neither death nor your power? But I know for a truth that if he is so powerful in human shape that he fears neither us nor death, then I know that he is so powerful in godhead that nothing may withstand him. And I know that there will be forever misery, world without end.'

Then Satan, prince of the place of living torment, answered Hell and spoke thus: 'Why do you doubt, or why do you fear to receive the Saviour, my adversary and yours also? For I tempted him and I arranged that all the Jewish people were aroused to anger and to malice against him. And I arranged that he was pierced with a spear, and I arranged that they gave him a drink mixed with gall and with vinegar, and I arranged that they prepared a wooden cross and hung him there and fastened him with nails. And now at last I will bring his death to you, and he shall be subjected to both me and you!' Then Hell spoke terribly thus: 'See that you arrange that he pluck not the dead from me; for here are many eager to leave me, so that they should not dwell in me. But I know that they will not leave me through their own strength, except that the Almighty God pluck them from me, who took Lazarus from me, whom I held fast bound in death for four days; and I gave him up again alive because of his command.'

Then Satan answered and said: 'It is the same who took Lazarus from both of us.' Hell then spoke to him thus: 'Behold, I adjure you by your power and by mine also, that you never permit him to enter into me. For when I heard the word of his command I was terrified with a great fear, and all my wicked thegns were afflicted and troubled together with me, so that we might not hold Lazarus; but he shook himself, just like an eagle when he wants to fly forth in swift flight, and he rushed out from us thus. And the earth, which held the dead body of Lazarus, gave it up again alive. And now I know that the man who did all that is strong and powerful in God; and if you bring him to me, he will in his divinity completely pluck from me and lead into life all those who are shut up here in this cruel prison.'

5. But while they spoke thus between themselves there was a voice and heavenly cry as loud as a clap of thunder, saying thus: *Tollite portas principes vestras, et elevamini porte eternales, et introibit rex glorie.*[1] That is in English: 'Take away these gates you princes, and lift up the everlasting gates, that the king of eternal glory may come in.' But when Hell heard that, then she said to Satan the prince: 'Leave me quickly, and get out of my dwelling; and if you are as powerful as you previously said, then fight now against the King of Glory, and let it be between you and him.' And then Hell drove Satan out of his seat, and said to the wicked thegns: 'Lock up the cruel and the brazen gates, and shut in front the iron bolts, and resist him strongly, and hold fast the captives, so that we be not captured.'

When the multitude of the saints who were there heard that, they all cried out with one voice, and said to Hell: 'Open up your gates, that the King of everlasting glory may come in.' Then David said moreover: 'Did I not prophesy to you when I was alive on the earth, when I said: "Praise the Lord for his mercy, for he will make known his wonderful works to the children of men, and shatter the brazen gates and the iron bolts; and he will deliver them from the path of their unrighteousness." '[2] Then after that the prophet Isaiah said to all the saints who were there: 'And did not I foretell to you, when I was alive on earth, that dead men should rise up and many graves be opened, and those who were on earth rejoice because salvation should come to them from the Lord?'[3] Then when all the saints heard this from the prophet Isaiah, they said to Hell: 'Open up your gates. Now shall you be weak and powerless and completely vanquished.'

While they spoke thus, there came the great voice like a clap of thunder and spoke thus: 'You princes, take away your gates and

[1] Psalm XXIII 7.
[2] Cf. Psalm CVI 15 ff.
[3] Cf. Isaiah, XXVI 19.

lift up the everlasting gates, that the king of eternal glory may come in.' But when Hell heard that, that it was cried out thus twice, then she cried out again, and spoke thus: 'Who is this king, who would be the King of Glory?' David answered her then and said: 'I recognize these words. And moreover I sang these words when I was on earth; and I said that the Lord himself would look down onto earth from heaven and there hear the lamentation of his servants in bonds.[1] But now, you most foul and you most foully-stinking Hell, open up your gates, that the King of everlasting glory may come in.' While David spoke thus, there came the glorious King that was our heavenly Lord in the likeness of a man, and then shone throughout the eternal gloom there. And then he there smashed all the bonds of sin, and he came to all our forefathers where for so long they had dwelt in the gloom.

6. But when Hell and Death and their wicked servants saw and heard that, they with their cruel servants were terrified, because they saw so great a brightness of light in their own kingdom. And suddenly they saw Christ sit upon the throne which he had taken for himself. And they cried out saying thus: 'We are vanquished by you; but we ask you, who are you, you who without any strife and without any stain brought our power low by your majesty? And who are you, so great and also so small, and so lowly and yet so exalted, and so wonderful as to overcome us in the form of a man? Behold, are you not he who lay dead in the tomb, and are come to us here alive, and at whose death all earth's creatures and all stars were shaken? And you, of all the other dead, have become free, and you have greatly troubled our whole troop. And who are you, who sent forth that light here, and with your divine power and brightness have blinded the sinful gloom, and have likewise greatly frightened also all this troop of these devils?'

And then all the devils cried out with one voice: 'Where do you come from, O Saviour, a man so strong and so bright in majesty, without any stain and so pure from any sin? All the earthly world was always subject to us until now. And we ask you earnestly, who are you who have come to us thus unafraid, and moreover here wish to pluck from us all those whom we long held in bonds? Or perhaps you are the same Saviour about whom Satan our lord spoke, saying that through your death he could have dominion over all the world?' But then the glorious King and our heavenly

---

[1] Cf. Psalm XXIII 8; CI 19–20.

Lord would have no more haranguing from the devils, but he trod down devilish death far below; and he seized Satan and bound him fast and delivered him into the power of Hell.

7. And she received him, just as she was ordered by our heavenly Lord. Then said Hell to Satan: 'So, you prince of all perdition, and so, you source and origin of every evil, and so, you father of all fugitives, and so, you who were the prince of all death, and so, author of all arrogance, how did you dare send that idea to the Jewish people that they should crucify this Saviour, and you know no fault in him? And now through that tree and through that cross you have destroyed all your joy; and because you hung this King of Glory, you acted perversely against yourself and against me. And realize now how many eternal tortures and endless torments you will be suffering in my eternal custody.' But then, when the King of Glory heard that, how Hell spoke to cruel Satan, he said to Hell: 'Let Satan be in your power, and yet both of you damned for eternity; and let that be for ever, world without end, in the place where you long held Adam and the children of the prophets.'

8. And then the glorious Lord stretched out his right hand, and said: 'All you my saints, you who bear my likeness, come to me; and you who were condemned by the fruit of the tree, you now see that through the tree of my cross on which I was hung you shall vanquish death and the Devil as well.' It was then that all the saints very rapidly drew near to the Saviour's hand. And then the Saviour took Adam by the right hand, and said to him: 'Peace be with you Adam, and with all your children.' Then falling down and kissing the Saviour's knees, and with tearful supplication and with a loud voice, Adam said thus: 'I praise you, Lord of heaven, that you wished to deliver me from this place of living torment.' And the Saviour then stretched out his hand and made the sign of the cross over Adam and over all his saints. And he plucked Adam out of hell by the right hand; and all the saints followed after them. And the holy David cried out thus with very loud voice, and said: 'Sing unto the Lord a new song of praise, for the Lord has revealed his wonderful works to all nations, and has made known his salvation in the sight of all nations and displayed his righteousness.'[1] Then all the saints answered him, and said: 'Praise be to the Lord for this, and glory to all his saints. Amen. Alleluia.'

---

[1] Cf. Psalm XCVII 1–2.

9. Then, holding Adam's hand and delivering them to the archangel Michael, the holy Lord himself journeyed into the heavens. All the saints followed after the archangel Michael, and he led them all into Paradise with glorious rejoicing. But as they were going inside, they met with two old men. And all the saints promptly questioned them, and spoke to them thus: 'Who are you, who were not in Hell with us and were not yet dead, and your bodies are together in Paradise notwithstanding?' The one answered them and said: 'I am Enoch, and I was brought here by the word of the Lord; and this is Elijah the Tishbite who is with me. He was conveyed here in a fiery chariot. And we two have not yet tasted death, but we must await Antichrist with divine signs and portents and fight against him; and we must be slain by him in Jerusalem, and he also by us. But within the space of three-and-a-half days we must be brought to life again and raised up in clouds.'[1]

10. But while Enoch and Elijah spoke thus, there came to them a certain man who was of wretched appearance, and bearing the sign of a cross upon his shoulders. And the saints then saw him straightaway, and said to him: 'Who are you, whose face is like a criminal's, and what is that sign that you bear upon your shoulders?' He answered them and said: 'You say truly that I was a criminal, doing all manner of evil on earth; but the Jews crucified me with the Saviour, and I saw then all those things that were done by the Saviour on the cross. And then I believed straight away that he was the Creator of all creation and the Almighty King; and I earnestly entreated him, and said thus: "O Lord, remember me when you come into your kingdom." And he immediately received my prayer, and he said to me: "Truly I say to you, today you will be with me in Paradise."[2] And he gave me this sign of the cross and said: "Go into Paradise with this sign, and if the angel who is the keeper at the gate of Paradise should refuse you entrance, show him this sign of the cross, and say to him that Christ the Saviour, God's Son who was now crucified, sent you there." And I then said all that to the angel who was the keeper there, and he immediately led me in on the right-hand side of the gate of Paradise; and he ordered me to wait, and said to me: "Wait here until all the race of men have gone in, the patriarch Adam

---

[1] Cf. Revelation, XI 9–12.
[2] Luke, XXIII 42–3.

with all his children and with all the saints who were with him in hell."'

And then all the patriarchs and the prophets, when they heard all the criminal's words, then they all said with one voice: 'Blessed be the Lord Almighty and the Everlasting Father who granted you such forgiveness of your sins and with such grace brought you to Paradise.' He answered and said: 'Amen!'

11. These are those divine and holy mysteries which the two prophets Carinus and Leuticus truly saw and heard, just as I said here previously when on this day they rose up from death with the Saviour, even as the Saviour woke them from death. And when they had written and completed all this, they got up and gave the papers that they had written to the elders. Carinus gave his paper to Annas and Caiaphas and Gamaliel; and similarly Leuticus gave his paper, delivered it into the hands of Nicodemus and Joseph; and said thus to them: 'Peace be with you all from the same Lord Saviour Christ and from the Saviour of us all.'

And then Carinus and Leuticus were suddenly as beautiful in appearance as the sun when it shines brightest; and in that brightness they departed from the people, so that the people did not know where they went. But when the elders and the priests read the document which Carinus and Leuticus had written, they were both written alike so that neither was the lesser or the greater than the other by one letter, nor even by one comma. And when the documents were read, all the Jewish people said between themselves: 'All these things which have here come to pass, are true; and blessed be the Lord for ever, world without end. Amen.' And each of the Jews went to his own home in great fear and beating his breast, inasmuch as they wished to make good what guilt they had with God. And then Joseph and Nicodemus went to Pilate the judge and told him all about the two prophets and about the documents which they wrote, and about all the proceedings which were previously hidden from him. So then in his judgement hall Pilate himself wrote down all those things that were done by the Saviour.

12. And afterwards he wrote a despatch and sent it to Rome to Claudius the King. And it was written thus:

'Pontius Pilate greets his lord King Claudius. And I make known to you what has recently happened: that because of their malice and because of their own humiliation, the Jews seized the Saviour and, moreover, delivered him to me, and greatly accused him and told many lies against him and said that he was a sorcerer, and also that he profaned each sabbath, for they saw that on the sabbath he brought light to blind men and healed lepers and drove out devils from men possessed and woke the dead, and wrought many other miracles. And I believed them, just as I ought not; and I ordered him to be scourged and afterwards gave him back to their own judgement; and afterwards they hung him on a wooden cross. And he was there dead, and afterwards he was buried; they placed forty-four soldiers at his tomb, who had to guard the body. But on the third day he rose up from death. And the guards told it all, and it could not be concealed. But when they heard that, the Jews gave the guards money to say that his disciples came and stole the body. And the guards took the money, and notwithstanding, could not keep silent the truth which had happened there. Now, dear king, I therefore advise you also, that you should never believe the lies of the Jews. Praise be to the Lord, and to the devils sorrow, ever world without end. Amen.'

WONDERS OF THE EAST

The description of legendary marvels in faraway places was a popular early genre, with probable origins in ancient Greek traveller's tales of the fabulous peoples of India. This particular compendium, which culls examples from a whole range of Classical authors, may ultimately derive from some such compilation as the so-called 'Epistle of Pharasmanes to the Emperor Hadrian'. Certain references, such as to the phoenix, the devilish horned serpents or the virtuous gold-mining ants, were well known to Church fathers like Augustine or the encyclopedist Isidore of Seville, who employed them in a figurative sense.

The Old English version possesses little enough literary merit, but is important in that it testifies to the interest of the Anglo-Saxons in the exotic orient. It consists of a series of brief sketches reporting those monstrous races and animals said by Classical and patristic authorities to inhabit the fringes of the world – especially the faraway east. There is added a paragraph (omitted in Knappe's edition) alluding to the Egyptian sorcerers Jamnis and Mambres and their attempts to counteract the miracles of Moses and Aaron.

The Old English text is preserved in two MSS. An abbreviated version, rather crudely illustrated, is included in the late tenth-century *Beowulf* manuscript: British Library MS. Cotton Vitellius A XV ff. 98^v–106^v. A rather better text is found in MS. Cotton Tiberius B V ff. 78^v–87^v, a handsomely illustrated miscellany, including writings by Cicero and Priscian, made probably at Canterbury in the first half of the eleventh century. In this the English is set out in alternate paragraphs with a Latin recension of the same text; its final pages are missing, but a full Latin version occurs in the early twelfth-century Bodleian Library, Oxford, MS. Bodley 614, ff. 36^r–51^v. The names of places or tribes are rarely identifiable. Although it follows no apparent geographical scheme, the language suggests that it may have derived from a world-map similar to the well-known Hereford Mappa Mundi; such a map is certainly included in the Tiberius MS. See generally J. B. Friedman, *The Monstrous Races in Medieval Art and Thought*, Cambridge, Mass., 1981.

The text was edited by Fritz Knappe, *Das angelsächsische Prosastück Die Wunder des Ostens*, Berlin, 1906, and a diplomatic transcript of the Vitellius text was printed by Stanley Rypins, *Three Old English Texts*, EETS., OS., CLXI, London, 1924, pp. 51–67. There are facsimile editions: of all three manuscripts by M. R. James, *Marvels of the East*, Oxford, 1929; and separately of the *Beowulf* MS. by Kemp Malone, *The Nowell Codex*, EEMF., XII, Copenhagen, 1963, and of the Tiberius MS. by P. McGurk *et al.*, *An Eleventh-Century Anglo-Saxon Illustrated Miscellany*, EEMF., XXI, Copenhagen, 1983.

1 The colony at the start of the country of Antimolima – which country is in number five-hundred of the lesser miles called *stadia*, and three-hundred-and-sixty-eight of the greater called *leagues*. On the island is a great host of sheep. And from there to Babylon it is a hundred-and-sixty-eight of the lesser *stadia* miles, and a hundred-and-fifteen of the greater miles called *leagues*.

2 The colony is much settled by merchants. Rams the size of oxen are born there. They dwell as far as the city of the Medes, the name of which city is Archemedon; it is the next greatest to the city of

Babylon. From Archemedon to there it is three-hundred of the lesser *stadia* miles, and two-hundred of the greater called *leagues*. The great wonders that are the works the great Macedonian, Alexander, ordered to be built are there. That country is in length and breadth two-hundred of the lesser *stadia* miles, and of the greater called *leagues* a hundred-and-thirty-three-and-a-half miles.

3   There is a place on the way to the Red Sea called Lentibelsinea, in which there are born hens like those among us, of a red colour. If anyone would catch or touches them, they immediately burn up all his body. Those are unheard-of sorceries.

4   Also wild animals are born there, which animals when they hear a man's voice, flee far away. Those animals have eight feet, and valkyrie's eyes and two heads. If anyone would seize them, they set fire to their bodies. Those are unheard-of animals.

5   Hascellentia is the name of the country through which men travel on the way to Babylonia; that is in length and breadth nine of the lesser miles called *stadia*. It is subject to the kingdom of the Medes. That country is wholly filled with good things. This place has serpents.

6   Those serpents have two heads whose eyes shine by night as bright as a lamp.

7   In a certain country are born asses which have horns as big as oxen's, and which are of the greatest fecundity. That is in the south part of Babylonia. They go to the Red Sea because of the many serpents that are in those places, which are called Corsias and which have horns as big as ram's. If they strike or touch anyone, then he expires immediately. In those lands is an abundance of pepper; that pepper the serpents protect in their zeal. One takes the pepper thus: by a man setting fire to the place, so that then the serpents flee from the hills into the earth. Therefore the pepper is black. From Babylonia to the Persian city where the pepper grows it is eight-hundred of the lesser miles called *stadia*, which makes six-hundred-and-twenty-three-and-a-half miles of the greater miles called *leagues*. The place is barren because of the hosts of serpents.

8 Also dog-headed men are born there who are called Conopoenas. They have a horse's mane, a boar's tusks and the

heads of dogs; and their breath is like a flame of fire. These lands are near the cities which are filled with all worldly wealth – that is in the south part of Egypt.

9 In a certain country men are born who are six feet tall in height. They have beards down to their knees and hair down to their heels. They are called *Homodubii*, that is, 'doubtfully men'; and they live on raw fish – and eat them.

10 Capi is the name of the river in the same place, which is called Gorgoneus, that is, 'son of the valkyrie'. Ants are born there as big as dogs. They have feet like grasshoppers. They are red and black in colour. Those ants dig up gold from the earth from before night until five o'clock of the day. Then men who are brave enough to take that gold bring with them camels: females with their foals, and males. The foals they tie up before they go over the river. They load the gold onto the females and themselves mount; and the males they leave. Then the ants find them, and while the ants are busy round the male camels, the men go over the river with the females and the gold. They are so swift that men imagine they are flying.[1]

11 Between these two rivers, that is, between the Nile and the Bryxontis, is situated a colony called Locotheo. The Nile is the chief of foul rivers and it goes through Egypt. And they call the river 'Archoboleta', which is to say, the Great Water. In these places are born the great hosts of elephants.

12 Men are born there who are fifteen feet tall, and they have a white body and two faces on one head, feet and knees very red, and a long nose and dark hair. When they want to reproduce, they travel in ships to India and there bring their kind into being.

13 Ciconia-in-Gallia is the name of the country where tricolored men are born. Their heads are maned like lions' heads and they are twenty feet tall and they have a great mouth like a fan. If they notice or see any man in those lands, or if anyone is following them, then they go far off and flee; and they sweat blood. These are thought to be men.

14 Beyond the river Bryxontis, east from there, men are born tall and big. They have feet and legs twelve feet long, sides and chest

---

[1] The Latin version points out that the females are keen to return to their foals.

seven feet long. They are of a black colour. And they are called *Hostes* – certainly whenever they seize anyone they devour him.

15   Then there are wild animals on the Bryxontis which are called *Lertices*. They have ass's ears, sheep's wool and bird's feet.

16   Then there is another island south of the Bryxontis on which men are born without heads, who have their eyes and mouth in their chests. They are eight feet tall and eight feet broad.

17   Dragons are born there which are in length one-hundred-and-fifty-feet long, and are as thick as great stone columns. Because of the size of the dragons, nobody can travel easily in that country.

18   From this place to another kingdom on the south side of the ocean, is measured three-hundred-and-twenty-three of the lesser *stadia* miles, and two-hundred-and-fifty-six of the greater called *leagues*. And *Homodubii*, that is 'doubtfully men', are born there. They have a human form down to the navel, and from there on the form of an ass. They have long legs like birds and a gentle voice. If they notice or see any man in those lands, then they go far off and flee.

19   Then there is another place in which there are foreign men. And they have kings under their power – a hundred-and-ten of them all told. Those are the worst men and the most foreign. Two lakes are there, one the sun's, the other the moon's. That which is the sun's is hot by day and cold by night. And that which is the moon's is hot by night and cold by day. Their width is two-hundred of the lesser miles called *stadia*, and a hundred-and-thirty-three-and-a-half of the greater called *leagues*.

20   In this place are kinds of trees which are similar to the laurel and the olive. From those trees the most precious oil, balsam, is all produced. The place is a hundred-and-fifty-one of the lesser miles called *stadia*, and fifty-one of the greater called *leagues*.

21   Then there is a certain island in the Red Sea where there is a race of men called by us Donestre. They are shaped like soothsayers from the head down to the navel, and the other part is similar to a man's body. And they know all human languages. When they see a man of foreign race, they call him and his fellows with the names of known men, and with lying words they deceive him and seize him. And then, after that, they devour all of him, except the head, and then they sit and weep over the head.

22 East from there, there are born men who in size are fifteen feet tall and ten feet in breadth. They have large heads, and ears like a fan. At night they spread one ear beneath them, and cover themselves with the other. Their ears are very light, and their bodies are as white as milk. And if they see or notice any man in those lands, then they take their ears in hand and flee rapidly – so quickly that it seems that they fly.

23 Then there is a certain island on which men are born whose eyes shine as brightly as if one had lit a great lamp on a dark night.

24 Then there is another island, which in length and in breadth is three-hundred-and-sixty of the lesser miles called *stadia*, and a hundred-and-ten of the greater called *leagues*. There was built there, in the days of Bel the king,[1] and Jove, a temple made out of wrought iron and of brass. And in the same place, east from there, is also another temple, sacred to the sun, in which is appointed a pious and gentle priest, and he guards the halls and takes care of them.

25 Then where the sun rises, there is a golden vineyard which has berries a hundred-and-fifty feet long. In those berries are produced something like pearls or gems.

26 Then there is another kingdom in the Babylonian lands where there is the biggest mountain between the Median mountain and Armenia. It is the biggest and highest of all mountains. Gentle men are there. They have for their kingdom and for their dominion the Red Sea. There precious jewels are produced.

27 Around these places are born women who have beards down to their chest; and they put on horses' skins for clothing. They have the name of great huntresses, and instead of dogs they train tigers and leopards, which are the fiercest animals. And they hunt all the kinds of wild animals which are born on the mountain.

28 Then there are other women who have boars' tusks and hair down to their heels and oxen's tails from their loins. These women are thirteen feet tall, and their bodies have the brightness of marble; and they have camel's feet and ass's teeth. Because of their uncleanliness they were slain by the great Macedonian,

---

[1] The god Baal, said to have been the founder of Babylon.

Alexander. When he could not take them alive, he killed them because they are foul in body and contemptible.

29 By the ocean is a race of wild animals called *Catini*. They are nobly beautiful animals. And men are there who live on raw flesh and honey.

30 In the left-hand part of the kingdom in which the *Catini* animals live, there are hospitable men – kings who have under them numerous princes to command. Their boundaries are near the ocean, and thence – from the left-hand part – come many kings.

31 This race of men lives many years, and they are generous men. And if anyone comes to them, then they give him a woman before they let him go away. The Macedonian, Alexander, when he came to them, was doubtful about their human nature. He did not wish to kill them nor to do them any harm.

32 Then there are kinds of trees upon which the most precious stones are produced, and from which they grow.

33 There is another race of men. They are of a black colour in appearance. One calls them Ethiopians.

34 Then there is a certain country in which vineyards grow profusely, where there is a couch made of ivory. It is three-hundred-and-six feet long.

35 Then there is a certain mountain called Adamans. On that mountain is the kind of bird called Griffin. Those birds have four feet, and a cow's tail, and an eagle's head.

36 In the same place is another kind of bird called a Phoenix. Those have crests on their heads like peacocks, and their nest – that they build from the most precious spices, which one calls cinnamon. And after a thousand years, it kindles a fire with its breath, and then rises up young again from the ashes.

37 Then there is another mountain where there are black men, and no other man may travel to those men because the mountain is all burning.

38 Here it tells how Mambres opened the magical books of his brother Jamnis, and to him was revealed the necromancy of his brother's devil-worship. Jamnis's soul answered him with these

words: 'You, brother! I am not unjustly dead, but I am truly and justly dead, and God's judgement goes against me because I in particular was wiser than all other magicians and I went against the two brothers called Moses and Aaron, who wrought those great tokens and portents.[1] Therefore I am dead and therefore I am brought to the midst of the kingdom of hell, where there is the great heat of eternal punishment and where there is a pool of perpetual torment from whence nobody ever ascends. Now, Mambres my brother, see that you do well to your sons and your friends in your life, because in hell there is nothing good, only gloom and darkness. And after you are dead, then you will come to hell, and your dwelling-place will be between dead men, down in the ground, and your pool will be two cubits wide and four long.'

39–50 The contents of the lost continuation of the text might be reconstructed from the Latin Bodley MS., which concludes with descriptions of: the rhinoceros/unicorn; mountains of gold guarded by dragons and griffins; the chameleon; two brothers in Asia, perpetually fighting and perpetually being healed by their sister; the race of Sciapodes, who use their single large foot as a sunshade; the Antipodes, whose feet point backwards; Hippodes, who have horse's feet; Hermaphrodites; a race with large lower lips which they use to shield their face from the sun; satyrs; parrots; and a group of Celtic British women condemned to dance forever.

[1] Cf. Exodus, VII 11f; 2 Timothy, III 8.

APOLLONIUS OF TYRE

The Apollonius story, which has affinities with other of the so-called 'Greek romances', probably originated during the second or third century in Hellenistic Asia Minor. But it was no doubt already well known in the West when Venantius Fortunatus, late sixth-century Bishop of Poitiers, alluded to the figure of Apollonius as a classic example of the exile (PL., LXXXVIII, 227). Translated into almost every language of medieval Europe, it was considered to be a 'mirror for princes' and a moral example for all Christians. Its popularity in England was enhanced by its inclusion in the Latin Gesta Romanorum, and it was treated at length in John Gower's Confessio Amantis VIII. Although described by Chaucer as a 'cursed story, a tale horrible for to rede' (The Man of Law's Tale, 80–4) it remained popular beyond the medieval period. It was the source of Shakespeare's Pericles.

The Old English version is found, together with several of Wulfstan's homilies, extracts from The Institutes of Polity, laws and other matters of interest to Wulfstan, in a mid-eleventh-century manuscript: Corpus Christi College, Cambridge, MS. 201B, pp. 131–45. At least one quire has been lost from the manuscript after p. 143, and the text is therefore incomplete at this point.

The text is edited, together with a parallel Latin text, by Peter Goolden, The Old English Apollonius of Tyre, Oxford, 1958.

Here begins the story about Antiochus, the wicked king, and about Apollonius the Tyrenian.

1. There was in the city of Antioch a certain king called Antiochus:[1] the city was called Antioch after the name of the king. This king's queen, by whom he had a very beautiful daughter of incredible loveliness, had departed from this life. When she came to marriageable age, many a great man longed for her, offering many splendid things. Then by an unhappy chance, it happened that when the father was thinking to whom he might best give her, his own heart fell in love with her with unlawful desire, to such an extent that he forgot fatherly piety and desired his own daughter for a wife. And that desire did not long delay, but at daybreak one day when he awoke from sleep, he broke into the chamber where she lay and commanded all his retinue to go away, as if he wanted some private conversation with his daughter. Well, then he engaged in that wicked sin, and with difficulty overcame the

[1] King of Syria 280–61 B.C.

struggling woman by greater strength – and wished to conceal the crime he had committed.

2. Then it happened that the girl's nurse went into the chamber and saw her sitting there in great perturbation, and said to her: 'Why are you so troubled in spirit, lady?' The girl answered her: 'Dear nurse, today two noble names have now perished in this chamber.' The nurse said: 'Of whom do you say that, lady?' She answered her and said: 'I am polluted with wicked sin before the day of my marriage.' Then said the nurse: 'Who ever was so rash of spirit that he dare defile a king's daughter before the day of her marriage, and not dread the king's wrath?' The girl said: 'Impiety has committed the crime against me.' The nurse said: 'Why do you not tell your father?' That girl said: 'Where is the father? Truly, in me, wretched one, my father's name has cruelly perished, and death therefore now is very desirable to me.' Then when the nurse heard that in fact the girl longed for her death, she addressed her with gentle speech and entreated her to turn her mind away from that wish and bow to her father's will, even though she were forced to it.

3. In fact the infamous king Antiochus persisted in this state of affairs, and with a feigned heart he represented himself to his citizens as though he were a pious father to his daughter, and among his household men he rejoiced that he was the husband of his own daughter. And so that he might enjoy his daughter's impious marriage-bed the longer and drive away from him those who longed for her in lawful marriage, he set them a riddle, saying: 'Let whichever man solves my riddle correctly take my daughter to wife, and let him who misinterprets it be beheaded.' Now what more is to be said but that kings and noblemen came from all sides on account of the girl's incredible beauty, and they scorned death and endeavoured to solve the riddle. But if any one of them, through the contemplation of book-like wisdom, solved the riddle correctly, then he was led out to execution in the same way as he who did not solve it correctly. And the heads were all set up over the gate.

4. While the cruel king Antiochus in fact persisted in this cruelty, there was a certain young man called Apollonius who was very wealthy and wise and was a nobleman in the province of Tyre,[1] who trusted in his wisdom and in book-learning and sailed

[1] The chief city of Phoenicia.

until he came to Antioch. He went into the king and said: 'All hail,
O king. Behold, now I come to you as a good and pious father. I
come in fact from a regal family, and I ask for your daughter as my
wife.' Then when the king heard that, he would not assent to his
wish. He looked on the young nobleman with a very angry face,
and said: 'Young man, do you know the condition of my
daughter's betrothal?' Apollonius said: 'I know the condition,
and I beheld it at the gate.' Then in wrath the king said: 'Now
hear the riddle: *Scelere vereor, materna carne vescor.*' That is in
English: 'I suffer crime, I enjoy mother's flesh.'[1] Again, he said:
'*Quaero patrem meum, meae matris virum, uxoris meae filiam
nec invenio.*' That is in English: 'I seek my father, my mother's
husband, my wife's daughter, and do not find them.' Then, truly,
having received the riddle, Apollonius turned himself a little from
the king, and when he had considered the sense he solved it with
wisdom, and with God's help he guessed the truth. Then he turned
to the king and said: 'You set a riddle, good king; hear then the
solution. When you said that you suffer crime, you are not lying in
that – look to yourself; and when you said "I enjoy mother's
flesh", you are not lying in that – look to your daughter.'

5. Then when the king heard that Apollonius had solved the
riddle correctly thus, he feared that it would be too widely known.
Then he looked at him with an angry face and said: 'You are far
from right, young man; you are wrong and what you say is
nonsense; so you have earned execution. Now I will allow you the
space of thirty days, so that you can think out the riddle correctly,
and then you shall receive my daughter to wife; and if you do not
do it you must undergo the sentence appointed.' Then Apollonius
became very anxious, and with his friends went on board ship and
sailed until he came to Tyre.

6. In fact after Apollonius had gone, Antiochus the king
summoned to him his steward, who was called Thaliarcus:
'Thaliarcus, my most trusty minister of all my secrets, you know
that Apollonius has solved my riddle correctly. Now quickly go
on board ship and go after him; and when you come to him, then
kill him with steel or with poison, that when you return you may
receive freedom.' Immediately Thaliarcus heard that, he took
with him both money and poison and went on board ship, and
went after the innocent Apollonius till he came to his native land.

[1] Both Latin and Old English versions of the riddle depend on the ambiguity inherent in
vescor/brucan, 'to feed on, taste', and 'to make use of, enjoy'.

But Apollonius came to his own first, however, and went into his house and opened his bookcase and contemplated the riddle in the light of the wisdom of all the philosophers and Chaldeans.[1] Then when he found nothing other than what he previously thought, he said to himself: 'What do you do now, Apollonius? You have guessed the king's riddle, and you have not received his daughter; wherefore you are now condemned to be killed.' And he went out then and ordered his ship to be loaded with wheat and with a great weight of gold and silver and with manifold and abundant garments; and thus with a few of the most loyal men he went on board at three o'clock in the morning, and set out to sea.

7. Then on the following day Apollonius was sought and asked for, but he was nowhere to be found. Then there rose up a great grief and excessive weeping, so that lamentation resounded throughout all the city. Indeed, all the citizens had so great a love for him that for a long time they went all unkempt and long-haired and abandoned their theatrical entertainments and locked up their baths. While these things were happening in Tyre, there came the aforesaid Thaliarcus who was sent by the king from Antioch in order to kill Apollonius. When he saw that all these places were locked up, he said to a boy: 'So you be healthy,[2] tell me for what reason this city abides in such great grief and woe.' The boy answered him, and spoke thus: 'Alas, what a wicked man you are, you who know what you ask about! Now what man is there who does not know that these citizens live in grief because since Apollonius the prince returned from Antiochus the king he has suddenly disappeared.' Then when Thaliarcus heard that, he returned to ship with great joy; and with sure sailing came to Antioch within one day, and went into the king and said: 'Lord king, be glad now and rejoice because Apollonius fears the power of your authority so that he dare not stay anywhere.' Then he, Antiochus the king, issued his proclamation, saying thus: 'Which-ever man brings Apollonius to me alive, I will give to him fifty pounds of gold; and he who brings me his head, I will give to him a hundred pounds of gold.' Then when this proclamation was thus issued, not only his enemies but also his friends were seduced by greed, and went after him and searched for him throughout all the earth, both in hill-country and in woodland and in hidden places. But he was nowhere to be found.

[1] A race noted for their astrology throughout medieval times.
[2] Whether this represents a greeting or a threat is unclear.

8. Then the king ordered ships to be prepared and go after him. But it was a long time before the ships were prepared, and before that Apollonius came to Tarsus.[1] Then one day he went along the beach. Whereupon one of his acquaintances who was named Hellanicus, who had come there first, saw him. Then he went up to Apollonius and said: 'Hail, Lord Apollonius.' Then, in the manner of powerful men, Apollonius scorned the humble man's greeting. Hellanicus immediately addressed him again, and said: 'Hail Apollonius, and do not scorn a humble man who is graced with honourable manners. But hear now from me what you yourself do not know. It is, in fact, very necessary for you to be on your guard, because you are condemned.' Then said Apollonius: 'Who could condemn me, a prince of my own nation?' Hellanicus said: 'Antiochus the king.' Apollonius said: 'For what reason has he condemned me?' Hellanicus said: 'Because you longed to be what the father is.' Apollonius said: 'Am I condemned harshly?' Hellanicus said: 'Whichever man brings you to him alive, he will receive fifty pounds of gold. He who brings him your head, will receive a hundred pounds of gold. I advise you to flee, therefore, and save your life.' After these words Hellanicus turned from him. And Apollonius ordered him to be called back to him, and said to him: 'You have done the worst by warning me. Now here, take a hundred pounds of gold from me and go to Antiochus the king and tell him that my head is cut from the neck. And bring that message to the delight of the king: then you will have reward and also hands clean of innocent blood.' Then said Hellanicus: 'Lord, it cannot be that I should take a reward from you for this business, because among good men neither gold nor silver compare with the friendship of a good man.' Then with these words they parted.

9. And Apollonius soon met another acquaintance coming towards him, whose name was called Stranguillo. 'Young Lord Apollonius, what are you doing in this country thus troubled in spirit?' Apollonius said: 'I heard tell that I was condemned.' Stranguillo said: 'Who condemned you?' Apollonius said: 'Antiochus the king.' Stranguillo said: 'For what reason?' Apollonius said: 'Because I asked for his daughter as my wife, of whom I may say, in truth, that she was his own wife. Wherefore, if I may, I will conceal myself in your country.' Then, said Stranguillo: 'Lord Apollonius, our city is impoverished and

---

[1] Capital of Cilicia.

cannot support your nobility, because we are suffering the severest and the cruellest famine, and there is no hope of salvation for my citizens, but the cruellest of deaths stands before our eyes.' Then Apollonius said: 'My dearest friend Stranguillo, thank God that he has led me to flee here to your borders. I will supply your citizens with a hundred thousand measures of wheat if you will conceal my flight.' When Stranguillo heard that, he prostrated himself at his feet and said: 'Lord Apollonius, if you help these hungry citizens, not only will we conceal your flight, but moreover, should need arise, we will fight for your safety.'

10. Then Apollonius mounted the tribunal in the street, and said to the citizens present: 'You citizens of Tarsus, I Apollonius, prince of Tyre, tell you that I believe you will remember this kindness and conceal my flight. You know also that Antiochus the king has driven me from my homeland; but by the aid of God, I have come here for your benefit. Truly, I will supply you with a hundred thousand measures of wheat for the price I bought it in my country.' Then when the people heard that, they were made joyful and earnestly thanked him and eagerly took up the wheat. Well, then Apollonius abandoned his royal rank and took the name of merchant rather than giver; and the price which he received for the wheat he immediately gave back again for the benefit of the city. Then the people became so joyful at his generosity and so grateful that they made a statue of him in bronze; and it stood in the street, and with the right hand held the wheat and with the left foot trod down the measure; and they wrote on it thus: 'The citizens of Tarsus gave this gift to Apollonius the Tyrenian, because he saved the people from famine and restored their city.'

11. After this, it happened that within a few months Stranguillo and his wife Dionysias advised Apollonius that he should go by ship to the Cyrenaican town of Pentapolis,[1] and said that he could be concealed there and stay there. And the people then led him to the ship with indescribable honour, and Apollonius bade them all farewell and went on board ship. Then when they had begun to sail and were advanced on their course, the serenity of the sea suddenly changed in the course of two hours and a great storm was stirred up, so that the sea beat against the stars of heaven and the rolling of the waves roared with the winds.

---

[1] Cyrene was a Hellenistic state in what is now Libya.

Moreover there came north-eastern winds and the dreadful south-western wind stood against them, and the ship completely broke up.

12. In this terrible storm all Apollonius' companions perished, and Apollonius alone by swimming came to the Cyrenaican land to Pentapolis, and there went up onto the beach. Then he stood naked on the beach, and gazed at the sea and said: 'Oh sea, Neptune, despoiler of men and deceiver of the innocent, you are more cruel than Antiochus the king! You have reserved this cruelty on my account, so that through you I should become poor and needy, and so that the cruellest king might destroy me the easier. Where can I go now? What can I ask for, or who will give sustenance to an unknown man?' While he was saying these things to himself, then suddenly he saw a certain fisherman walking along, towards whom he looked, and sorrowfully spoke thus: 'Take pity on me, old man, whoever you are; take pity on me, naked, shipwrecked, who was not born of poor birth; and so that you may clearly know in advance on whom you take pity, I am Apollonius, prince of Tyre.' Then immediately the fisherman saw that the young man lay at his feet, he lifted him up with compassion and brought him with him to his house and laid before him those dainties that he had to offer. Since he wanted to show him still more kindness, insofar as it lay in his power, he then tore his cloak in two and gave the half part to Apollonius, saying thus: 'Take what I have to give, and go into the city. Perhaps you may meet someone who will take pity on you. If you find no one who will take pity on you, turn back here and let my few possessions suffice for us both, and come fishing with me. However, I charge you, if through the aid of God you recover your former dignity, that you do not forget my poor garment.' Then said Apollonius: 'If I do not remember you when things go better for me, I hope that I may again suffer shipwreck, and not find someone like you again.'

13. After these words, he went along the way that was pointed out to him till he came to the city gate and went in there. While he was wondering whom he might ask for sustenance, he saw a naked youth running through the street, who was smeared with oil and girded with a cloth and carried in his hands young men's games appropriate to the gymnasium, and cried out in a loud voice and said: 'Listen you citizens, listen you strangers, free and slave, noble and common; the gymnasium is open!' Then when

Apollonius heard that, he stripped himself of the half-cloak he had on, and went into the bath; and while he gazed at each one of them in their occupation, he looked for his equal but he could not find him there among the company. Then suddenly there came Arcestrates, king of all that people, with a great crowd of his men, and went into the bath. Then with his companions the king began to play with a ball; and as God willed, Apollonius joined in the king's game; and running caught the ball, and striking with very great speed, sent it back to the playing king. Again he sent it back; he struck swiftly so that he never allowed it to fall. Then when the king perceived the young man's agility, so that he knew that he had not his equal in that game, he said to his companions: 'Go away. It seems to me this lad is my equal.' Then when Apollonius heard that the king praised him, he quickly ran and approached the king and with skilled hand whipped the top with such great rapidity that it seemed to the king as if he were changed from old age to youth; and after that he ministered to him agreeably on his throne. And then when he went out of the bath, he led him by the hand, and afterwards returned the way he had previously come.

14. Then after Apollonius had gone, the king said to his men: 'I swear by the common salvation that I never bathed better than I did today, because of which young man's service I know not.' Then he turned to one of his men and said: 'Go and find out who the young man is who served me so well today.' Then the man went after Apollonius. When he saw that he was dressed in a dirty cloak, he went back to the king and said: 'The young man whom you asked after, is a shipwrecked man.' Then the king said: 'How do you know that?' The man answered him and said: 'Although he should be silent about himself, his dress reveals it.' Then said the king: 'Go quickly and say to him that the king bids you come to his feast.' When Apollonius heard that, he obeyed and went along with the man until he came to the king's hall. Then the man went in first to the king and said: 'The shipwrecked man for whom you sent has come, but he cannot, for shame, enter without clothing.' Then the king ordered him to go immediately in to the feast. Then Apollonius went in and sat where he was directed, opposite the king. Then the service was carried in there, and after that a royal feast. And Apollonius ate nothing although all other men ate and were happy; but he gazed at the gold and the silver and the costly apparel and the tables and the royal plate. While he gazed at all this in sadness, a certain old and envious nobleman

was sitting by the king. When he saw that Apollonius sat so sorrowfully and gazed at all things and ate nothing, then he said to the king: 'Good king, behold, this man whom you have so much favoured is very envious of your wealth.' Then said the king: 'You are mistaken. In fact this young man envies nothing that he sees there. But he reveals that he has suffered great loss.' Then with a cheerful face Arcestrates the king turned to Apollonius and said: 'Young man, be happy with us and trust to God that you may yourself come to better things.'

15. While the king was saying these words, by chance the king's young daughter came in and kissed her father and those sitting around. Then when she came to Apollonius, she turned back to her father and said: 'Good king, and my dearest father, who is this young man who sits opposite you in so honourable a seat with a sorrowful face? I do not know what he is troubled about.' Then said the king: 'Dear daughter, this young man is shipwrecked; and he pleased me best of all men in the game, so I invited him to this feast of ours. I do not know who he is nor where he comes from. But if you want to know who he is, ask him, because it is proper that you should know.' Then the girl went to Apollonius and with respectful words said: 'Although you are silent and unhappy, I still see in you your noble birth. Now therefore, if it does not seem too grievous, tell me your name and relate to me what has happened to you.' Then Apollonius said: 'If you needs must ask for my name, I tell you that I lost it at sea. If you want to know my nobility, know that I left it in Tarsus.' The girl said: 'Tell me more exactly, so that I can understand.'

16. Then Apollonius told her truly all his circumstances, and at the end of the speech tears fell from his eyes. When the king saw that, he turned himself towards his daughter and said: 'Dear daughter, you have done wrong. In wanting to know his name and what has happened to him, you have now renewed his old sorrow. But I bid you give him whatever you will.' Then when the girl heard that her father permitted what she herself already wished to do, then said she to Apollonius: 'Apollonius, you are truly one of us! Leave your grief; and now I have my father's leave, I will make you wealthy.' Apollonius thanked her for this. And the king rejoiced at his daughter's kindness, and said to her: 'Dear daughter, order your harp to be fetched, entertain your friends and take away the young man's sadness.' Then she went out and ordered her harp to be fetched; and as soon as she began to play,

she accompanied the sound of the harp with beautiful song. Then all the men began to praise her for her musical skill, and Apollonius alone kept silent. Then said the king: 'Apollonius, now you are doing wrong, because all men praise my daughter for her musical skill and you alone censure her by remaining silent.' Apollonius said: 'Oh you good king, if you will forgive me, I say that I perceive that your daughter has fallen into the way of musical skill, but she has not learned it well. But order the harp to be given to me now; then you will understand what you do not yet understand.' Arcestrates the king said: 'Apollonius, I know truly that you are well taught in all things.' Then the king ordered Apollonius to be given the harp. Then Apollonius went out and dressed himself and set a garland on his head and took the harp in his hand and went in and stood thus, so that the king and all those sitting around imagined that he was not Apollonius but that he was Apollo, the god of the heathens. Then there was stillness and silence within the hall. And Apollonius took his plectrum and began to strike the harp-strings with skill, and accompanied the sound of the harp with beautiful song. And the king himself and all who were present there called out with a loud voice and praised him. After this Apollonius left the harp and played and performed there many pleasing things, which were unknown and unfamiliar in that country; and each of the things he performed pleased them all greatly.

17. Truly, when the king's daughter saw that Apollonius was so well educated in all accomplishments, then her heart fell in love with him. Then at the end of the entertainment, the girl said to the king: 'Dear father, a little earlier you gave me permission to give Apollonius whatever I wanted from your treasure.' Arcestrates the king said to her: 'Give him whatever you want.' She then went out very happy and said: 'Master Apollonius, with my father's permission, I give you two hundred pounds in gold and four hundred pounds weight of silver, and a great quantity of costly clothing, and twenty serving-men.' And she then said to the serving men thus: 'Carry with you these things which I have promised my master Apollonius, and lay them within the chamber in front of my friend.' Then this was done thus according to the princess' command, and all those men who saw her gifts praised them. Then in fact the entertainment ended, and everybody got up and addressed the king and the queen, and bade them farewell, and went home. Similarly Apollonius said: 'Farewell

good king and pitier of the poor, and you princess, lover of learning.' Then he turned to the serving-men that the girl had given him, and said to them: 'Take these things with you that the princess has given me, and let us go and seek our lodgings so that we may rest.' Then the girl was afraid that she might not see Apollonius again as soon as she would wish, and went then to her father and said: 'Good king, are you content that Apollonius, who has been enriched by us today, should go hence and that evil men should come and rob him?' The king said: 'You are right. Bid them find him a place where he may rest most honourably.' Then the girl did as she was commanded, and Apollonius accepted the dwelling that was assigned to him, and entered, thanking God who had not denied him regal dignity and comfort.

18. But the girl had a restless night, inflamed with love of the works and songs that she had heard from Apollonius. And when it was day she could wait no longer, but as soon as it was light went and stood beside her father's bed. Then said the king: 'Dear daughter, why are you awake so early?' The girl said: 'The accomplishments which I heard yesterday kept me awake. Now I entreat you, therefore, that you entrust me to our guest Apollonius for instruction.' Then the king was very pleased, and ordered Apollonius to be fetched and said to him: 'My daughter longs to be instructed by you in the delightful arts you possess; and if you will agree to this, I swear to you by the power of my kingdom, that whatever you lost at sea I will restore to you on land.' Then when Apollonius heard that, he accepted the girl for instruction, and taught her as well as he himself had learned.

19. Then it happened a few hours after this, that Arcestrates the king held Apollonius hand in hand and thus went out into the city street. Then at length there came walking towards them three learned and nobly-born men, who for a long time had desired the king's daughter. Then they all three together greeted the king with one voice. Then the king smiled and turned to them and said thus: 'What is it, that you greet me with one voice?' Then one of them answered and said: 'We asked for your daughter long ago and you have continually tormented us by delay. Therefore we have come here today together thus. We are your citizens, born of noble family. Now we entreat you to choose which of us three you want to have as son-in-law.' Then said the king: 'You have not hit upon a good time. My daughter is now very busy with her studies. But lest I should delay you longer, write down your names and her

marriage-gift in a letter; then I will send the letters to my daughter so that she herself may choose which of you she wants.' Then the young men did so, and the king took the letters and sealed them with his ring and gave them to Apollonius, saying thus: 'Now Master Apollonius, if you do not object, take and carry them to your pupil.'

20. Then Apollonius took the letters and went to the royal hall. Then when the girl saw Apollonius she said: 'Master, why do you come alone like this?' Apollonius said: 'Lady, you are not yet a woman of ill repute! Take and read these letters which your father sends you.' The girl took them and read the names of the three young men, but she did not find there the name she wanted. When she had read over the letters, then she turned to Apollonius and said: 'Master, wouldn't it grieve you if I should choose a husband thus?' Apollonius said: 'No. But I should rejoice much more if you could, through the instruction which you have received from me, yourself declare in writing which one of them you want. My wish is that you should choose a husband whom you yourself wish.' The girl said: 'Oh master, if you loved me, you would be sorry about it.' After these words she, with a resolute mind, wrote another letter and sealed it and gave it to Apollonius. Apollonius then carried it out into the street and gave it to the king. The letter was written thus: 'Good king, and my dearest father, now that your kindness has given me permission to choose for myself what husband I wanted, I say to you truly, I want the shipwrecked man; and if you should wonder that so modest a woman wrote those words so shamelessly, then know that I have declared by means of wax, which knows no shame, what I could not for shame say to you myself.'

21. Then when the king had read over the letter, he did not know which shipwrecked man she meant. Then he turned to the three young men and said: 'Which of you has been shipwrecked?' Then one of them who was called Arcadius said: 'I have been shipwrecked.' Another answered him and said: 'You keep quiet! Plague take you, so that you be neither whole nor sound! You studied book-learning with me, and you have never been outside the city gates without me. Where did you suffer shipwreck?' When the king could not find which of them had been ship-wrecked, he turned to Apollonius and said: 'Apollonius, you take this letter and read it. It may well be that you who were present there may know what I do not know.' Then Apollonius took and

read the letter, and as soon as he realized that he was loved by the girl his face completely reddened. When the king saw that, then he took Apollonius' hand and went with him a little apart from the young men, and said: 'Do you know the shipwrecked man?' Apollonius said: 'Good king, if you please, I know him.' When the king saw that Apollonius was all suffused with blushes, then he understood the remark and said to him thus: 'Rejoice, rejoice, Apollonius, for my daughter desires that which is my will! Nor truly, may anything happen in such matters except by the will of God.' Arcestrates turned to the young men and said: 'What I said to you earlier – that you did not come at a suitable time to ask for my daughter – is true; but when she can be freed from her studies, then I will send you word.' Then they went home with this answer.

22. And Arcestrates the king therefore held Apollonius' hand, and led him home with him, not as if he were a visitor, but as if he were his son-in-law. Then eventually he let go of Apollonius' hand and went alone into the chamber where his daughter was and spoke thus: 'Dear daughter, whom have you chosen as a husband?' The girl then fell at her father's feet and said: 'Kind father, listen to your daughter's desire. I love the shipwrecked man who was betrayed by misfortune. But lest you are unclear as to those words, I want Apollonius, my teacher, and if you will not give him to me you forsake your daughter.' Then truly the king could not bear his daughter's tears, but raised her up and said to her: 'Dear daughter, do not be afraid for anything. You have chosen the man that pleases me well.' Then he went out and turned to Apollonius and said: 'Master Apollonius, I have enquired into the desire of my daughter's heart. Weeping she then told me these things, saying thus among other words: "You swore to Apollonius that if he would assent to my wish and teach me, you would restore to him whatever the sea took away from him. Now, because he was obedient to your command and my wish, I went after him . . ." '

At this point several chapters have been lost from the manuscript, but the plot may be restored from the Latin versions:

Apollonius marries the princess, who is called Arcestrate after her father, and she becomes pregnant. He learns of the death of King Antiochus and that he himself is now King of Tyre. During a storm on the return journey to Antioch, his wife prematurely gives birth to a girl, and apparently dies. Her body is sealed in a chest and dropped overboard, and is subsequently washed up at Ephesus. She is found to be alive, and chooses to become a priestess in the temple of Diana.

Apollonius puts in at Tarsus and entrusts his daughter, whom he names Thasia, to the care of a nurse called Dionysias and her husband Stranguillo. Some years later Dionysias, discomfited because her own daughter seems ugly compared with the teenage Thasia, orders her steward to kill the princess and throw her body into the sea. On the beach she is allowed to pray before dying, and in the interval she is abducted by pirates. The steward reports that the princess has been killed, and a monument is erected to her memory. The pirates sell Thasia to a brothel in Mitylene.[1] But by relating her sad story to its clients, she manages to retain her virginity.

Returning to Tarsus, Apollonius is told that his daughter is dead. On his return journey he is driven out of his way by a storm and arrives at Mitylene. He remains on board grieving. Thasia is sent to see if she can console him with music and riddles. In the course of conversation, Thasia's own story is revealed and she is thus recognized by Apollonius at his lost daughter. The brothel-keeper is burnt alive; and Thasia is married to Athenagoras, prince of Mitylene, who had previously fallen in love with her.

About to return to his own country together with his daughter and son-in-law, Apollonius is instructed by an angel in a dream to visit the temple of Diana at Ephesus. There they ask to see the priestess.

48. . . . Then it was made known to her who was the leader there, that a certain king with his son-in-law and with his daughter had come there with great gifts. When she heard that, she decked herself in regal dress and clothed herself with purple and adorned her head with gold and with jewels; and surrounded by a large company of women came towards the king. She was indeed very beautiful and because of her great love of purity they all said that there was none so pleasing to Diana as she. When Apollonius saw that, he ran to her with his son-in-law and daughter, and all fell at her feet, and imagined that she were the goddess Diana because of her great radiance and beauty. Then the temple was opened and the offerings were brought in; and Apollonius then began to speak and say: 'From childhood I was named Apollonius, born in Tyre. When I came to full understanding, there was no art that was practised by kings or by noblemen that I did not know. I solved the riddle of Antiochus the king so that I might receive his daughter as my wife. But he himself was united with her in the foulest filth, and then plotted to kill me.

---

[1] Capital of the island of Lesbos.

Then when I fled from that, I was shipwrecked at sea and came to Cyrene. Then the king, Arcestrates, harboured me with such great love that eventually I merited being given his only-begotten daughter as wife. She then went with me to take up my kingdom; at sea she gave birth to this my daughter – whom I have presented before thee, Diana – and she gave up her spirit. Then I clothed her in regal dress and laid her in a chest with gold and a letter, so that he who found her should bury her honourably. And I entrusted this my daughter to the most wicked of people to nurse. Then in grief I travelled for fourteen years in the land of Egypt. Then when I returned, they told me that my daughter was dead and my sorrow was completely renewed in me.'

49. When he had related all these things, Arcestrate – his wife in fact – rose up and embraced him. Apollonius did not then know nor believe that she was his wife, but pushed her away from him. Then she cried out with a loud voice and said with weeping: 'I am Arcestrate your wife, daughter of Arcestrates the king, and you are Apollonius my teacher, who taught me; you are the shipwrecked man that I loved, not for lust but for wisdom. Where is my daughter?' Then he turned to Thasia, and said: 'This is she.' And then they all wept and rejoiced also. And the word spread throughout all the land that Apollonius, the famous king, had found his wife; and there was tremendous rejoicing and the organs were played and the trumpets blown, and a joyful feast was prepared by the king and the people. And she[1] made her disciple who attended her, priestess; and with the joy and weeping of all the province of Ephesus she went with her husband and with her son-in-law and with her daughter to Antioch, where the kingdom was kept for Apollonius.

50. Then afterwards he went to Tyre and placed Athenagoras, his son-in-law, as king there. Then indeed, from there he went to Tarsus with his wife and with his daughter and with a royal army, and ordered Stranguillo and Dionysias to be immediately seized and led in front of him where he sat on his throne. Then when they were brought, he said before all the assembly: 'You citizens of Tarsus, would you say that I Apollonius, ever did you any harm?' Then they all answered with a single voice and said: 'We always said that you were our king and father, and that we would gladly die for you because you saved us from famine.' Then Apollonius

---

[1] Arcestrate.

said: 'I entrusted my daughter to Stranguillo and Dionysias, and they would not then give her back to me.' That wicked woman said: 'Do not you well know, lord, that you read the inscription on her tomb yourself?' Then Apollonius called out very loud and said: 'Dear daughter Thasia, if there be any understanding in hell leave that infernal hall and listen to your father's voice.' The girl then stepped forth clothed in regal dress and uncovered her head and said loudly to the wicked woman: 'Hail to you Dionysias. I greet you now, summoned from hell.' Then the guilty woman trembled in all limbs when she looked at her; and the citizens marvelled and rejoiced. Then Thasia commanded Theophilus, Dionysias' steward, to be led before her, and said to him: 'Theophilus, in order to save yourself, say in a loud voice who ordered you to kill me.' The steward said: 'Dionysias, my lady.' So, then the citizens led Stranguillo and his wife out of the city and stoned them to death, and wanted to slay Theophilus also. But Thasia interceded for him and said: 'If this man had not granted me an interval to pray to God, I should not have come to this honour.' Then indeed, she extended her hand to him and bade him go in safety; and Thasia took to herself Philothemia, the daughter of the guilty woman.

51. Apollonius then, indeed, gave the people great gifts to rejoice them; and their walls were restored. Then he stayed there six months and afterwards went by ship to the Cyrenaican town of Pentapolis, and came to Arcestrates the king; and the king rejoiced in his old age that he saw his granddaughter with her husband. They remained together for fully one year. And afterwards Arcestrates the king, very old, died among them all, and bequeathed his kingdom half to Apollonius and half to his daughter.

All these things being thus done, Apollonius the famous king walked by the sea. Then he saw the old fisherman who had previously harboured him when naked. Then the king ordered him to be suddenly seized and led to the royal hall. Then when the fisherman saw that the soldiers wanted to take him, he imagined at first that they were to slay him. But then when he came into the king's hall, the king ordered him to be led before the queen, and said thus: 'Oh happy queen, this is my standard-bearer, who harboured me when naked, and directed me so that I came to you.' Then Apollonius the king turned to the fisherman and said: 'Oh kind old man, I am Apollonius the Tyrenian, to whom you gave half your cloak.' Then the king gave him two hundred gold pence, and kept him as a retainer for as long as he lived. Then Hellanicus – who had previously made known to him what Antiochus the king had decreed concerning him – also came to him, and he said to the king: 'Lord king, remember Hellanicus, your servant.' Then Apollonius took him by the hand and raised him up and kissed him, and made him wealthy and placed him as one of his retainers.

After all this, Apollonius the king begot a son by his wife, whom he set as king in the kingdom of Arcestrates his grandfather. And he himself lived benevolently with his wife for seventy-seven years and held the kingdom in Antioch and in Tyre and in Cyrene; and he lived in peace and happiness all the days of his life after his hardship. And he himself composed two books about his adventure, and put one in the temple of Diana, the other in the library.

Here ends both the misery and happiness of Apollonius the Tyrenian; let him who wishes read it. And if anyone read it, I beg that he will not blame the translation, but that he will conceal whatever may be blameworthy in it.

A COLLECTION OF PROVERBS

This Old English collection of apophthegms was based largely on selections from the so-called *Distichs of Cato*, although it includes also sentences from the Alfredian Boethius and the Book of Deuteronomy, as well as native proverbial lore. Attributed to the Republican statesman Marcus Porcius Cato, the *Distichs* seem in reality to have been composed some time during the third or fourth centuries A.D. It became a favourite medieval school-book, used to teach grammar, rhetoric and metrics, and familiar to authors like Alcuin and Chaucer. Several Middle English verse translations exist, and it was drawn upon by the so-called *Proverbs of Alfred*.

Three twelfth-century copies of the Old English version exist: Trinity College, Cambridge, MS. R.9.17, ff. 45–8ᵛ; British Library MSS. Cotton Vespasian D.XIV, ff. 7–11ᵛ and Cotton Julius A.II, ff. 141–4ᵛ; the first added to a copy of Ælfric's Grammar, and the second included in a collection of homilies largely by Ælfric.

The Vespasian text was printed by R. D. N. Warner, *Early English Homilies*, EETS., O. S., CLII, London, 1917, pp. 3–7; and there is a full critical edition by R. Cox in *Anglia*, 90 (1972), 1–42.

In the wisdom of his heart a man ought to adorn himself with wise precepts.

Don't be too keen on sleeping and fond of idleness, because sleep and idleness nourish bad habits and sickness of the body.

We declare that the best thing in the sight of God is that a man be discreet, and appreciate how to moderate both his speech and his silence, and know when he has been answered.

When you blame another man, remember that no one is without sin.

If your wife accuse anyone to you, don't believe it too quickly, because she often makes many a one her enemy because they are more faithful to her lord than her; because she often hates what her lord loves.

Don't argue with an obstinate man, or a verbose one; it is given to many to be able to speak, and to very few to be discreet.

Be more grateful for what you have, than for what men promise you; nor hope too much for what men promise you: where little is promised, there is little lying.

Don't be too obstinate, because it is better that you be confuted with right than that you confute another man with wrong; the greatest honour is that a man know what is right, and then want to submit to it.

Speak about other men's good deeds more often than about your own, and tell them to many men.

When you're old and asked for many old sayings and proverbs, then make them known to the young.

If a man accuse you of any wrong, and you know yourself innocent, don't pay attention to what they discuss or whisper; they denounce what they themselves are thinking.

When you are happiest then remember that you may suffer misfortune, if it should come upon you: because the end and the beginning are not always alike.

Don't hope for another man's death: who will live longest is unknown.

If a poor friend give you a little, take it with great thanks.

If you become poor, remember to put up with it willingly: remember that your mother gave birth to you naked.

Don't fear death too much; man can't live happily as long as he fears death. But don't forget it completely, lest you lose the life eternal.

If a man repay the good you do with evil, don't blame it on God, but look to yourself.

A man will more often keep what he has if he is afraid of losing it; the man who doesn't want to ruin himself spends sparingly.

If you have children, teach them trades so that they may live by them; how property may fall to them is uncertain. A trade is better than property.

Don't promise anything twice: why should it be promised again, unless it were a lie before?

Don't consider what you anticipate a certainty: give greater thanks for what you have than for what you hope to have.

Don't be too irascible: out of anger grows hatred, and out of gentleness, love.

Where you must needs be angry, still be moderate.

Often forbear where you may easily take revenge: patience is halfway to happiness.

Help both the known and the unknown where you can; who will have need of another is unknown.

Don't wish to know about heavenly matters beyond your ability; since you are an earthly man, enquire about that.

Don't be too stubborn in your anger, for anger often distracts a man's mind so that he cannot tell what is right.

Be satisfied with what you have. It is less dangerous in a little ship and a little water than in a great ship and a great water.

Don't imagine that the evil man gains any benefit from his evil, because although it be concealed for a while, at a certain time it will be revealed.

When you scorn a younger man than you are, or a less wise or a less prosperous one, then remember how often a man may surpass the one who previously surpassed him; just as they say in the old proverb: 'Sometimes it's the servant's time, sometimes another's.'

Don't try to find out what is going to happen to you by casting lots, but do the best you can; God will easily decide his will respecting you and your need, although he doesn't tell it you beforehand.

Avoid being envious of another man's good fortune, because you'll distress yourself more than him.

Don't despair too much if you be judged wrongly; few men rejoice for long in what they defraud another.

If you should have a dispute with someone and then become reconciled again, don't refer to the earlier wrongs unless they renew them again.

Do neither: don't praise yourself nor belie yourself; both of those are the habit of foolish men who toil after vain-glory.

It is sublime wisdom that a wise man should profess folly, and it is the greatest folly that a foolish man should profess wisdom.

The more a man talks, the less people believe him.

If you should do something wrong when drunk, don't blame it on the ale, because you yourself had control of it.

Have no zeal for evil, whatever displease you; often fate will bring about what you wish, which in the event brings recompense.

Never come to so ill a pass that you don't hope for improvement, for that hope will never let you perish.

Choose no man for his wealth, neither dissipate your own; many a man has much hair on his forehead, and yet suddenly becomes bald.

Concern yourself with certain men, because every man's life is a lesson for someone.

Don't keep silent about a wrong that is done, lest men suppose that it pleases you.

If anyone should condemn you justly, bear it well and be well content with it.

Speak with moderation and also behave thus, lest men accuse you of lying, where you imagine that you display your virtues.

Don't listen to the words of an indiscriminate man, for many a man has the bad habit that he does not know how to speak to any purpose, and yet cannot keep silent.

It is foolish for a man to speak before he think.

Pay no attention to the words of an angry woman, because she will often deceive you with weeping.

Don't fear death too much on any account; while you won't think it wholly good, it is the end of every evil, and it never comes twice.

Renounce the pride of this world if you want to be rich in your spirit; for those who covet wealth are always impoverished and pitiful in their spirit; but be content with your condition: then you will always have enough.

If you should harm your own, don't blame it on God, but look to yourself.

Enjoy your possessions while you're healthy; the sick miser owns money but does not own himself.

Suffer very gladly the anger of your lord and your teacher, and his words, though he chide you.

If you think that you're too lecherous blame it on your throat, because the throat is a friend to the belly, where the worthless desires come from.

It is a foolish man who fears the beasts and wolves but doesn't fear the man who teaches him well.

If you have strength, use it to advantage.

If you want to be of good report, don't rejoice in any wrong.

Always learn something; though your wealth should desert you, your trade will not desert you.

Don't be too loquacious, but listen to each man's words very keenly: because words reveal each man's disposition and his manners, though they should conceal them for a time.

If you know any skill, follow it keenly; just as sorrow and anxiety enhance a man's spirit, so a skill adds to his honour.

Always learn something from the wise, so that you can teach the unwise; either is a very useful and proper activity.

If you want to be healthy, drink in moderation; all surfeit and all idleness nourishes sickness.

Don't leave unpraised what you plainly perceive to be estimable. Where you are in doubt, praise in moderation, lest they accuse you of lying.

Don't trust calm water, neither scorn a gentle man: quiet water often breaks down the bank.

Embark upon what you can accomplish, for it is safer to row by the shore than to sail out on the sea.

If, in prosperity, anything amiss should happen to you, ask yourself whether anything similar has occurred before; then you might endure it the more easily.

Don't quarrel with a righteous man and with the guiltless, for God avenges unjust judgements.

If your old friend should anger you, don't forget that he always pleased you before.

Plough with your oxen and sacrifice with your incense: those men are foolish who imagine that they please God when they slaughter their oxen.

Every day you are afraid, you ought to thank God for your life.

Though many a man praise you, don't believe them too much, but consider what the truth of it is yourself. Avoid being put to shame by the reputation, if a man should lie about you; be glad if someone tell the truth, even if in moderation.

Mix happiness with sorrow; because if either of them exists for long without the other, then it is unbalanced, and you might endure what comes upon you the less easily; for neither of them can be perfect without the other, any more than wetness can exist without dryness, or warmth without cold, or light without darkness.

Study many books and listen to many accounts; but know what you should believe: men write many things without believing.

Don't spoil what you have, lest you should have need of another man's.

Don't worry too much how fortune may wander; he who wholly scorns this world does not greatly fear death.

Whenever it is most peaceful, then fear discord; and when it seems most dangerous, then hope for comfort and good fortune.

Always be more faithful than men believe you to be, lest they suppose that your word is only to be relied upon when your reputation is at stake.

He who is always afraid, is like him who is always dying.

If you want to make yourself superior to many, then make

yourself inferior to one. If you want many to flatter you, then very keenly flatter a particular one. If you don't want to flatter anyone, then abandon all that you possess, except for food and clothing and such tools as you use – then flatter God alone and don't wish for any man's flattery.

If you want to get what you like from many men, you must also put up with what you don't like from many men. If you want to get what you like from any men, you must often allow what you don't like in them. You cannot have the good from any man unless you can sometimes allow for his bad; for nothing is wholly good but God alone.

But correct each wrong as best you may, however, so that you don't bring it to a worse pass; that wrong is in no way improved which is brought to a worse pass.

Moderation looks for nothing better.

If any man be the less honourable because many a wise man despises him, then every foolish man will be the less honourable the greater power he has.

In every river, the worse the ford the better the fish.

Which of the two should praise the merchandise: he who has to sell it or he who wants to buy it?

Woe to the nation that has a foreign king – immoderate, eager for money and hard-hearted – for his greed will be on the nation and the discontent of his heart on his land.

He who wants power over his lord wants it for two reasons. One of two: either he wants the lord to lie below him, to ensure that he himself sits the higher; or he would raise the lord up over himself, and himself step up afterwards and hang onto him also, but always push the lord in front.

Don't ask the advice of any wizard, or seek direction from the dead; truly God shuns such things.

Take no bribe, for it blinds the thoughts of wise men and perverts the words of the righteous.

BALD'S LEECHBOOK

The tenth-century Winchester manuscript, British Library Royal MS. 12 D xvii, known as Bald's Leechbook, consists of three collections of medical and quasi-medical prescriptions. Each is preceded by a detailed list of contents. The first comprises a series of eighty-eight remedies for particular disorders, beginning with those of the head and working downwards. The second is a rather more learned account of internal disorders, including symptoms and attempts at diagnosis. This ends on f. 109 with a Latin colophon which tells how the book was written by the scribe Cild at the instance of a certain Bald. The third part is apparently an addition, covering much the same ground as that of the first part, although including more openly magical material. The final prescriptions are missing, and perhaps this part also originally ended with a descriptive colophon.

The Leechbook displays considerable original knowledge of native plants. Other information derives from Classical manuals like that of the sixth-century Byzantine physician Alexander of Tralles. But it also includes prescriptions sent to King Alfred by Elias, Patriarch of Jerusalem, c. 879–907, as well as others developed by native physicians two of whom, Dun and Oxa, are mentioned by name.

A complete facsimile of the manuscript was edited by C. E. Wright, *Bald's Leechbook*, EEMF., V, Copenhagen, 1955. The text was edited by T. O. Cockayne, *Leechdoms, Wortcunning, and Starcraft of Early England*, London, 1864–6, vol. II, and G. Leonhardi, *Kleinere angelsächsische Denkmäler*, 1, in Grein's Bibliothek der angelsächsischen Prosa, VI, Hamburg, 1905. A modern edition is being prepared for publication by Marilyn Deegan.

I 36. For the sickness which they call 'shingles': take the bark of quickbeam, and aspen, and apple, maple, elder, willow, sallow, myrtle, wych-elm, oak, blackthorn, birch, olive, dogwood; there should be most of the ash-tree, and except for hawthorn and alder, some from every tree which one can get – of most of the trees which are written here; and also: bog-myrtle and butcher's broom, house-leek, elecampane, radish, dwarf elder, the great nettle, wormwood, centaury. Then take a ten-amber cauldron, put in a third part of the barks and of the herbs, boil strongly in unfermented beer, if you have it (if you haven't got it, boil hard in water), then remove the barks and put fresh ones into the same juice; do thus three times, then strain the potion clean, very hot, and then add a basin-full of butter, very hot, and stir together. Let it stand for two or three days, then remove the butter. And then take bog-myrtle catkins, and bunches of ivy berries, tansy and betony, elecampane, knapweed, basil; beat together; boil in the butter; then remove the herbs from the butter completely, so far as one can; then take fine barley-flour and burnt salt; then make a pottage with the butter and stir it without heat, and add pepper. Then let him eat the pottage first, fasting for a night. Then afterwards let him drink the potion and no other liquid for ten days, thirty if he can. Then take mistletoe from an oak, beat it fine and dry it and rub down to flour; then weigh out a penny-weight; put that into the best wine; let him drink that for nine days, and eat neither new cheese, nor fresh goose, nor fresh eel, nor fresh pork, nor anything which comes from a wine-decoction, nor fishes without shells, nor web-footed birds; if he eat any of these, let it be salted; and let him not drink beer, and wine and ale only in moderation. If one follows this remedy, then the man will be healthy.

For shingles, take water dock, beat it very fine, boil a good handful in an old wine decoction, remove the herbs, add a second handful of the same herb again; boil hard again, then remove the herbs; then take sulphur, beat it very fine, then add it to the salve until it is as thick as pottage; then anoint the blotches with the salve until he is well.

I 68. In case a poisonous spider — that is the stronger one — should bite a man, cut three incisions close to and running away from it; let the blood run into a green hazel-wood spoon, then throw it away over the road so there will be no injury. Again; cut one incision on the wound, pound a plantain, lay it on; no harm will come to him. For the bite of a weaving-spider, take the lower part of æferthe and lichen from a black-thorn; dry it to powder, moisten with honey; treat the wound with that. For the bite of a poisonous spider: black snails fried in a hot pan and ground to powder, and pepper and betony; one is to eat that powder, and drink it and apply it. For the bite of a poisonous spider: take the lower part of mallow; apply it to the wound. Again: cut five incisions, one on the bite and four around about; in silence, cast the blood with a spoon over the waggon-road.

I 69. For the bite of a mad dog: mix agrimony and plantain with honey and the white of an egg; treat the wound with that. For a wound from a dog: boil burdock and groundsel in butter; anoint with that. Again: bruise betony; apply it to the bite. Again: beat plantain; apply it. Again: seethe two or three onions; roast them on ashes; mix with fat and honey, apply it. Again: burn a pig's jaw to ashes; sprinkle on. Again: take plantain root; pound it with fat; apply it to the wound so it casts out the poison.

I 70. If a man be over-virile, boil water agrimony in welsh ale; he is to drink it at night, fasting. If a man be insufficiently virile, boil the same herb in milk; then you will excite it. Again: boil in ewe's milk: water agrimony, alexanders, the herb called Fornet's palm, so it will be as he most desires.

I 71. For the dorsal muscle; seethe green rue in oil and in wax; anoint the dorsal muscle with it. Again: take goat hair; let it smoke under the breeches against the dorsal muscle. If a heel-sinew be broken, take Fornet's palm, seethe it in water, foment the limb with it, and wash the limb with it; and make a salve of butter; anoint after the fomentation.

I 72. At which time blood-letting is to be avoided, and at which to be allowed. Blood-letting is to be avoided for a fortnight before Lammas and for thirty-five days afterwards, because then all poisonous things fly and injure men greatly. Those doctors who were wisest taught that no one should drink a potion in that month, nor anywhere weaken his body, unless there were great need for it – and then to stay inside during the middle of the day, since the air is most infected then. Therefore the Romans and all southern people made earth-houses for themselves because of the air's heat and poisonousness. Doctors also say that flowering herbs are then best to work, both for potions and salves and powder.

How one should avoid blood-letting on each of the six 'fives' of the month; and when it is best. Doctors also teach that no one should let blood at a five-night-old moon, and again at a ten-night, and fifteen and twenty and twenty-five and a thirty-night-old moon, but between each of the six 'fives'. And there is no time so good for blood-letting as in early spring when the evil humours which are imbibed during winter are gathered together, and best of all in the month of April, when trees and plants first sprout, when the bad pus and the bad blood increases in the cavities of the body.

If a bloody wound in a man should turn bad, then take mallow, boil it in water, foment with that; and pound the lower part – apply that. If you wish to prevent blood in a cut, take cauldron soot, rub it to powder; sprinkle on the wound. Again: take rye and barley straw; burn it to powder. If you cannot staunch a bloody wound, take new horse-dung; dry it in the sun or by the fire; rub it to powder very thoroughly; lay the powder very thick on a linen cloth; bind the bloody wound with that for a night. If you cannot staunch a flowing vein, take the same blood which runs out, burn it on a hot stone and rub it to powder; lay that powder on the vein and bind it up tight. If one cut into a sinew while blood-letting, mix together wax and pitch and sheep's grease; lay it on a cloth and on the wound.

I 87. If a man's hair fall out, make him a salve; take great hellebore and viper's bugloss, and the lower part of burdock, and gentian; make the salve from that plant and from all these, and from butter on which no water has come. If hair fall out, boil the polypody fern, and foment the head with that very hot. If a man should be bald, the great doctor Pliny prescribes this remedy: take dead bees, burn them to ashes – linseed also – add oil to it; seethe very long over the coals, then strain and wring out; and take willow leaves, pound them, pour into the oil, boil again for a while over the coals, then strain; anoint with it after the bath.

A head-bath for that: boil willow leaves in water; wash with that, before you anoint it; and pound the leaves strongly boiled; bind on at night, until it be dry, so that you can afterwards anoint with the salve; do so for thirty nights, longer if there be need of it.

In order that hair should not grow: take ants' eggs; rub them down; smear on the place; no hair will ever come there. If hair should be too thick, take a swallow, burn it to ashes under a tile and have the ashes sprinkled on.

II 17. For all liver diseases, their origins and consequences, and concerning the six things which cause pain in the liver; and remedies for all those, and plain symptoms respecting both urine and lack of appetite, and their colour. The liver extends on the right side as far as the pit of the stomach; it has five lobes and cleaves to the loins; it is the blood's material, and the blood's dwelling and nourishment. When foods are digested and attenuated, they come to the liver; then they change their colour and turn into blood; and then it casts out the impurities which are there and collects the pure blood and sends it through four arteries; chiefly to the heart, and also throughout the whole body to the furthest members.

Respecting six things which cause liver-pain: first swelling, that is, a tumour of the liver; second is the bursting of the swelling; third is a wound of the liver; fourth is surging heat with sensitiveness and with a sore swelling; fifth is a hardening of the stomach with sensitiveness and with soreness; sixth is a hardening of the liver without sensitiveness and without soreness. You may discern a swelling or tumour of the liver thus: the swelling in the liver occurs first under the soft rib on the right side, and there the man first feels heaviness and pain; and from that place the pain ascends over all the side as far as the collar-bone and as far as the right shoulder; and his urine is blood-red, as if it were bloody; he is afflicted with lack of appetite and his colour is pale, and he is somewhat feverish and constantly feels cold, and trembles as one does with typhus; he cannot keep food down; the liver enlarges and one cannot touch the pain with the hands, so severe is it; and when it is most severe one has no sleep. When the swelling bursts, then the urine is purulent like pus; if it runs out the pain is less.

II 18. For a swelling or tumour of the liver. If the passage should block, one must first let blood from a vein on the left side; then make him a fomentation and a salve thus: from oil and rue and dill, and as much as you think of wild celery seed; seethe all with the oil, and then with the juice foment the right side for a long time with soft wool, and then lay the wool on, and bandage tightly for about three days. Again: make him a salve to be applied, and on the thickest cloth or on a skin lay barley-meal soused with wine and then boiled and all rubbed down with vinegar and with honey, and boiled again – swathe with that, very warm, and bind over the soreness; and from time to time draw off with a cupping-glass or with a horn. If the passage be blocked, draw it out with a herbal potion. Make it from wormwood and from centaury and from rue seed; add sufficient strained honey; give a spoonful, fasting for a night.

III 1. In case a man ache in the head: take the lower part of crosswort, put it on a red fillet; let him bind the head with it. For the same: take mustard seed and rue, rub into oil, put into hot water; wash the head frequently in that water; he will be healthy. For an old headache, take penny royal, boil in oil or butter; with that anoint the temples and over the eyes and on top of the head; even though his mind be turned, he will be healthy. For a very old headache, take salt and rue and bunches of ivy berries; pound all together, put into honey, and with it anoint the temples and the forehead and on the top of the head. For the same: look for little stones in the stomachs of swallow chicks; take care that they do not touch earth or water or other stones; sew up three of them in whatever you wish; put them on the man who is in need; he will soon be well; they are good for headache and for eye pain and for the Devil's temptations, and goblins, and typhus, and incubus and herbal seizure and bewitching and evil enchantments; it must be big chicks in which you will find them. If a man ache in one side of his head, thoroughly pound rue, put it into strong vinegar, and with that let the head be anointed right on top. For the same: dig up plantain, without iron, before the rising of the sun; bind the roots around the head with a moist red fillet; he will soon be well.

III 36. For a cancerous eruption: take the bile of a goat and honey; mix together equal quantities of both, and apply to the wound. For the same: burn a fresh dog's head to ashes and apply that to the wound. If that doesn't work, take human excrement, dry it thoroughly, rub it to dust and apply. If you can't cure it with this, you'll never be able to do it at all.

III 38(b). If a woman suffer from too great a menstrual discharge: take fresh horse-dung, lay it on hot coals and allow it to steam a lot up between the thighs under the clothes, so that the person sweats a lot.

III 57. Against a woman's chatter: eat a radish at night, while fasting; that day the chatter cannot harm you.

III 61. Make thus a salve against the race of elves, goblins and those women with whom the Devil copulates: take the female hop-plant, wormwood, betony, lupin, vervain, henbane, dittander, viper's bugloss, bilberry plants, cropleek, garlic, madder grains, corn cockle, fennel. Put those plants in a vat; place under an altar; sing nine masses over it; boil it in butter and in sheep's grease; add much holy salt;[1] strain through a cloth; throw the herbs into running water. If any evil temptation come to a man, or elf or goblin, anoint his face with this salve, and put it on his eyes and where his body is sore, and cense him and frequently sign him with the cross; his condition will soon improve.

---

[1] For 'holy salt' see above, pp. 73, 113.

THE DEVELOPMENT OF THE FOETUS

Anglo-Saxon knowledge of human anatomy was in part empirical and in part derived from Classical, ultimately Hippocratic, sources; a mixture of the relatively sophisticated and the superstitious. One mid-eleventh-century Canterbury miscellany includes, amidst all sorts of traditional folkloric prognostications, fragments of an account of foetal development: British Library MS. Cotton Tiberius A III, ff. 40ᵛ–1, 42ᵛ–3. The same hand was responsible also for a continuous gloss to a text of the Benedictine Rule and to Ælfric's Colloquy (see above, pp. 169). The text was printed by T. O. Cockayne, *Leechdoms, Wortcunning and Starcraft of Early England*, London, 1864–6, III, pp. 144–6.

Here it begins to tell about the nature of a man, how he becomes man in his mother's inside. First the man's brain is formed in his mother's inside, then in the sixth week that brain is covered with a membrane on the outside. In the second month the veins are formed — they are separated into three-hundred-and-sixty-five shorter and longer; and the blood then flows to the feet and into the hands; and he is then articulated in limbs and is altogether developed. In the third month he is man, except for the soul. In the fourth month he is firm in limbs. In the fifth month he is lively and grows, and the mother is at her wit's end; and then when the ribs are formed, numerous pains occur, when the body of the foetus is shaping in her inside. In the sixth month he forms skin, and bones are growing. In the seventh month the toes and the fingers are growing. In the eighth month his breast parts are growing, and heart and blood, and he is all firm-set. In the ninth month it is clearly known to the woman whether she can give birth. In the tenth month the woman will not escape with her life if the child is not born, because it turns to a mortal sickness in the abdomen — most often on a Tuesday night.

[At this point a passage of indeterminate length is lost.]

Again, another thing with these matters, is that you might know which kind of child a pregnant woman will give birth to. If she walks slowly and has hollow eyes, she will give birth to a boy; if she walks quickly and has swollen eyes, she will give birth to a girl. Again another thing. Take two plants in hand, that is, a lily and a rose; carry them to a pregnant woman; ask her to take whichever of the plants she wishes; if she takes a lily she will give birth to a boy, if she takes a rose she will give birth to a girl. Again, another method is that if the woman steps more with her heels on the earth she will give birth to a boy; if she steps more with her toes on the earth she will give birth to a girl. Again, another thing is: if the woman's belly is high up she will give birth to a boy; if it is sunk down she will give birth to a girl. Again, another thing: if a woman be pregnant four or five months, and then she frequently eats nuts or acorns or any fresh fruits, then sometimes it happens that as a result of that the child is stupid. Again, another thing about that is: if [she] eats bull's flesh or ram's or buck's or boar's or cock's or gander's, or any of the animals that can procreate, then sometimes it happens that as a result of that the child is hump-backed and bent.

BYRHTFERTH:
PROLOGUE TO THE MANUAL

Byrhtferth was a monk at the monastery of Ramsey in Huntingdonshire during the late tenth and early eleventh century. A pupil of Abbo of Fleury (see p. 158) he seems to have studied for a period at Canterbury and at the monastery of Echternach – an early English foundation in what is now Luxembourg. He is credited with several Latin works, including commentaries on the scientific books of Bede (*PL.*, XC 188. ff) as well as Lives of St Dunstan, Archbishop of Canterbury (960–88), and St Oswald, founder-abbot of Ramsey and later Archbishop of York (972–91).

This scientific manual is composed partly in Latin and partly in Old English. It is concerned primarily with astronomy and the computation of the calendar, involving such difficult matters as lunar ferials, epacts and embolismic years. Internal evidence indicates that it was written in 1011. Byrhtferth draws freely on a wide variety of sources, including: Isidore, Gregory, Alcuin, Hrabanus Maurus, Helperic of Auxerre, Haymo of Fulda, and in particular on Bede's two treatises *De Natura Rerum* and *De Temporum Ratione*.

Only one copy of Byrhtferth's Manual survives: Bodleian MS. Ashmole 328, a mid-eleventh-century manuscript apparently copied from a rather disordered exemplar. It is illustrated throughout with diagrams. The complete text was edited, together with facsimile plates of several of the diagrams, by S. J. Crawford. *Byrhtferth's Manual*, EETS., OS., CLXXVII, London, 1929; and the Old English text only, by F. Kluge, *Anglia*, 8 (1885), 298–337.

Here begins the science of computation according to the Romans, and according to the Greek and Jewish and Egyptian and English nations, and many others.

As determined by the skill of eminent men, the year which is called 'the solar year' is composed of three hundred and sixty-five days and six hours. From these days there are composed twelve months, in which there are fifty-two weeks, according to the course of the sun. (The names of the months are here distinguished.)

If anyone is pleased to know what a 'quadrans', that is a quarter, may be, then he should realize, by true reckoning, that a 'quadrans' is the fourth part of the day, or of other things which one may properly divide into four.

There is a circle, which philosophers call the 'zodiac', or 'horoscope', or 'mazaroth', or 'sidereal'. Through it run the sun and the moon and the stars, Saturn and Jupiter, Mars and Venus and Mercury. This circle is divided into twelve; and the sun runs through those twelve compartments within twelve months, and stays in each of the signs for thirty days and ten-and-a-half hours. There are also twelve signs in the aforesaid circle through which the sun passes, and it stays in each sign just as we now stated, that is for thirty days and ten-and-a-half hours. Take twelve times thirty; add them together; then you will have three-hundred-and-sixty days. Take the ten days which are left, and say 'twelve times ten': then there will be a hundred-and-twenty hours. Take those hundred-and-twenty hours and make five days.

We will explain these things more plainly than the Latin does. In a day and a night there are twenty-four hours; and in two days there are forty-eight hours; and in three days there are seventy-two; in four days, ninety-six; in five days there are a hundred-and-twenty hours. Take those five days and add them to the three-hundred-and-sixty days; then you will have the days of the twelve months with perfect reckoning. The reading says that there is still half an hour in each sign. Take those and add the six half-hours to the six half-hours; then there will be fairly collected six hours. From these six hours the quadrans very successfully arises and very proudly advances within four years, just as a king steps from his bridal chamber, arrayed.

Further, I warn him who wishes to investigate this with understanding, that he omit these six hours in the first year after the leap-year; and the second and also the third; and I instruct him – listen if he will – that the fourth year he collect together all these six hours, so that there be four times six hours, which learned philosophers call 'quadrantes' in Latin. 'Quadrans' in Latin is termed 'tetrarcha' in Greek.

[diagram of the zodiac]

Now that the circle which is called zodiac is marked out here, and the names of the twelve months, we will now enlarge further, by the power of God.

When the greatness of Almighty God had wonderfully created all things, he established all things in measurement and in number and in weight. He made two great lamps, as Genesis, that is the first book in the Bible, tells. He created sun and moon, and planets and stars; and he established two solstices, the one on the 21st of December, and the other on the 20th of June; and he dignified and set in order the twelve months with two equinoxes, which are

established on the 21st of March and on the 20th of September.
Moreover, with his own power he adorned the year with four
elements, as this figure displays to all who look at it.

[diagram of solstices, equinoxes and the four elements]

Besides these things of which we speak, there are noted down
significations and qualities and the names of the four winds and
the four seasons – spring, summer, autumn and winter – and also
the parallels, that is, childhood, and youth, and mature age and
very old age. Spring-time and childhood correspond; and youth
and summer are alike; and autumn and mature age are associated;
and winter and old age make an end. Spring-time is wet and
warm; the air is wet and warm; childhood is wet and warm, and
their blood is wet and warm. 'Aestas' is summer; it is warm and
dry. Fire is warm and dry; youth is warm and dry. 'Colera rubea',
that is red bile, occurs in summer; it is warm and dry. 'Autumnus',
that is the autumn; its nature is to be cold and dry. Earth is cold
and dry; mature age is dry and cold. In autumn there occurs
'colera nigra', that is black bile; it is dry and cold. 'Hiemps' is
winter; it is cold and wet; water is cold and wet; as the old man is
cold and snuffly. 'Phlegm', that is snot or mucus, affects the old
and infirm.

[diagram illustrating the foregoing dicta]

We have stirred with our oars the waves of the deep gulf; we
have also looked on the mountains around the salt sea strand; and
with extended sail and prosperous winds we have pitched camp
on the coasts of the most beautiful land. The waves symbolize this
deep science, and the mountains also symbolize the magnitude of
this science. It says, therefore: 'Where we saw the flower of the
lily,'[1] that is the beauty of computation, 'there we received the
nectar of roses', that is, we perceived the profundity of computation. In that place the noble plain furnished us with honey, sweet
and pleasant in flavour. In that same place we received myrrh, that
is, a famous spice with which they anoint the bodies of great men,
so that they cannot decay, and 'gutta', that is, a honey-sweet drop
(which if the sick tastes, he will immediately arise), and 'thus', that
is, incense. Through the merciful grace of God we found these
things at Ramsey. Wherefore I will not keep silent on account of

---

[1] A commonplace image; cf. Aldhelm, *MGH. Auct., Antiq.*, XV (1919), 231–2, and
Byrhtferth's own preface to Bede's *De Temporibus* (*Speculum*, 3 (1928), 516).

the eloquence of authors or on account of learned men who do not need to ponder these things between them; but we have touched the deep sea and the mountains of this work. Now by the will of God we will cultivate this work we have undertaken with abundant fruit.